W9-BXU-931

SPRINGDALE PUBLIC LIBRARY
405 S. Pleasant
Springdale, AR 72764

SPRINGDALE PUBLIC LIBRARY
405 S. Pleasant
Springdale, AR 72764

sasha kagan
crochet *inspiration*

sasha kagan
crochet *inspiration*

sixth&spring books

SPRINGDALE PUBLIC LIBRARY
405 S. Pleasant
Springdale, AR 72764

To my beloved children, Tanya, Jacob, Ambrose and Rowan. Thank you for being there for me and supporting my creativity.

Vice President, Publisher
Trisha Malcolm

Editorial Director
Elaine Silverstein

Art Director
Chi Ling Moy

Graphic Designers
Kim Howie
Sheena T. Paul

Book Division Manager
Erica Smith

Associate Editors
Erin Walsh
Amanda Keiser

Instructions Editor
Pat Harste

Instructions Checker
Elaine Gross

Technical Consultants
Carla Scott
Mary Kathryn Simon

Copy Editor
Kristina Sigler

Yarn Editor
Tanis Gray

Technical Illustrations
Karen Manthey

Photography
Jack Deutsch Studio
Marcus Tullis

Fashion Stylists
Misty Gunn
Laura Maffeo

Hair and Makeup
Elena Lyakir

Bookings Manager
Rachael Stein

Creative Director
Joe Vior

Production Manager
David Joinnides

President, Sixth&Spring Books
Art Joinnides

Copyright © 2007 Sasha Kagan

All rights reserved. No part of this publication may be reproduced or used in any form or by any means—graphic, electronic, or mechanical, including photocopying, recording, or information storage-and-retrieval systems—without written permission of the publisher.

The written instructions, photographs, designs, projects and patterns are intended for the personal, noncommercial use of retail purchaser and are under federal copyright laws; they are not to be reproduced in any form for commercial use. Permission is granted to photocopy patterns for the personal use of the retail purchaser.

Images on page 12 reproduced with permission of Rowan Yarns.

Resource information is current at time of publication. We have made every effort to ensure the accuracy of the contents of this publication. We are not responsible for any human or typographical errors.

3 5 7 9 10 8 6 4 2

Manufactured in China

Library of Congress Control Number: 2006931203

ISBN: 1-933027-12-6

ISBN-13: 978-1-933027-12-8

Table of *Contents*

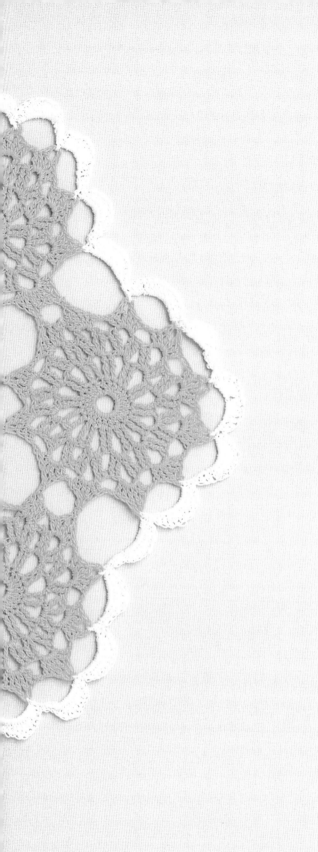

Introduction

Fibers are my flexible friends, and when I took up the challenge of writing this book they twisted and turned in the most unexpected ways, dancing with the crochet hook guiding their path.

Take the triple treble, for instance: Yarn three times 'round the hook, dip down into the previous row, pull yarn through; one wrap, two wraps, three wraps; one final wrap to the top, and off we go again! Beware: Crochet is a mesmerizing and totally addictive activity.

It wasn't until I started to explore crochet in depth that I began to understand just how many stitches are possible. Now, on reflection, I realize that I have only just scratched the surface of the infinite variety of stitch combinations that the medium has to offer.

In *Crochet Inspiration* I will take you with me on my journey of exploration. Many talented teachers, both known and unknown, have traveled this path, each adding their own nuance, twist or interpretation to fabric made with hook and yarn. With this book, I offer you my spin so far.

Each chapter features original designs using some of my favorite stitches to give you examples of what is possible. Who knows? You may, like me, find yourself "hooked" for life! Happy crocheting!

Sasha Kagan

How to Use this Book

The following abbreviations and stitch key are used in the swatch, charts and garment instructions.

Stitches unique to a swatch are noted within swatch instructions.

U.K. and Australian readers will find a chart for converting the U.S. instructions.

Abbreviations

approx approximately

beg begin, beginning

CC contrasting color

ch chain(s)

ch-sp space created by chains

cm centimeters

cont continue, continuing

dec decrease, decreasing

dc double crochet

dtr double treble

hdc half double crochet

inc increase, increasing

lp(s) loop(s)

m meter

MC main color

mm millimeter(s)

oz/g ounce(s)/gram(s)

pat(s) pattern(s)

rem remain, remains or remaining

rep repeat, repeating

rev sc reverse single crochet

RS right side

rnd(s) round(s)

sc single crochet

sk skip, skipping

sl st slip st

sp space

st(s) stitch(es)

t-ch turning chain

tog together

tr treble crochet

tr tr triple treble

WS wrong side

yd/m yard(s)/meter(s)

yo yarn over

* Repeat directions following * as many times as indicated

[] Repeat the directions inside brackets as many times as indicated

() Work directions inside parentheses into stitch indicated

U.S. Term	U.K./AUS Term
sl st slip st	**sc** single crochet
sc single crochet	**dc** double crochet
hdc half double crochet	**htr** half treble crochet
dc double crochet	**tr** treble crochet
tr treble crochet	**dtr** double treble crochet
dtr double treble crochet	**trip tr** or **trtr** triple treble crochet
trtr triple treble crochet	**qtr** quadruple treble crochet
rev sc reverse single crochet	**rev dc** reverse double crochet
yo yarn over	**yoh** yarn over hook

Stitch Key

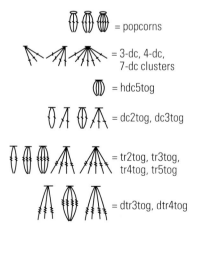

◯ = chain (ch)

• = slip st (sl st)

+ = single crochet (sc)

T = half double crochet (hdc)

= double crochet (dc)

= treble crochet (tr)

= double treble crochet (dtr)

= triple treble crochet (ttr)

= quadtr

= quintr

= FPdc

= BPdc

= picots

= sc2tog

= loop st

= spike st 2 or more rows below

— = worked in back loop

— = worked in front loop

= Solomon's knot

or = Marguerite sts

= bullion st

= linked dc (LDC)

= linked dtr (LDTR)

= bobble

= popcorns

= 3-dc, 4-dc, 7-dc clusters

= hdc5tog

= dc2tog, dc3tog

= tr2tog, tr3tog, tr4tog, tr5tog

= dtr3tog, dtr4tog

beginnings

Chapter 1

My earliest memory of crochet was, at age 4 or 5, sitting on a three-legged stool on the doorstep of my parents' tumble-down thatched cottage in Hertfordshire making a baby's matinee jacket. The yarn was a beautiful peach color and the crochet hook was pale green plastic. I was fascinated by the way the rows of stitches interlocked with each other in a shell pattern. I could hardly bear to put it down, promising myself "just one more row!" In the end, the jacket turned out far too small for all but a fairy babe to wear, so my doll was the grateful recipient.

Years went by and I found myself in the wonderland called art school. Self-expression through clothing was a major part of the zeitgeist of 1960s Britain, and the arts of handcrafting and hand-altering garments were at the height of trendiness.

I became obsessed with clothes, spending all my grant money on fabric and yarn to make up ever more eccentric garments to wear at college. Liberty lawn minidresses were smocked and embroidered,

and colored leather was punched and lashed together with thongs. Cherished 1940s fabric from my mother's stash was sewn into patchwork cushions; sweaters, jackets, tank tops and hats were knitted by hand; and for evening, a Lurex crochet shift dress was a must for parties.

Ah, the crocheted dress—out came the hook again. Starting with an Irish crocheted rose, I ad-libbed my way through a box of silver Lurex, and two days later I had produced a sleeveless floor-length gown and matching cloche cap. This outfit was worn with purple tap shoes from Anello and Davide, false eyelashes and a very white face!

The next twist of fate happened when I visited a girlfriend's home in Lincolnshire. As it it turned out, her father manufactured the Lurex of my gown! He put me in touch with a lady at his head office in London and suggested I show her some of my designs. Thus began my career as a fiber artist. I moved on to study at the Royal College of Art,

majoring in fine-art printmaking. I subsidized my escalating clothes habit through sales of my textile designs.

It wasn't until I moved to Wales to set up my knitwear business, by that time with a young family in tow, that my dress sense calmed down from "art-student wacky" to my more wearable country-classic look.

As the babies came and my business grew, exciting packages would arrive from my mother containing exquisite baby clothes: knit and crocheted rompers, jackets, booties, hats, mittens, shawls and cot blankets. These pieces kept the children warm throughout the winter months in cold, wet, windy Wales. I loved these pieces and treasure the remaining ones to this day.

For my twice-yearly hand-knitted collections, I often use crochet as a final trim and accent color. Picot and shell edgings are perfect to balance out a color or to highlight the proportions of a jacket. "Tiny

Tiny Flower   *Flirty Top*

Flower" from Rowan's *Yorkshire Fable* book, "Flirty Top" from Rowan Magazine 37, and "Victorian Rose Peplum" from my third book *Country Inspiration*—voted People's Favorite at my solo exhibition at the Victoria and Albert Museum in 2000—all illustrate this versatile use of crochet.

In 2005, I was out and about giving a lecture tour in the United States for Westminster Fibers. For me, the highlight of this tour was meeting Tatiana Mirer at the Big Apple Knitting Guild's annual retreat. I was delighted to meet her, as she had translated my first two books, *The Sasha Kagan Sweater Book* and *Sasha Kagan's Big and Little Sweaters*, into Russian (my father's native tongue). She taught me how to make a crochet rose and we spent many happy hours together musing on knitting, crochet, textiles and life.

Enter colleague and good friend Trisha Malcolm with an idea for us to work more closely together. Leafing through her extensive textile library, we found ourselves drawn to the intricate lace and heirloom pieces in her crochet collection. Thus the idea was born for this book.

In a way, I have come full circle, exploring painting, printmaking, sewing, embroidery and knitting before returning to the child making her first crocheted piece.

It has been, and still is, a fascinating journey of discovery, especially now that so much fabulous yarn is available. I hope that you too will enjoy playing with the dancing hook, and that you can use my spin on crochet to inspire your own creations.

crochet fabric

Chapter 2

Variations on *Single Crochet*

1 *Single Crochet—Basic*

Chain any number; plus 1 for foundation row.

Foundation row (RS) Sc in 2nd ch from hook and in each ch across. Ch 1, turn.

Row 1 Skip first st, working through both lps, sc in each st across, end sc in top of t-ch of row below. Ch 1, turn.

Rep row 1 for basic sc.

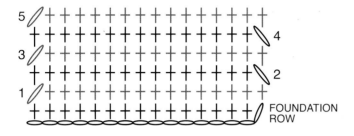

2 *Single Crochet—Front Loop*

Chain any number; plus 1 for foundation row.

Foundation row (RS) Sc in 2nd ch from hook and in each ch across. Ch 1, turn.

Row 1 Skip first st, working through front lps only, sc in each st across, end sc in top of t-ch of row below. Ch 1, turn.

Rep row 1 for front loop sc.

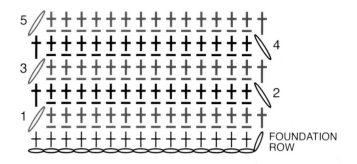

3 *Single Crochet—Back Loop*

Chain any number; plus 1 for foundation row.

Foundation row (RS) Sc in 2nd ch from hook and in each ch across. Ch 1, turn.

Row 1 Skip first st, working through back lps only, sc in each st across, end sc in top of t-ch of row below. Ch 1, turn.

Rep row 1 for back loop sc.

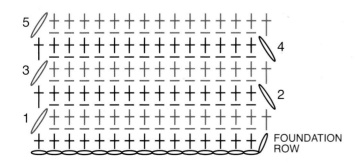

4 *Single Crochet—Back Loop—Striped*

With A, chain any number; plus 1 for foundation row.

Note When changing colors, draw new color through last 2 lps on hook to complete last st, then chain and turn. Cut and join colors as needed.

Foundation row (RS) Work as for back loop sc.

Row 1 Work as for back loop sc, changing to B at end of row. Rep row 1, working in stripe pat as follows: *2 rows B, 2 rows C and 2 rows A; rep from * throughout.

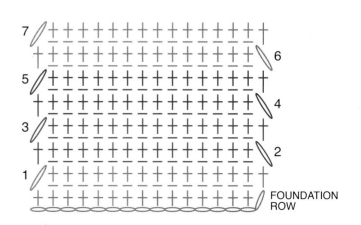

5

6

7

8

5 *Single Crochet—Back and Front Loop*

Chain an odd number; plus 1 for foundation row.

Foundation row (RS) Sc in 2nd ch from hook and in each ch across. Ch 1, turn.

Row 1 Skip first st, *sc in back lp of next st, sc in front lp of next st; rep from * across, end sc in top of t-ch of row below. Ch 1, turn.

Rep row 1 for back and front loop sc.

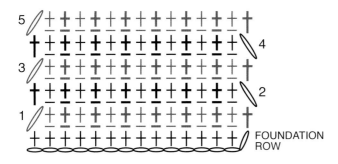

6 *Single Crochet—Crossed*

Chain a multiple of 2 sts, plus 1; plus 2 for foundation row.

Foundation row (RS) Sc in 3rd ch (counts as 1 sc and ch 1) from hook, *ch 1, skip next ch, sc in next ch; rep from * across. Turn.

Row 1 Ch 2 (counts as 1 sc and ch 1), insert hook in first ch-1 sp, yo and draw up a lp, insert hook in next ch-1 sp, yo and draw up a lp, yo and draw through all 3 lps on hook, *ch 1, insert hook in last ch-1 sp worked, yo and draw up a lp, insert hook under next ch-1 sp, yo and draw up a lp, yo and draw through all 3 lps on hook; rep from * across, ending with last leg of last sc2tog in 2nd ch of t-ch. Turn.

Rep row 1 for crossed sc.

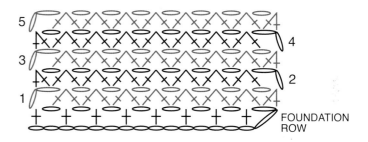

7 *Single Crochet Daisy—Solid*

Chain a multiple of 2 sts; plus 1 for foundation row.

Daisy cluster (DCL)

Insert hook into bottom lp of ch 1 just made, yo and draw up a lp, draw up a lp in same st as last lp of daisy cluster just made, draw up a lp in each of next 2 ch (or sts), yo and draw through all 5 lps on hook.

Foundation row (RS) Draw up a lp in 2nd, 3rd, 4th and 5th ch from hook, yo and draw through all 5 lps on hook, ch 1, *work DCL, ch 1; rep from * across. Turn.

Row 1 Ch 1, sc in each st and ch across. Turn.

Row 2 Ch 3, draw up a lp in 2nd ch from hook, then in 3rd ch from hook, draw up a lp in each of next 2 sts, yo and draw through all 5 lps on hook, ch 1, *work DCL, ch 1; rep from * across. Turn.

Rep rows 1 and 2 for solid sc daisy.

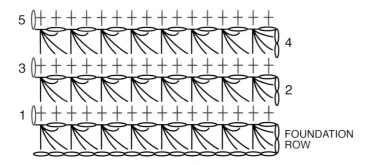

8 *Granite Stitch*

Chain a multiple of 2 sts, plus 1; plus 3 for foundation row.

Foundation row (RS) Sc in 4th ch (counts as 1 sc, ch 1 and skip 1 ch) from hook, *ch 1, skip next ch, sc in next ch; rep from * across. Turn.

Row 1 Ch 2 (counts as 1 sc and ch 1), sc in first ch-1 sp, *ch 1, sc in next ch-1 sp; rep from * across. Turn.

Rep row 1 for granite st.

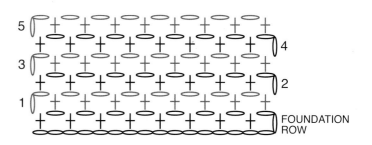

9

10

9 Single Crochet—Bricks

Chain a multiple of 4 sts plus 3; plus 1 for foundation row.

Long single crochet (long sc) Insert hook in st of row below, yo and draw up a long lp, yo and draw through 2 lps on hook (long sc made).

Note Take care not to work the sc directly behind the long sc.

Foundation row (RS) Sc in 2nd ch from hook and in each ch across. Ch 1, turn.

Row 1 Working through back lps only, sc in each st across. Ch 1, turn.

Row 2 *Sc in back lp of next 3 sts, long sc in next st of row below; rep from *, end sc in back lp of last 3 sts. Ch 1, turn.

Row 3 Rep row 1.

Row 4 Sc in back lp of first st, work long sc in next st of row below, *sc in back lp of next 3 sts, long sc in next st of row below; rep from *, end sc in back lp of last st. Ch 1, turn.

Rep rows 1–4 for sc bricks.

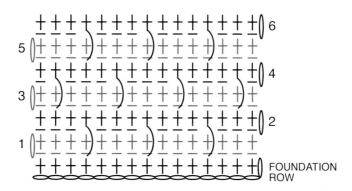

10 Single Crochet—Waffle

Chain an odd number; plus 1 for foundation row.

Single crochet 2 together (sc2tog) Draw up a lp in each of next 2 ch (or sts), yo and draw through all 3 lps on hook.

Foundation row (RS) Draw up a lp in 2nd, then 3rd ch from hook, yo and draw through all 3 lps on hook,

ch 1, *sc2tog, ch 1; rep from *, end sc in last ch. Turn.

Row 1 Ch 1, insert hook to the right of first vertical bar between last sc and ch-1 of row below, yo and draw up a lp, insert hook to the left of same vertical bar, yo and draw up a lp, yo and draw through all 3 lps

on hook, ch 1, *insert hook to the right of vertical bar between next 2 sc2tog's of row below, yo and draw up a lp, insert hook to the left of the same vertical bar, yo and draw up a lp, yo and draw through all 3 lps on hook, ch 1; rep from *, end sc in last st.

Rep row 1 for sc waffle.

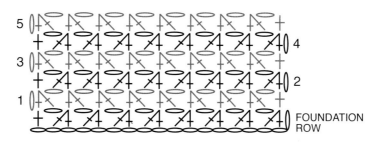

With A, chain a multiple of 2 sts; plus 1 for foundation row.

Note When changing colors, draw new color through 2 lps on hook to complete last sc, then turn.

Cut and join colors as needed.

Foundation row (RS) Work as for solid sc daisy.

Row 1 Work as for solid sc daisy, changing to B.

Row 2 Work as for solid sc daisy.

Rep rows 1 and 2 of solid sc daisy, working in stripe pat as follows: 1 row B, *2 rows C, 2 rows D, 2 rows E, 2 rows A and 2 rows B; rep from * to end.

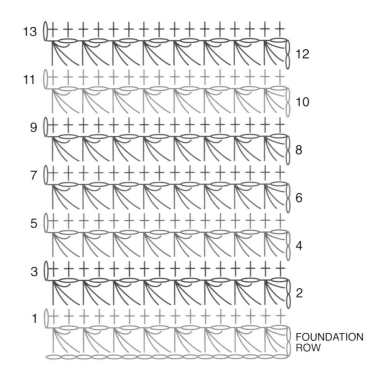

12 *Single Crochet—Zigzag*

With A, chain a multiple of 13 sts, plus 1; plus 1 for foundation row.

Note When changing colors, draw new color through last 2 lps on hook to complete last st, then chain 1 and turn. Cut and join colors as needed.

Foundation row (RS) Work 2 sc in 2nd ch from

hook, *sc in next 5 ch, skip next 2 ch, sc in next 5 ch, work 3 sc in next ch; rep from *, end last rep with work 2 sc in last ch, changing to B. Ch 1, turn.

Row 1 Work 2 sc in first st, sc in next 4 sts, *skip next 2 sts, sc in next 5 sts, work 3 sc in next st, sc in next 5 sts; rep from *, end skip next 2 sts, sc sc in

next 4 sts, work 2 sc in last st, changing to C. Ch 1, turn.

Rep row 1 for zigzag sc, working in stripe pat as follows: 1 row C, 1 row A and 1 row B.

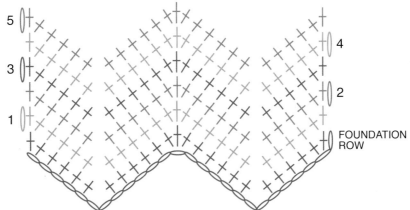

13

14

15

16

Stitches get *Taller*

13 *Half Double Crochet—Basic*

Chain any number; plus 2 for foundation row.

Half double crochet (hdc) Insert hook in 3rd ch from hook, yo and draw up a lp, yo and draw it through first loop only, yo and draw through rem two loops.

Foundation row (RS) Hdc in 3rd ch from hook and in each ch across. Ch 2, turn.

Row 1 Skip first st, working through both lps, hdc in each st across, end hdc in top of t-ch of row below. Ch 2, turn.

Rep row 1 for basic hdc.

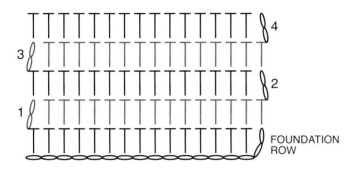

14 *Half Double Crochet—Front Loop*

Chain any number; plus 2 for foundation row.

Foundation row (RS) Hdc in 3rd ch from hook and in each ch across. Ch 2, turn.

Row 1 Skip first st, working through front lps only, hdc in each st across, end hdc in top of t-ch of row below. Ch 2, turn.

Rep row 1 for front loop hdc.

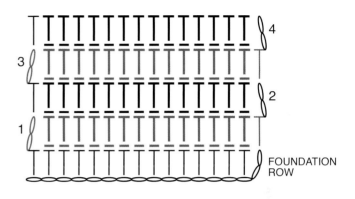

15 *Half Double Crochet—Back Loop*

Chain any number; plus 2 for foundation row.

Foundation row (RS) Hdc in 3rd ch from hook and in each ch across. Ch 2, turn.

Row 1 Skip first st, working through back lps only, hdc in each st across, end hdc in top of t-ch of row below. Ch 2, turn.

Rep row 1 for back loop hdc.

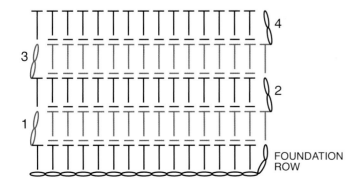

16 *Half Double Crochet—Back and Front Loop*

Chain any odd number; plus 2 for foundation row.

Foundation row (RS) Hdc in 3rd ch from hook and in each ch across. Ch 2, turn.

Row 1 Skip first st, *hdc in back lp of next st, hdc in front lp of next st; rep from * across, end hdc in top of t-ch of row below. Ch 2, turn.

Rep row 1 for back and front loop hdc.

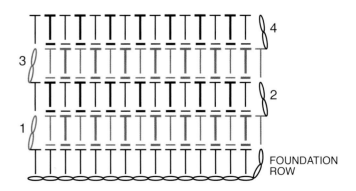

17

18

19

20

17 Double Crochet—Basic

Chain any number; plus 3 for foundation row.

Double crochet (dc) Yo; insert hook in 4th ch from hook and draw up a loop (3 loops on hk). Yo and draw loop through first 2 lps (2 lps rem). Yo and draw lp through 2 lps.

Foundation row (RS) Dc in 4th ch from hook and in each ch across. Ch 3, turn.

Row 1 Skip first st, working through both lps, dc in each st across, end dc in top of t-ch of row below. Ch 3, turn.

Rep row 1 for basic dc.

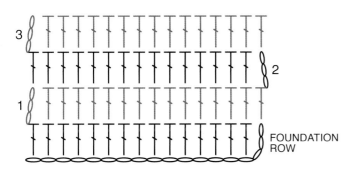

18 Double Crochet—Diagonal

Chain a multiple of 4 sts plus 1; plus 1 for foundation row.

Foundation row (RS) Sc in 2nd ch from hook and in each ch across. Ch 3, turn.

Row 1 *Skip first st, dc in next 3 sts, working from front to back, insert hook into skipped st, yo and draw up a long lp, yo and draw through 2 lps on hook; rep from *, end dc in last st. Ch 1, turn.

Row 2 Sc in each st across. Ch 3, turn.

Rep rows 1 and 2 for diagonal dc.

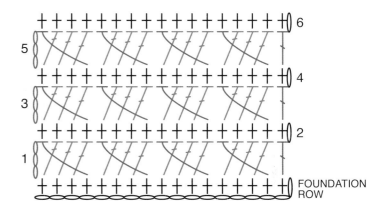

19 Double Crochet—Crossed

Chain a multiple of 2 sts; plus 4 for foundation row.

Foundation row (RS) Skip first 4 ch, dc in next ch, then dc in last skipped ch, *skip next ch, dc in next ch, dc in skipped ch; rep from *, end dc in last ch. Ch 3, turn.

Row 1 Skip first 2 sts, dc in next st, dc in 2nd st skipped, *skip next st, dc in next st, dc in skipped st; rep from *, end dc in top of t-ch of row below. Ch 3, turn.

Rep row 1 for crossed dc.

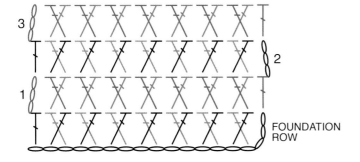

20 Treble Crochet—Basic

Chain any number; plus 4 for foundation row.

Treble crochet (tr) Yo twice, insert hook in 5th ch from hook. Draw lp through chain (4 lps rem), yo and draw through 2 lps (3 lps rem), yo and draw through 2 lps (2 lps rem), yo and draw through last 2 lps.

Foundation row (RS) Tr in 5th ch from hook and in each ch across. Ch 4, turn.

Row 1 Skip first st, working through both lps, tr in each st across, end tr in top of t-ch of row below. Ch 4, turn.

Rep row 1 for basic tr.

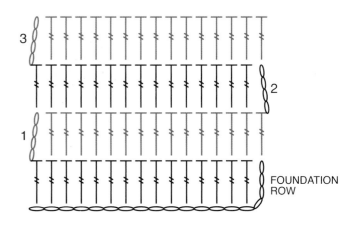

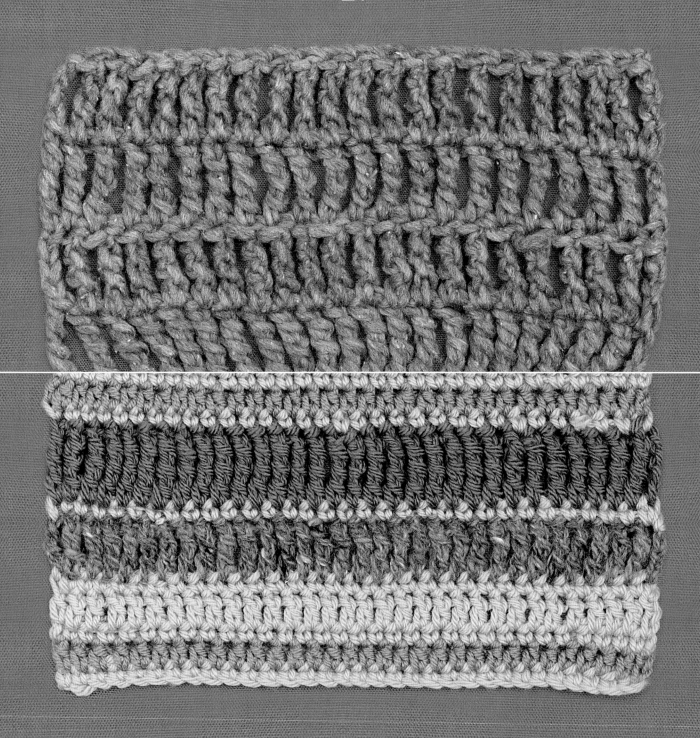

21

22

21 *Double Treble Crochet—Basic*

Chain any number; plus 5 for foundation row.

Double treble (dtr) Yo 3 times, insert hook in 6th ch from hook, draw lp through ch (5 lps rem), continue to yo and draw through 2 lps until one lp rems.

Foundation row (RS) Dtr in 6th ch from hook and in each ch across. Ch 5, turn.

Row 1 Skip first st, working through both lps, dtr in each st across, end dtr in top of t-ch of row below.

Ch 5, turn.

Rep row 1 for basic dtr.

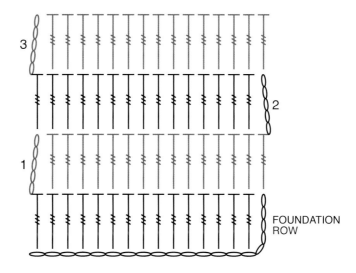

22 *Big and Little Stripes*

With A, chain any number; plus 1 for foundation row.

Note When changing colors, draw new color through last 2 lps on hook to complete last st, then chain and turn. Cut and join colors as needed.

Foundation row (RS) Sc in 2nd ch from hook and in each ch across, changing to B in last ch. Ch 2, turn.

Row 1 Skip first st, hdc in each st across, end hdc in top of t-ch of row below changing to A. Ch 1, turn.

Row 2 Skip first st, sc in each sc across, end sc in top of t-ch of row below changing to C. Ch 3, turn.

Row 3 Skip first st, dc in each st across, end dc in top of t-ch of row below changing to A. Ch 1, turn.

Row 4 Rep row 2, changing to D. Ch 4, turn.

Row 5 Skip first st, tr in each st across, end tr in top of t-ch of row below changing to A. Ch 1, turn.

Row 6 Rep row 2, changing to E. Ch 5, turn.

Row 7 Skip first st, dtr in each st across, end dtr in top of t-ch of row below changing to A. Ch 1, turn.

Row 8 Rep row 2, changing to B. Ch 2, turn.

Rep rows 1–8 for big and little stripes.

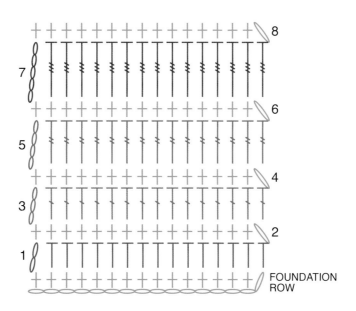

Bobbles

23 *Easy Mock Bobbles I*

Chain a multiple of 2 sts plus 1; plus 1 for foundation row.

Foundation row (RS) Sc in 2nd ch from hook and in each ch across. Ch 1, turn.

Row 1 (WS) Sc in first st, *tr in next st, sc in next st; rep from * across. Ch 1, turn.

Rows 2, 3 and 4 Sc in each st across. Ch 1, turn.

Rep rows 1–4 for easy mock bobbles I.

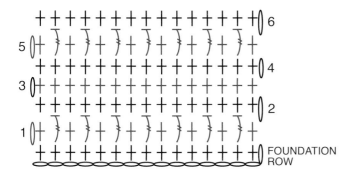

25 *Bullion Stitch—Striped*

With A, chain a multiple of 2 sts; plus 2 for foundation row.

Bullion stitch Wrap yarn around hook 5 times, insert hook into st, yo and draw up a lp, yo and draw through all lps on hook one at a time.

Note Cut and join B as needed. Carry color not in use loosely across WS of work.

Foundation row (RS) Hdc in 3rd ch from hook and in each ch across. Ch 3, turn.

Row 1 *With B, bullion st in next st, with A, dc in next st; rep from * across. Ch 2, turn.

Row 2 With A, hdc in each st and ch across. Ch 3, turn.

Repeat rows 1 and 2 for bullion st stripes.

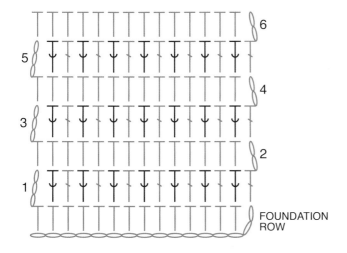

24 *Easy Mock Bobbles II*

Chain a multiple of 2 sts plus 1; plus 1 for foundation row.

Foundation row (RS) Sc in 2nd ch from hook and in each ch across. Ch 1, turn.

Row 1 (WS) Sc in first st, *tr in next st, sc in next st; rep from * across. Ch 1, turn.

Row 2 Sc in each st across. Ch 1, turn.

Row 3 Sc in first 2 sts st, *tr in next st, sc in next st; rep from *, end sc in last st. Ch 1, turn.

Row 4 Rep row 2. Ch 1, turn.

Rep rows 1–4 for easy mock bobbles II.

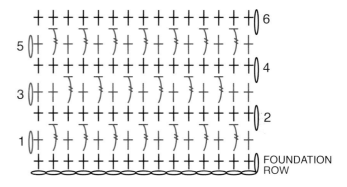

26 *Baby Bobbles*

Chain a multiple of 3 sts plus 1; plus 1 for foundation row.

Bobble In same st work [yo, insert hook into st and draw up a lp. Yo and draw through 2 lps on hook] 5 times, yo and draw through all 6 lps on hook.

Foundation row (RS) Sc in 2nd ch from hook and in each ch across. Ch 1, turn.

Row 1 (WS) Sc in first st, *work bobble in next st, sc in next 2 sts; rep from * across. Ch 1, turn.

Row 2 Sc in each st across. Ch 1, turn.

Row 3 Sc in first 2 sts, *work bobble in next st, sc in next 2 sts; rep from * across, end work bobble in next st, sc in last st. Ch 1, turn.

Row 4 Rep row 2.

Rep rows 1–4 for baby bobbles.

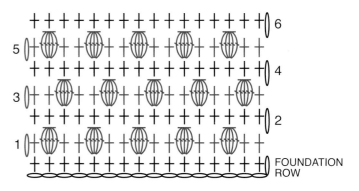

27

28

Chain any number; plus 3 for foundation row.

Note This stitch is worked with RS facing throughout. Each row of astrakhan st is worked in two halves. After the foundation row is worked (from right to left), the first half of the stitch (the furry ch-7 lps) is worked from left to right, then the second half

(the dc row to which you will attach the ch-7 lps) is worked from right to left.

Foundation row (RS) Skip first 3 ch (counts as 1 dc), dc in next ch and in each ch across. Do not turn.

Row 1 (first half—worked from L to R) Working in front lps of row below, work as follows: *ch 7, sl

st in front lp of next dc to the right; rep from *, end ch 7, sl st in top of ch-3 of row below. Do not turn.

Row 1 (second half—worked from R to L) Ch 3 (counts as 1 dc), working in back lps of 2 rows below, dc in each st across. Do not turn.

Rep row 1 for astrakhan st.

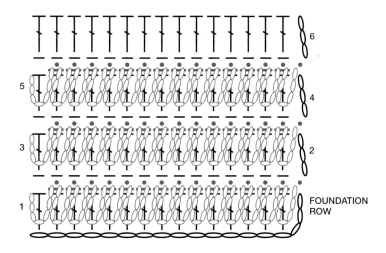

Chain a multiple of 4 sts plus 1; plus 3 for foundation row.

Bobble In same st work [yo, insert hook into st and draw up a lp. Yo and draw through 2 lps on hook] 5 times, yo and draw through all 6 lps on hook.

Foundation row (RS) Dc in 4th ch from hook and in each ch across. Ch 1, turn.

Row 1 (WS) Sc in first st, *work bobble in next st, sc in next 3 sts; rep from * across. Ch 1, turn.

Row 2 Sc in each st across. Ch 1, turn.

Row 3 Sc in first 3 sts, *work bobble in next st, sc in next 3 sts; rep from *, end work bobble in next st, sc in last st. Ch 1, turn.

Row 4 Rep row 2.

Rep rows 1–4 for giant bobbles.

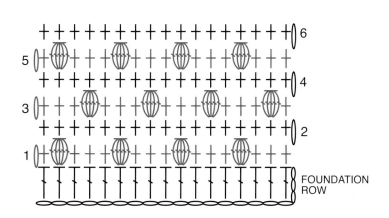

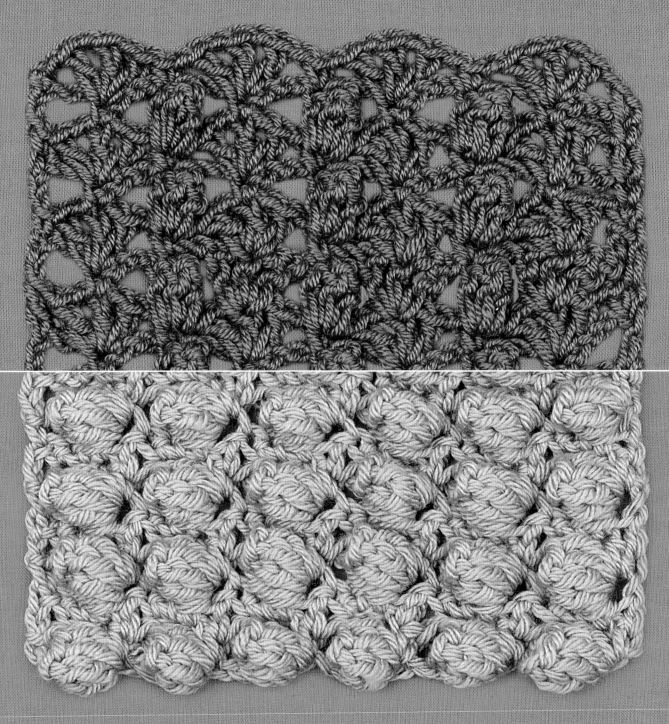

29

30

Chain a multiple of 8 sts plus 1; plus 1 for foundation row.

Popcorn Work 4 dc in same st, drop lp from hook. Working from front to back, insert hook into both lps of first dc, pick up dropped lp and draw through dc, then ch 1 to secure popcorn.

Foundation row (RS) Sc in 2nd ch from hook, *ch 1, skip next 3 ch, work (dc, ch 1, dc, ch 1, dc) in next ch, ch 1, skip next 3 ch, sc in next ch; rep from * across. Turn.

Row 1 Ch 6 (counts as 1 dc and ch 3), sc in center dc of first fan, *ch 3, work popcorn in next sc, ch 3, sc in center dc of next fan; rep from * across, end ch 3, dc in last sc. Turn.

Row 2 Ch 1, sc in first dc, *ch 1, work (dc, ch 1, dc, ch 1, dc) in next sc, ch 1, sc in top of popcorn; rep from * across, end ch 1, work (dc, ch 1, dc, ch 1, dc) in last sc, ch 1, sc in 3rd ch of ch-6 of row below. Turn.

Rep rows 1 and 2 for popcorn fans.

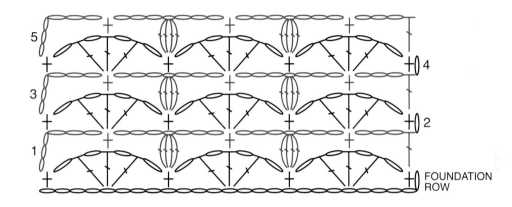

Chain a multiple of 4 sts plus 1; plus 1 for foundation row.

Popcorn Work 5 dc in same st, drop lp from hook. Working from front to back, insert hook into both lps of first dc, pick up dropped lp and draw through dc, then ch 1 to secure popcorn.

Foundation row (RS) Sc in 2nd ch from hook, *ch 3, popcorn in same ch as last sc, skip next 3 ch, sc in next ch; rep from * across. Turn.

Row 1 Ch 3 (counts as 1 dc), skip first sc, *sc in next 2 ch, hdc in next ch, dc in next sc; rep from * across. Turn.

Row 2 Ch 1, sc in first st, *ch 3, work popcorn in same st as last sc, skip next 3 sts, sc in next dc; rep from * across, end ch 3, work popcorn in same st as last sc, skip last 3 sts, sc in top of ch-3 of row below. Turn.

Rep rows 1 and 2 for popcorn grid.

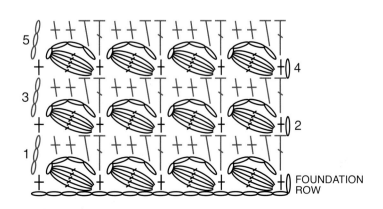

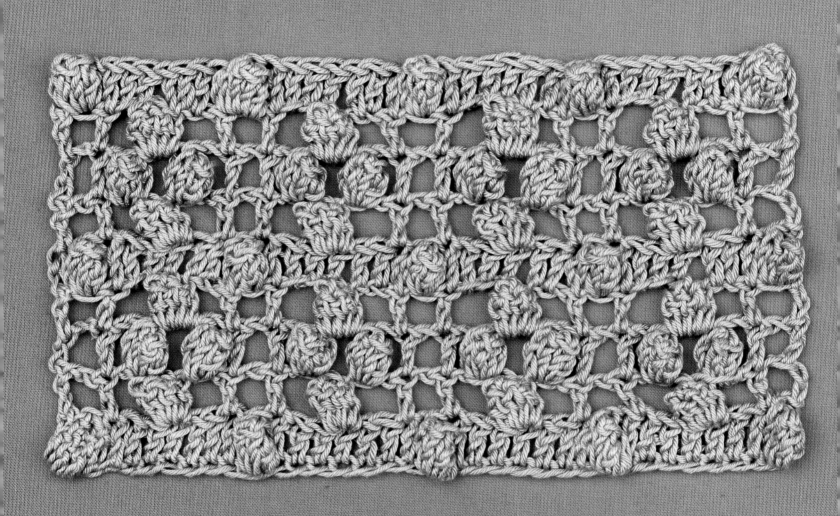

31

Chain a multiple of 8 sts plus 3; plus 2 for foundation row.

Popcorn Work 5 dc in same st, drop lp from hook. Working from front to back, insert hook into both lps of first dc, pick up dropped lp and draw through dc, then ch 1 to secure popcorn.

Note Popcorns are made on RS rows and WS rows. Push those made on WS rows to the RS as you make them.

Foundation row (RS) Work popcorn in 4th ch from hook, *dc in next 7 ch, work popcorn in next ch; rep from *, end dc in last ch. Turn.

Row 1 Ch 4 (count as 1 dc and ch 1), skip first st and first popcorn, dc in next st, *ch 2, skip next 2 sts, work popcorn in next st, ch 2, skip next 2 sts, dc in next st, ch 1, skip next popcorn, dc in next st; rep from *, end last rep with dc in 3rd ch of ch-4 t-ch. Turn.

Row 2 Ch 4 (counts as 1 dc and ch 1), skip first st and first ch, dc in next st, *ch 1, skip next ch, work popcorn in next ch, ch 1, skip next popcorn, work popcorn in next ch, [ch 1, skip next ch, dc in next st] twice; rep from *, end last rep with dc in 3rd ch of ch-4 t-ch. Turn.

Row 3 Ch 4 (counts as 1 dc and ch 1), skip first st and first ch, dc in next st, *ch 2, work popcorn in ch-sp between next 2 popcorns, ch 2, dc in next dc, ch 1, skip next ch-1, dc in next st; rep from *, end last rep with dc in 3rd ch of ch-4 t-ch. Turn.

Row 4 Ch 3 (counts as 1 dc), skip first st, work popcorn in next ch, *dc in next dc, dc in next 2 ch, dc in next popcorn, dc in next 2 ch, dc in next dc, work popcorn in next ch; rep from *, end last rep with dc in 3rd ch of ch-4 t-ch. Turn.

Rep rows 1–4 for popcorn lace.

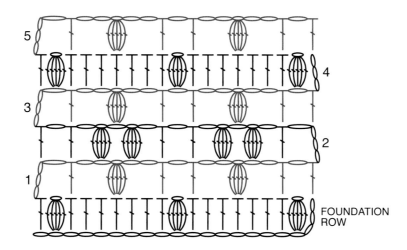

32

33

34

35

Shells and *Clusters*

32 *Shell Stitch—Solid*

Chain a multiple of 6 sts plus 1; plus 1 for foundation row.

Foundation row (RS) Sc in 2nd ch from hook, *skip next 2 ch, work 5 dc in next ch (whole shell made), skip next 2 ch, sc in next ch; rep from * across. Turn.

Row 1 Ch 3 (counts as 1 dc), work 2 dc in first st (half shell made), *skip next 2 dc, sc in next dc, skip next 2 dc, work 5 dc in next sc; rep from *, end last rep with 3 dc in last sc (half shell), skip t-ch. Turn.

Row 2 Ch 1, sc in first dc, *skip next 2 dc, work 5 dc in next sc, skip next 2 dc, sc in next dc; rep from *, end last rep with sc in top of t-ch of row below. Turn. Rep rows 1 and 2 for solid shell st.

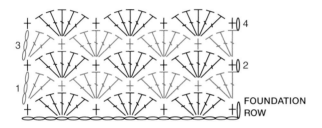

34 *Shell Stitch—Lacy*

Chain a multiple of 6 sts plus 1; plus 1 for foundation row.

Foundation row (RS) Sc in 2nd ch from hook, *skip next 2 ch, work 5 dc in next ch (shell made), skip next 2 ch, sc in ch; rep from * across. Turn.

Row 1 *Ch 5, sc in center dc of next shell; rep from *, end ch 2, dc in sc of row below. Turn.

Row 2 Sc in first dc, *work 5 dc in next sc, sc in next ch-5 lp; rep from *, end last rep with, sc in 3rd ch of ch-5 of row below. Turn. Rep rows 1 and 2 for lacy shell st.

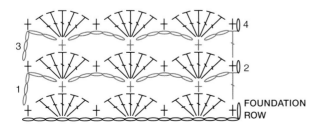

33 *Shell Stitch—Striped*

With A, chain a multiple of 6 sts plus 1; plus 1 for foundation row.

Note When changing colors, draw new color through last 2 lps on hook to complete last st, then turn. Cut and join colors as needed.

Foundation row (RS) Work as for shell st solid, changing to B at end of row. Rep rows 1 and 2 of shell st solid, working in stripe pat as follows: 1 row B, 1 row C and 1 row A.

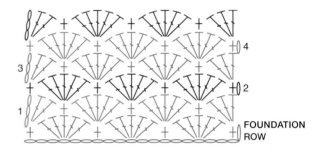

35 *Thistle Stitch*

Chain a multiple of 8 sts; plus 4 for foundation row.

Foundation row (RS) Work 5 tr in the 8th ch from hook, skip next 3 ch, tr in next ch, *skip next 3 ch, work 5 tr in next ch, skip next 3 ch, tr in next ch; rep from * across. Turn.

Row 1 Ch 4 (counts as 1 tr), work 2 tr in first tr, skip next 2 tr, tr in next tr, *skip next 2 tr, work 5 tr in next tr, skip next 2 tr, tr in next tr; rep from * to last 3 sts, end skip next 2 tr, work 3 tr in top of t-ch of row below. Turn.

Row 2 Ch 4 (counts as 1 tr), *skip next 2 tr, work 5 tr in next tr, skip next 2 tr, tr in next tr; rep from *, end last rep with tr in top of ch-4 of row below. Turn. Rep rows 1 and 2 for thistle st.

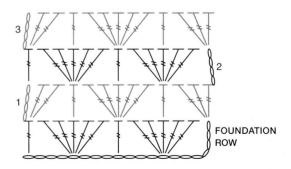

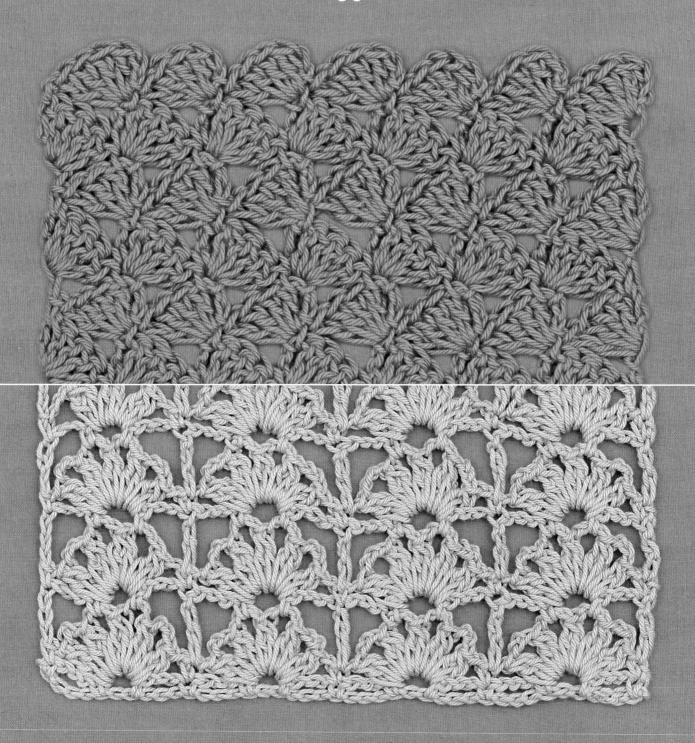

36

37

Chain a multiple of 6 sts plus 1; plus 1 for foundation row.

Foundation row (RS) Work 4 dc in 4th ch from hook, skip next 3 ch, sc in next ch, *ch 2, work 4 dc in same ch as last sc, skip next 3 ch, sc in next ch; rep from * across, end sc in last ch. Turn.

Row 1 Ch 5, work 4 dc in 4th ch from hook, *skip next 4 dc, sc between last dc skipped and next ch-2 sp, ch 2, work 4 dc in side edge of sc just made; rep from * to last 4 dc, skip last 4 dc, sc in next ch. Turn.

Rep row 1 for diagonal shell st.

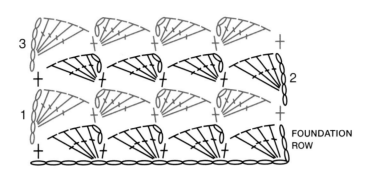

Chain a multiple of 10 sts plus 1; plus 1 for foundation row.

Double crochet 2 together (dc2tog) In same ch-3 sp, [yo, insert hook in ch-3 sp, yo and draw up a lp, yo, draw through 2 lps on hook] twice, yo and draw through all 3 lps on hook.

Foundation row (WS) Sc in 2nd ch from hook, *ch 3, skip next 3 ch, sc in next ch, ch 3, skip next ch, sc in next ch, ch 3, skip next 3 ch, sc in next ch; rep from * across. Turn.

Row 1 Ch 1, sc in first sc, *ch 1, skip next ch-3 sp, work dc2tog in next ch-3 sp, then in same sp work [ch 3, dc2tog] 4 times, ch 1, skip next ch-3 sp, sc in next sc; rep from * across. Turn.

Row 2 Ch 7 (counts as 1 tr and ch 3), skip first ch-3 sp, sc in next ch-3 sp, ch 3, sc in next ch-3 sp, ch 3, tr in next sc, *ch 3, skip next ch-3 sp, sc in next ch-3 sp, ch 3, sc in next ch-3 sp, ch 3, tr in next sc; rep from * across. Turn.

Row 3 Ch 1, sc in first tr, *ch 1, skip next ch-3 sp, work dc2tog in next ch-3 sp, then in same sp work [ch 3, dc2tog] 4 times, ch 1, sc in next tr; rep from *, end last rep with sc in 4th ch of ch-7 of row below. Turn.

Rep rows 2 and 3 for boxed shell st.

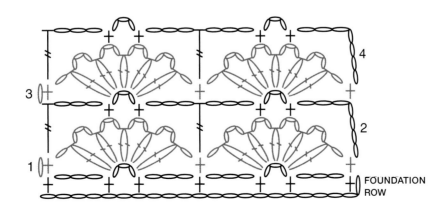

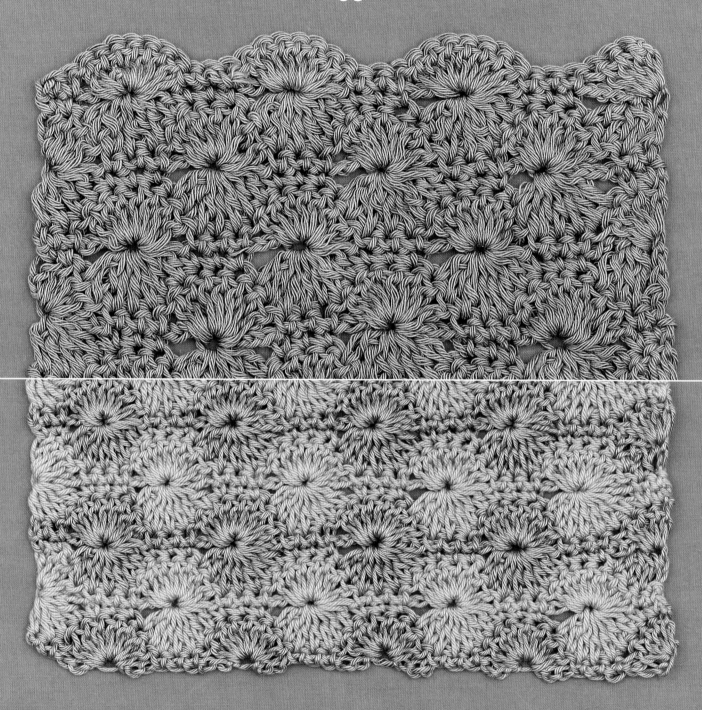

Chain a multiple of 10 sts plus 6; plus 1 for foundation row.

Cluster 7 stitches (CL7) [Yo, insert hook into next st, yo, draw up a lp, yo, draw through 2 lps on hook] 7 times, yo draw through all 8 lps on hook.

Cluster 4 stitches (CL4) [Yo, insert hook into next st, yo, draw up a lp, yo, draw through 2 lps on hook] 4 times, yo draw through all 5 lps on hook.

Cluster 3 stitches (CL3) [Yo, insert hook into next st, yo, draw up a lp, yo, draw through 2 lps on hook]

3 times, yo draw through all 4 lps on hook.

Foundation row (WS) Sc in 2nd ch from hook, sc in next ch, *skip next 3 ch, work 7 dc in next ch, skip next 3 ch, sc in next 3 ch; rep from * to last 4 ch, end skip next 3 ch, work 4 dc in last ch. Turn.

Row 1 Ch 1, sc in first 2 sts, *ch 3, CL7, ch 3, sc in next 3 sts; rep from * to last 4 sts, end ch 3, CL4, skip t-ch. Turn.

Row 2 Ch 3 (counts as 1 dc), work 3 dc in first st, *skip next ch-3 sp, sc in next 3 sc, skip next ch-3 sp,

work 7 dc in lp which closed next CL; rep from *, end skip last ch-3 sp, sc in last 2 sc, skip t-ch. Turn.

Row 3 Ch 3 (counts as 1 dc), skip first st, CL3, *ch 3, sc in next 3 sts, ch 3, CL7; rep from *, end ch 3, sc in last st, sc in top of t-ch. Turn.

Row 4 Ch 1, sc in first 2 sc, *skip next ch-3 sp, work 7 dc in lp which closed next CL, skip next ch-3 sp, sc in next 3 sc; rep from *, end skip last ch-3 sp, work 4 dc in top of t-ch. Turn.

Rep rows 1–4 for solid Catherine wheel.

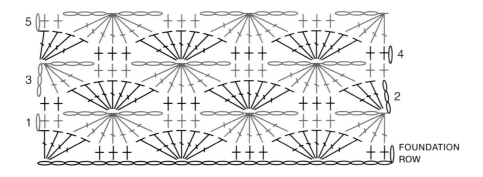

39 *Catherine Wheel—Bicolor*

With A, chain a multiple of 10 sts plus 6; plus 1 for foundation row.

Note When changing colors, draw new color through last 2 lps on hook to complete last st, then

turn. Cut and join colors as needed.

Foundation row Work as for solid Catherine wheel, changing to B at end of row. Rep rows 1–4 of Catherine wheel solid, working in stripe pat as

follows: 1 row A, *2 rows B, 2 rows A; rep from * throughout.

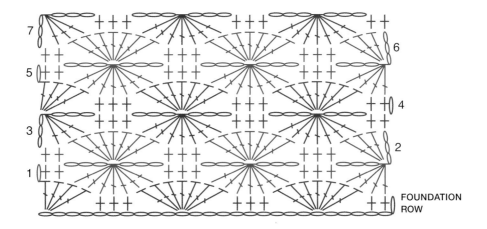

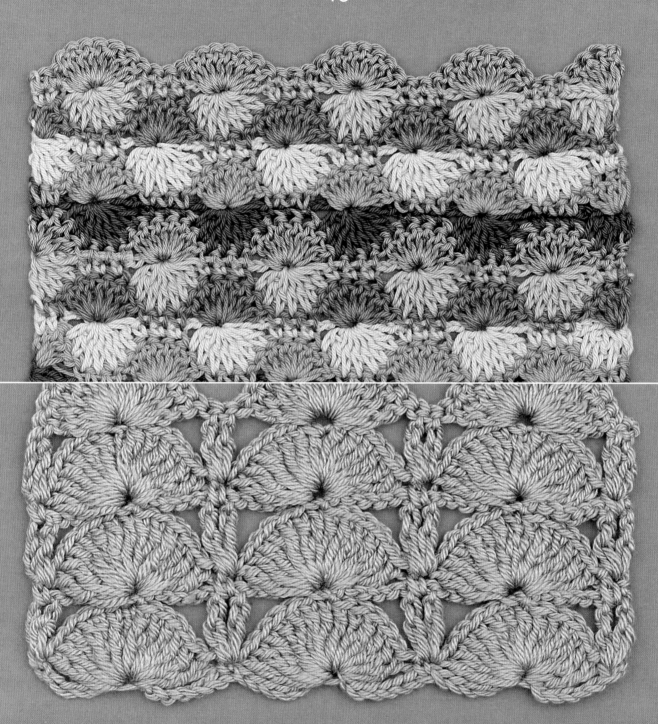

40 *Catherine Wheel—Multicolor*

With A, chain a multiple of 10 sts plus 6; plus 1 for foundation row.

Note When changing colors, draw new color through last 2 lps on hook to complete last st, then turn. Cut and join colors as needed.

Foundation row Work as for solid Catherine wheel, changing to B at end of row. Rep rows 1–4, working in stripe pat as follows: 1 row B, 1 row C, 1 row D, 1 row E, 1 row F and 1 row A.

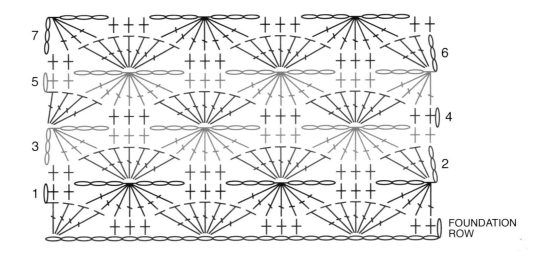

41 *Peacock Stitch*

Chain a multiple of 12 sts plus 1; plus 1 for foundation row.

Foundation row (RS) Sc in 2nd ch from hook, *skip next 5 ch, work 13 tr in next ch, skip next 5 ch, sc in next ch; rep from * across. Turn.

Row 1 Ch 4 (counts as 1 tr), tr in first sc, * ch 5, skip next 6 tr, sc in next tr, ch 5, skip next 6 tr, work 2 tr in next sc; rep from * across. Turn.

Row 2 Ch 1, *sc between next 2 tr, work 13 tr in next sc; rep from * across, end sc between last tr and ch-4 of row below. Turn.

Rep rows 1 and 2 for peacock st.

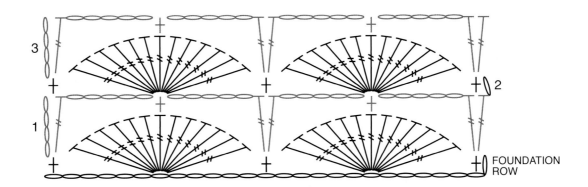

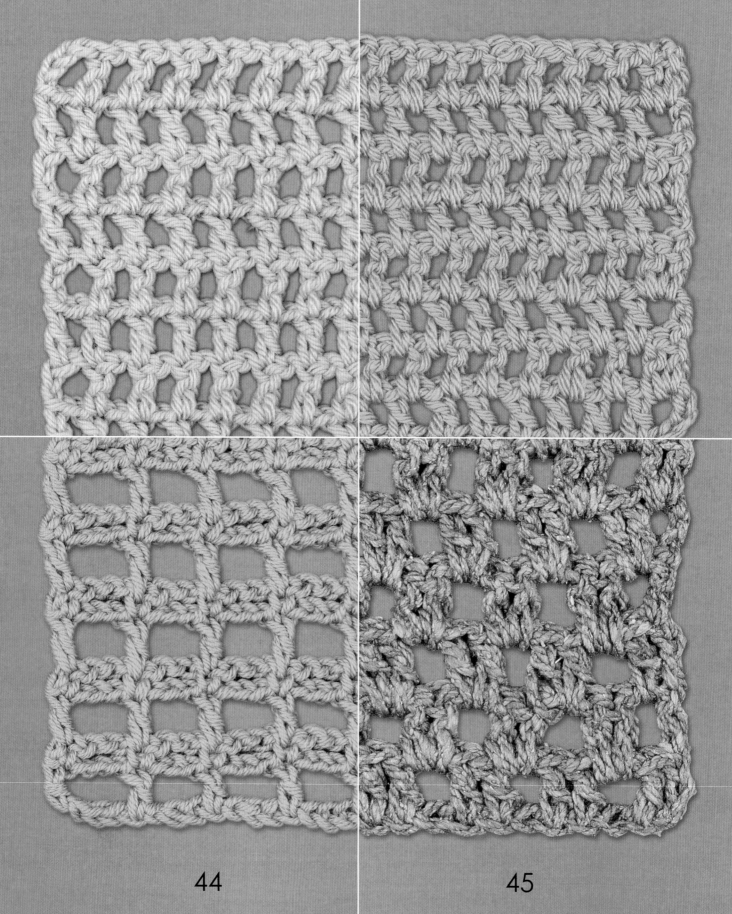

Variations on *Mesh*

42 *Mesh Stitch—Basic*

Chain a multiple of 2 sts; plus 4 for foundation row.

Foundation row (RS) Dc in 6th ch (counts as 1 dc, ch 1 and skip 1 ch) from hook, *ch 1, skip next ch, dc in next ch; rep from * across. Turn.

Row 1 Ch 4 (counts as 1 dc and ch 1), skip first dc, *dc in next dc, ch 1; rep from *, end dc in 3rd ch of t-ch of row below. Turn.

Rep row 1 for basic mesh st.

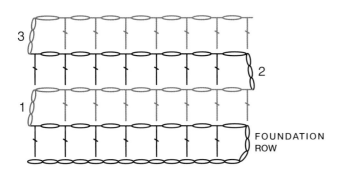

43 *Mesh—Offset*

Chain a multiple of 2 sts; plus 4 for foundation row.

Foundation row (RS) Dc in 6th ch (counts as 1 dc, ch 1 and skip 1 ch) from hook, *ch 1, skip next ch, dc in next ch; rep from * across. Turn.

Row 1 Ch 4 (counts as 1 dc and ch 1), *dc in next ch-1 sp, ch 1; rep from * across. Turn.

Rep row 1 for offset mesh st.

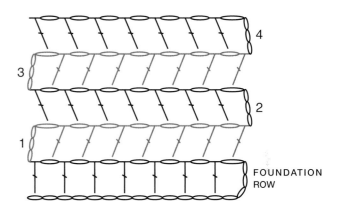

44 *Mesh—Double Bars*

Chain a multiple of 4 sts; plus 6 for foundation row.

Foundation row (RS) Dc in 10th ch (counts as 1 dc, ch 3 and skip 3 ch) from hook, *ch 3, skip next 3 ch, dc in next ch; rep from * across. Turn.

Row 1 Ch 1, sc in first dc, *ch 3, sc in next dc; rep from *, end ch 3, sc in 4th ch of t-ch. Turn.

Row 2 Ch 6 (counts as 1 dc and ch 3), skip first sc, dc in next sc, *ch 3, dc in next sc; rep from * across. Turn.

Rep rows 1 and 2 for double bars mesh st.

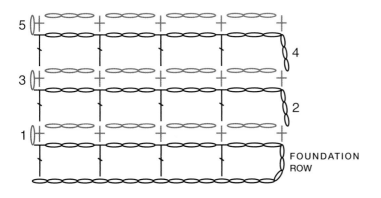

45 *Mesh—Double Check*

Chain a multiple of 3 sts, plus 1; plus 3 for foundation row.

Foundation row (RS) Dc in 4th ch (counts as 1 dc) from hook, *ch 1, skip next ch, dc in next 2 ch; rep from * across. Turn.

Row 1 Ch 4 (counts as 1 dc and ch 1), *work 2 dc in next ch-1 sp, ch 1; rep from *, end dc in 3rd ch of t-ch. Turn.

Row 2 Ch 3 (counts as 1 dc), dc in first ch-1 sp, *ch 1, work 2 dc in next ch-1sp; rep from *, end ch 1, dc in last ch-1 sp, dc in 3rd ch of t-ch. Turn.

Rep rows 1 and 2 for double check mesh.

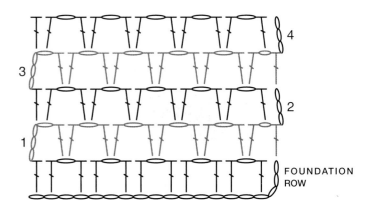

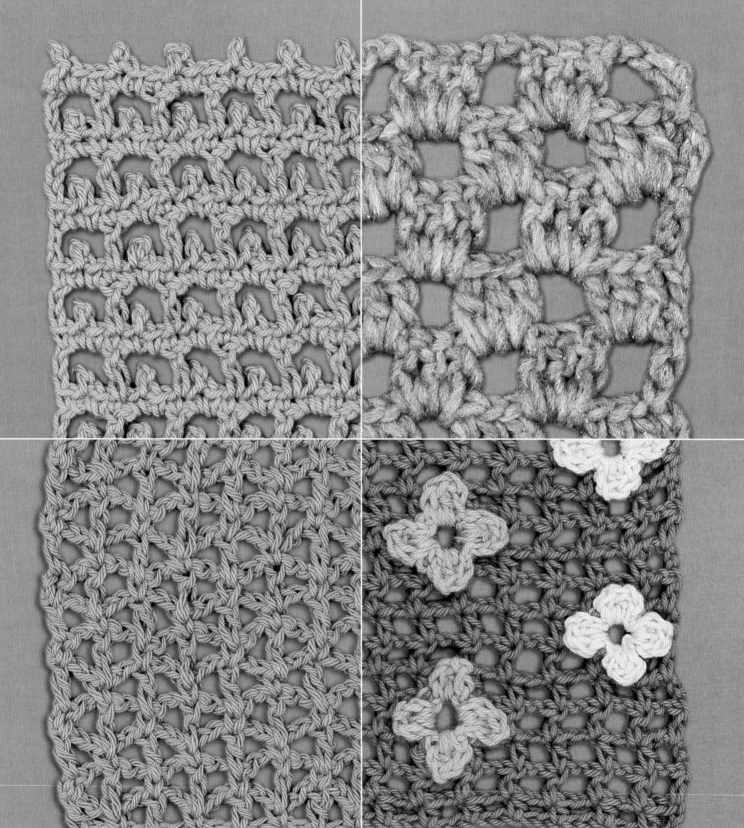

46 *Picot*

Chain a multiple of 3 sts, plus 1; plus 1 for foundation row

Foundation row (RS) Sc in 2nd and 3rd ch from hook, *ch 4, sl st in 4th ch from hook (picot made), sc in next 3 ch; rep from *, end ch 4, sl st in 4th ch from hook, sc in last 2 ch. Turn.

Row 1 Ch 5 (counts as 1 dc and ch 2), skip first 2 sc, dc in next sc, *ch 2, skip next 2 sc, dc in next sc; rep from * across. Turn.

Row 2 Ch 1, sc in first dc, *work (sc, picot, sc) in next ch-2 sp, sc in next dc; rep from *, end work (sc, picot, sc) in last ch-2 sp, sc in 3rd ch of t-ch of row below. Turn.

Rep rows 1 and 2 for picot.

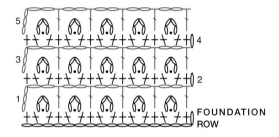

48 *Archways*

Chain a multiple of 4 sts, plus 3; plus 1 for foundation row.

Foundation row (RS) Sc in 2nd ch from hook, ch 2, skip next ch, dc in next ch, *ch 2, skip next ch, sc in next ch, ch 2, skip next ch, dc in next ch; rep from * across. Turn.

Row 1 Ch 1, sc in first dc, ch 2, dc in next sc, *ch 2, sc in next dc, ch 2, dc in next sc; rep from * across. Turn.

Rep row 1 for archways.

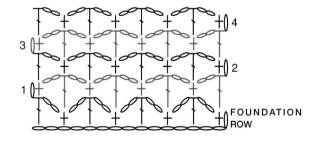

47 *Mesh—Triple Check*

Chain a multiple of 5 sts, plus 3; plus 3 for foundation row.

Foundation row (RS) Dc in 4th ch (counts as 1 dc) from hook, dc in next 2 ch, *ch 2, skip next 2 ch, dc in next 3 ch; rep from * across. Turn.

Row 1 Ch 5 (counts as 1 dc and ch 2), *work 3 dc in next ch-2 sp, ch 2; rep from *, end dc in 3rd ch of t-ch of row below. Turn.

Row 2 Ch 3 (counts as 1 dc), *work 3 dc in next ch-2 sp, ch 2; rep from *, end work 3 dc in last ch-2 sp. Turn.

Rep rows 1 and 2 for triple check mesh.

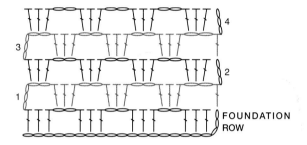

49 *Tiny Flowers*

Background mesh

With background yarn, chain a multiple of 3 sts; plus 4 for foundation row.

Foundation row (RS) Hdc in the 7th ch (counts as 1 hdc, ch 2 and skip 2 ch) from hook, *ch 2, skip next 2 ch, hdc in next ch; rep from * across. Turn.

Row 1 Ch 4 (counts as 1 hdc and ch 2), skip first hdc, *hdc in next hdc, ch 2; rep from *, end hdc in 2nd ch of t-ch of row below. Turn.

Rep row 1 for mesh background.

Tiny flowers

With RS facing, join flower yarn with a sl st in top bar of a mesh square leaving a 6"/15cm-long tail.

First petal Ch 3 (counts as 1 dc), work (2 dc, sl st) over same bar. Turn work counterclockwise to bar at left. **Second petal** Work (sl st, ch 3, 2 dc, sl st) over same bar. Turn work counterclockwise to bar at left. **Third petal** Work as for second petal. Turn work counterclockwise to bar at left. **Fourth petal** Work as for second petal. Join round with a sl st in first sl st. Fasten off. On WS, use yarn tail to close center of flower. Place flowers over mesh background where desired.

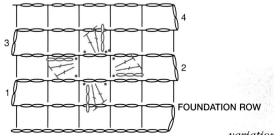

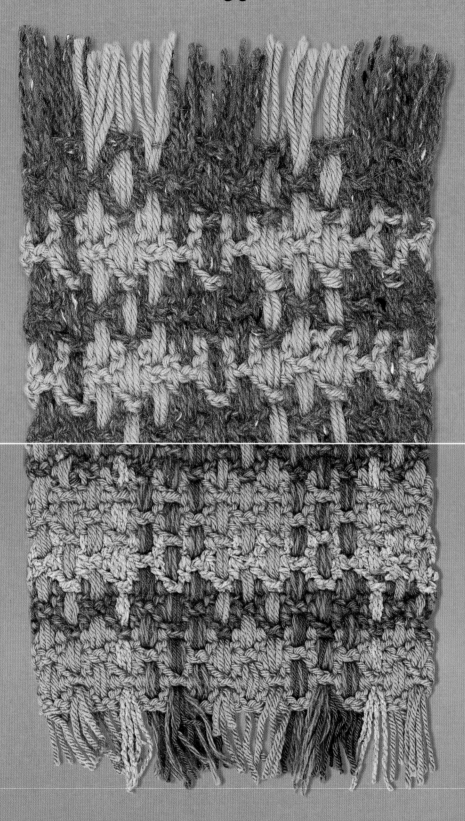

51

With A, chain a multiple of 2 sts; plus 4 for foundation row.

Note When changing colors, draw new color through last 2 lps on hook to complete last st, then turn. Cut and join colors as needed.

Background mesh

Foundation row (RS) Work as for basic mesh st.

Row 1 Work as for basic mesh st, changing to B at end of row. Rep row 1 of basic mesh st, working in stripe pat as follows: *3 rows B and 3 rows A; rep from *across.

Weaving

Cut yarn strands 8"/20.5cm longer than desired finished length to allow 4"/10.25cm fringe at both ends. Working color sequence from left to right, weave rows from bottom edge to top edge as follows:

Row 1 With 4 strands of A in tapestry needle, weave strands over and under the ch-sps.

Row 2 With 4 strands of A in tapestry needle, weave strands under and over the ch-sps.

Rows 3 and 4 Rep rows 1 and 2 using B. Rep rows 1–4 for weaving pat. Trim fringe at each end to desired length.

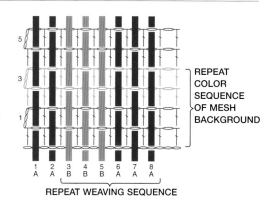

REPEAT COLOR SEQUENCE OF MESH BACKGROUND

| 1 | 2 | 3 | 4 | 5 | 6 | 7 | 8 |
| A | A | B | B | B | A | A | A |

REPEAT WEAVING SEQUENCE

With A, chain a multiple of 2 sts; plus 4 for foundation row.

Note When changing colors, draw new color through last 2 lps on hook to complete last st, then turn. Cut and join colors as needed.

Background mesh

Foundation row (RS) Work as for basic mesh st. Rep row 1 of basic mesh st for 2 rows using A, changing to B at end of second row. Continue to rep row 1, working in stripe pat as follows: *2 rows B, 2 rows C and 3 rows A; rep from * across.

Weaving

Cut yarn strands 8"/20.5cm longer than desired finished length to allow for 4"/10.25cm fringe at both ends. Work color sequence from left to right, weaving rows from bottom edge to top edge as follows:

Row 1 With 4 strands of A in tapestry needle, weave strands over and under the ch-sps.

Row 2 With 4 strands of A in tapestry needle, weave strands under and over the ch-sps.

Row 3 Rep row 1 using B.

Row 4 Rep row 2 using C.

Rows 5 and 6 Rep rows 1 and 2 using C.

Rows 7 and 8 Rep rows 1 and 2 using A.

Row 9 Rep row 1 using A.

Row 10 Rep row 2 using C.

Rows 11 and 12 Rep rows 1 and 2 using C.

Row 13 Rep row 1 using B.

Beg with row 2 (to keep continuity of weaving), continue in same color sequence as follows: 2 rows A, 1 row B, 3 rows C, 3 rows A, 3 rows C and 1 row B; rep from * across. Trim fringe at each end to desired length.

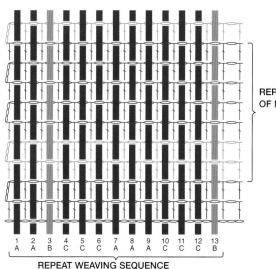

REPEAT COLOR SEQUENCE OF MESH BACKGROUND

| 1 | 2 | 3 | 4 | 5 | 6 | 7 | 8 | 9 | 10 | 11 | 12 | 13 |
| A | A | B | C | C | C | A | A | A | C | C | C | B |

REPEAT WEAVING SEQUENCE

Filets

Reading Filet Charts

Open square Each open square equals 2 dc (the two vertical lines on each side of the open square) and a ch-2 sp (the horizontal line that connects the two vertical lines).

Block square over an open square Each single block square over an open square equals 4 dc made up of 2 dc (the two vertical lines on each side of the block square) and 2 dc worked into a ch-2 sp (the horizontal line that connects the two vertical lines). When there are two or more block squares side by side, work 1 dc in each dc and 2 dc in each ch-2 sp.

Block square over a block square Each single block square over a block square equals 4 dc made up of 2 dc (the two vertical lines on each side of the block square) and 2 dc (1 dc in each of the 2 dc of the row below). When there are two or more block squares side by side, work 1 dc in each dc across to next ch-2 sp.

Lacets and bars Both lacets and bars are worked over 2 squares of the chart grid and are used in conjunction with each other.

Lacet One lacet equals ch 3, skip 2 sts (or ch), sc in next st (or ch), ch 3, skip 2 sts (or ch), dc in next dc.

Bar One bar equals ch 5, skip next lacet (or next ch-2 sp), dc in next dc. To reestablish grid pattern after a bar, work ch 2, dc in 3rd ch of next ch-5, ch 2, dc in next dc.

STITCH KEY

Bar =

Lacet =

CHART KEY

☐ = Space

▣ = Block

☐ = Bar

◡ = Lacet

How to Begin and End Rows

When there is:

A space over a space at the *beginning* **of the row** Ch 5 (counts as 1 dc and ch 2), skip first st and first ch-2 sp, dc in next dc, then continue across the row following chart.

A space over a space at the *end* **of the row** Dc in next to last dc, ch 2, skip last ch-2 sp, dc in 3rd ch of ch-5 t-ch.

A space over a block at the *beginning* **of the row** Ch 5 (counts as 1 dc and ch 2), skip first 3 sts, dc in next dc, then continue across the row following chart.

A space over a block at the *end* **the row** Dc in 3rd dc from the end of the row, ch 2, skip next 2 dc, dc in top of ch-3 t-ch.

A block over a space at the *beginning* **of the row** Ch 3 (counts as 1 dc), skip first st, dc in next ch-2 sp, dc in next dc, then continue across the row following chart.

A block over a space at the *end* **of the row** Dc in last dc, then dc in next 3 ch of ch-5 t-ch.

A block over a block at the *beginning* **of the row** Ch 3 (counts as 1 dc), skip first st, dc in next 3 dc, then continue across the row following chart.

A block over a block at the *end* **of the row** Dc in last 3 dc, then dc in top of ch-3 t-ch.

Decreasing spaces

To decrease one or more spaces at the *end* **of the row** Work to end of chart row, then turn to prepare for next row, leaving remaining sts unworked.

To decrease one or more spaces at the *beginning* **of the row** Sl st in top of last dc worked at end of row below, then sl st in each ch and dc until you have decreased the desired number of spaces.

Decreasing blocks

To decrease one or more blocks at the *end* **of the row** Work to end of chart row, then turn to prepare for next row, leaving remaining sts unworked.

To decrease one or more blocks at the *beginning* **of the row** Sl st in top of last dc worked at end of row below, then sl st in each dc until you have decreased the desired number of blocks.

Increasing spaces

To increase one space at the *end* **of the row** Ch 2, then work a dtr in same place as last dc worked. The length of the dtr is equal to 1 dc and ch 2.

To increase more than one space at the *end* **of the row** Ch 2, then work a dtr in same place as last dc worked (first inc space made), *ch 2, dtr in the middle of last dtr made; rep from * for each additional space.

To increase one space at the *beginning* **of the row** Ch 7 (counts as skip 2 ch, 1 dc and ch 2), then dc in first dc of row, then continue across the row following chart.

To increase two spaces at the *beginning* **of the row** Ch 10 (counts as skip 2 ch, first dc and ch 2 for first space, and skip 2 ch for second space). Then work dc in 8th ch from hook, ch 2, skip next 2 ch, dc in first dc of row, then continue across the row following chart.

To increase three or more spaces at the *beginning* **of the row** Ch 7 for first space, then ch 3 for each additional space, up to but not including the space before first dc of row, ch 2 for this space. Then work dc in 8th ch from hook, *ch 2, skip next 2 ch, dc in next ch; rep from * to last 2 ch, end skip 2 ch, dc in first dc of row, then continue across the row following chart.

Increasing blocks

To increase one or more blocks at the *end* **of the row** Work a tr in same place as last dc worked, then [work a tr in bottom section of last tr made] twice (one block inc made), [work a tr in bottom section of last tr made] 3 times for each additional block to be increased.

To increase one block at the *beginning* **of the row** Ch 5, skip first 3 ch (counts as 1 dc), then dc in next 2 ch and first dc of row, then continue across the row following chart.

To increase more than one block at *beginning* **of the row** Ch 5 (for first block), then ch 3 for each additional block, then skip first 3 ch (counts as 1 dc), then dc in next and each remaining ch to first dc of row, dc in first dc, then continue across the row following chart.

SPRINGDALE PUBLIC LIBRARY
405 S. Pleasant
Springdale, AR 72764

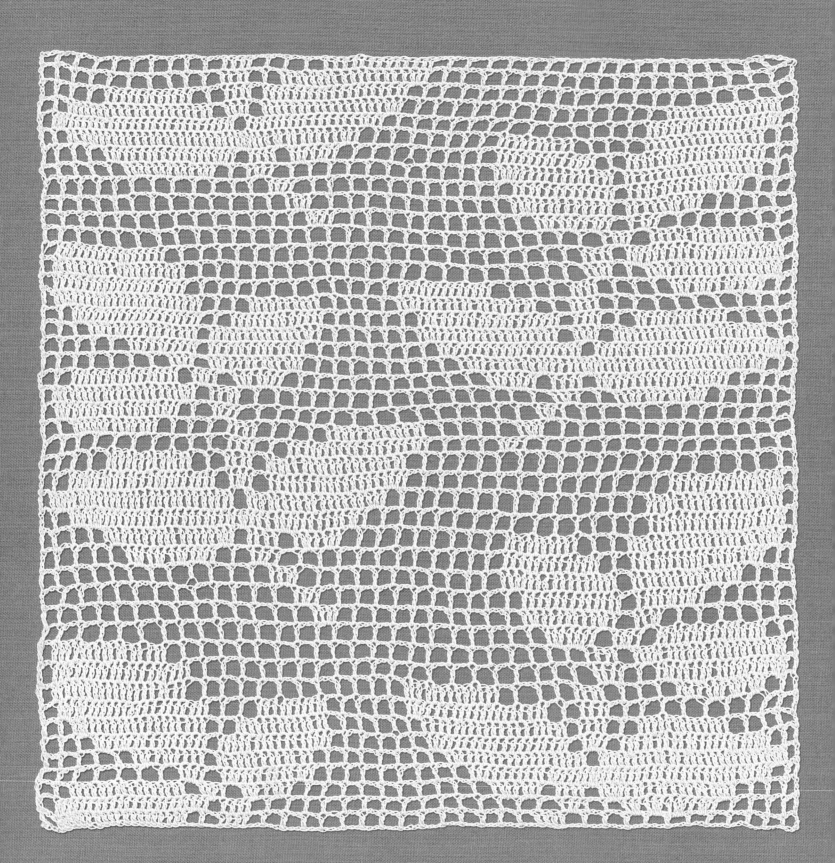

52

(38 squares by 46 rows)

Chain 119.

Row 1 (RS) Dc in 8th ch from hook, [ch 2, skip next 2 ch, dc in next ch] 11 times, dc in next 3 ch, [ch 2, skip next 2 ch, dc in next ch] 15 times, dc in next 3 ch, [ch 2, skip next 2 ch, dc in next ch] twice, dc in next 18 ch, ch 2, skip next 2 ch, dc in last ch. Turn. Beg with row 2, continue to work chart to row 46.

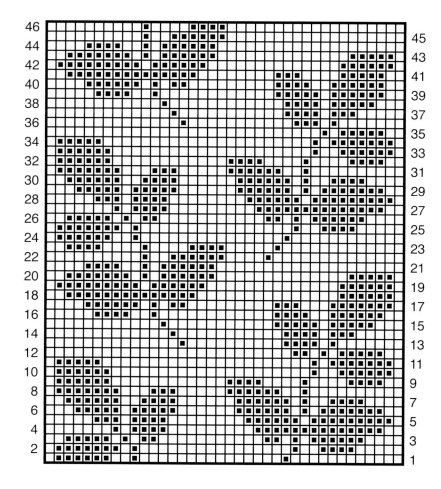

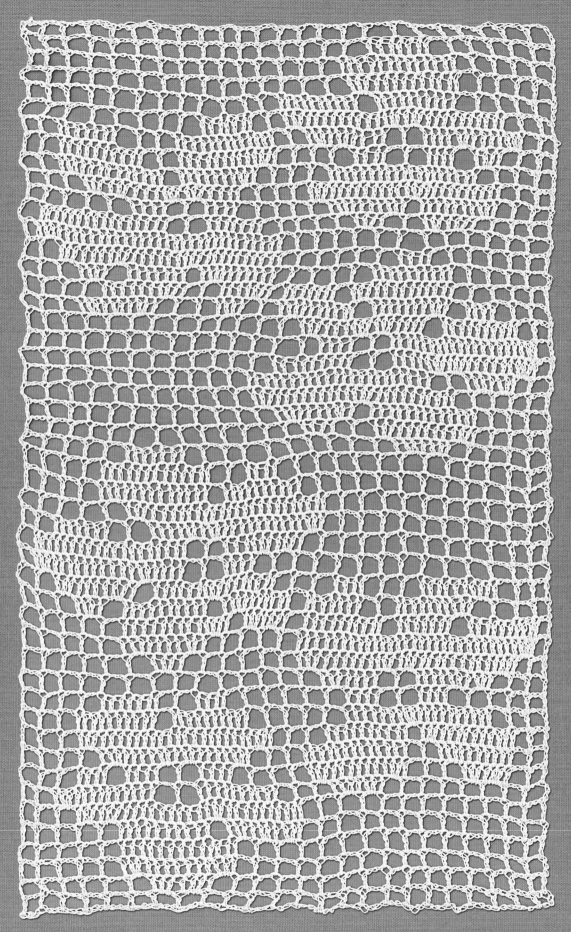

53

(24 squares by 49 rows)

Chain 77.

Row 1 (RS) Dc in 8th ch from hook, [ch 2, skip next 2 ch, dc in next ch] 23 times. Turn. Beg with row 2, continue to work chart to row 49.

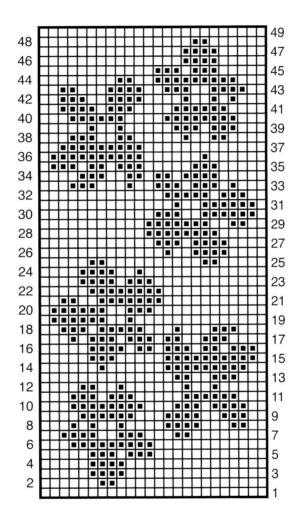

54

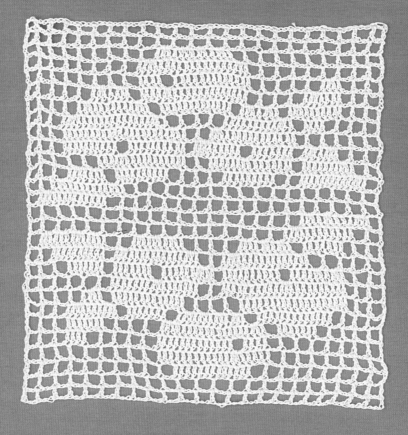

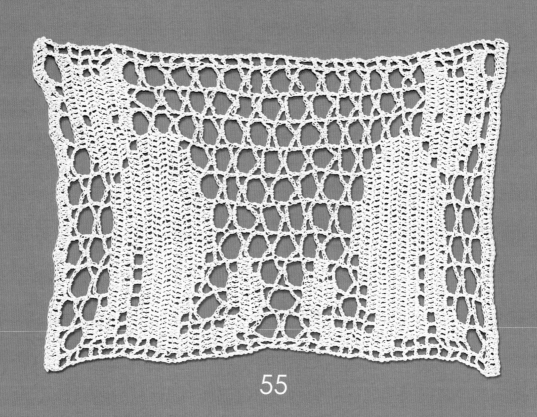

55

54 *Snowberry Circle*

(23 squares by 28 rows)

Chain 74.

Row 1 (RS) Dc in 8th ch from hook,

[ch 2, skip next 2 ch, dc in next ch] 22 times.

Turn. Beg with row 2, continue to work chart to row 28.

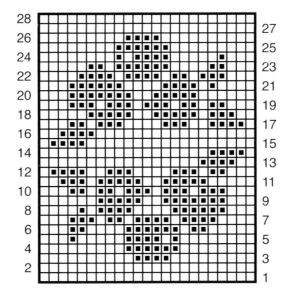

55 *Cats*

(22 squares by 41 rows)

Chain 69.

Note This chart is worked sideways.

Row 1 (RS) Skip first 3 ch (counts as 1 dc), dc in next ch and in each ch across—66 dc. Turn. Beg with row 2, continue to work chart to row 41.

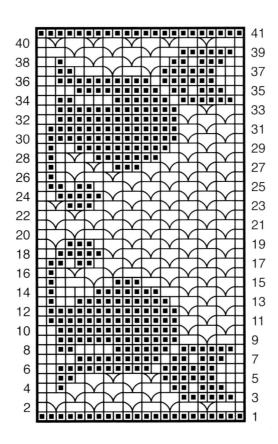

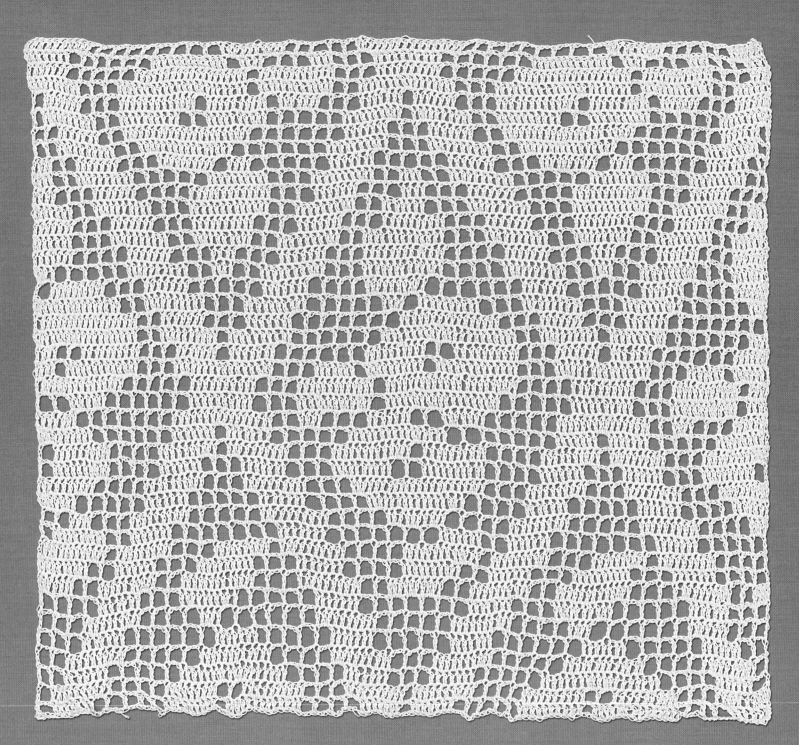

56

(44 squares by 42 rows)

Chain 135.

Row 1 (RS) Dc in 4th ch from hook and in next 5 ch, [ch 2, skip next 2 ch, dc in next ch] 4 times, dc in next 12 ch, ch 2, skip next 2 ch, dc in next 10 ch, [ch 2, skip next 2 ch, dc in next ch] 5 times, dc in next 6 ch, ch 2, skip next 2 ch, dc in next 7 ch, [ch 2, skip next 2 ch, dc in next ch] 4 times, dc in next 12 ch, ch 2, skip next 2 ch, dc in next 10 ch, [ch 2, skip next 2 ch, dc in next ch] 5 times, dc in next 6 ch, ch 2, skip next 2 ch, dc in last ch. Turn. Beg with row 2, continue to work chart to row 42.

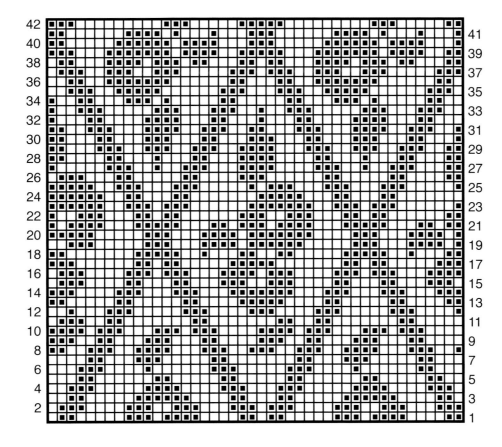

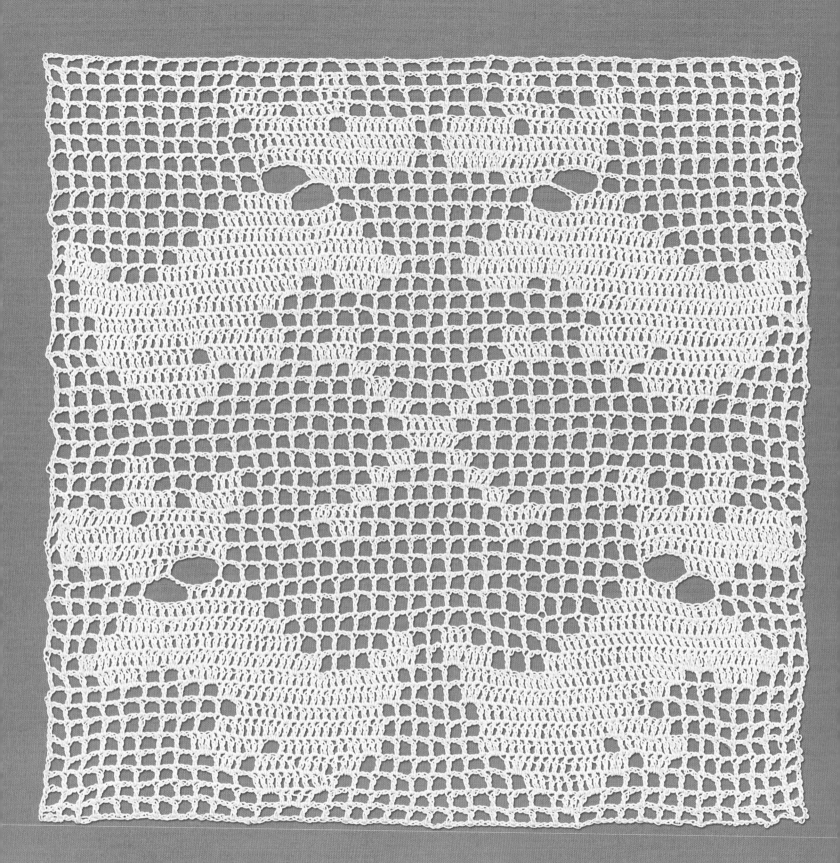

57

(38 squares by 44 rows)

Chain 119.

Row 1 (RS) Dc in 8th ch from hook, [ch 2, skip next

2 ch, dc in next ch] 37 times. Turn. Beg with row 2,

continue to work chart to row 44.

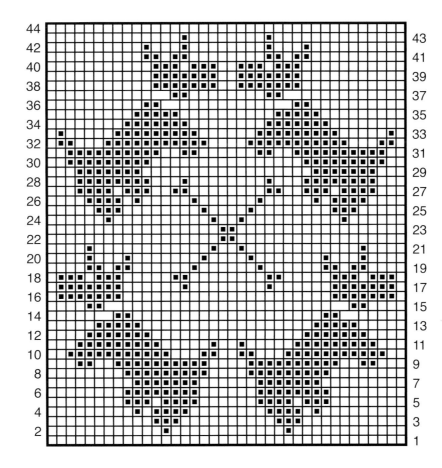

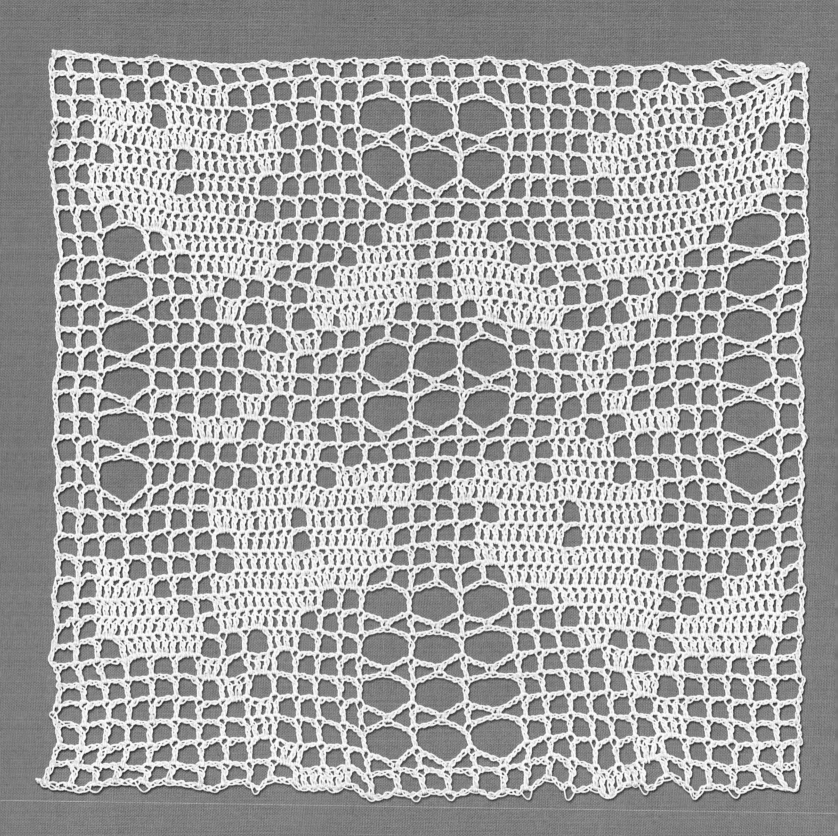

58

(30 squares by 32 rows)

Chain 95.

Row 1 (RS) Dc in 8th ch from hook, [ch 2, skip next 2 ch, dc in next ch] 8 times, dc in next 6 ch, [ch 2, skip next 2 ch, dc in next ch] 8 times, dc in next 6 ch, [ch 2, skip next 2 ch, dc in next ch] 9 times. Turn. Beg with row 2, continue to work chart to row 32.

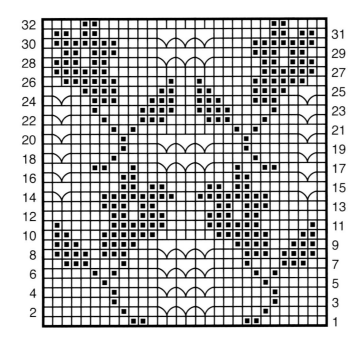

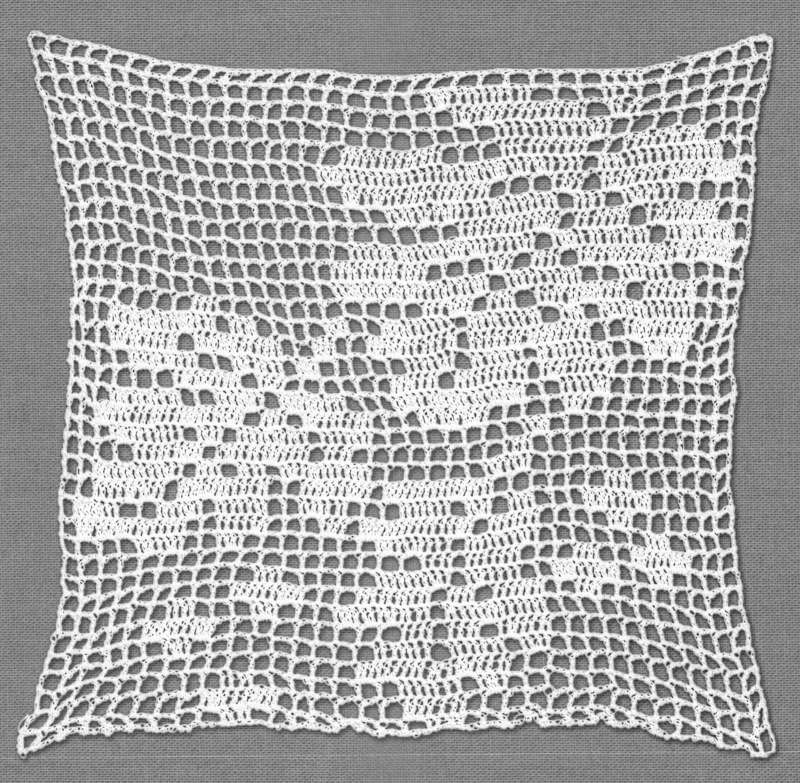

59

59 *Hawthorn*

(34 squares by 36 rows)

Chain 107.

Row 1 (RS) Dc in 8th ch from hook, [ch 2, skip next 2 ch, dc in next ch] 33 times. Turn. Beg with row 2, continue to work chart to row 36.

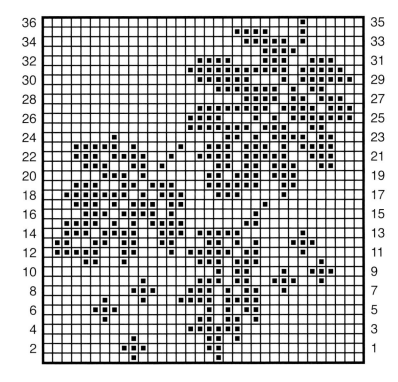

60

(71 squares by 71 rows)

Chain 38.

Row 1 (RS) Dc in 8th ch from hook, [ch 2, skip next 2 ch, dc in next ch] 10 times. Turn.

Beg with row 2, continue to work chart to row 71.

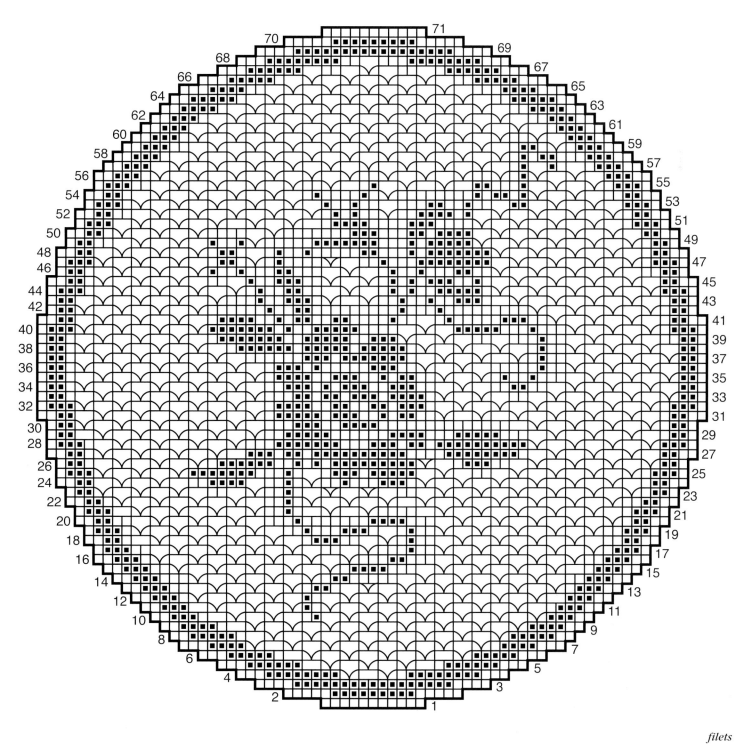

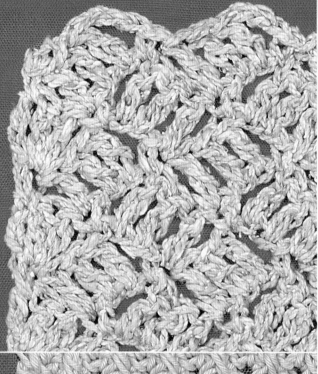

61

62

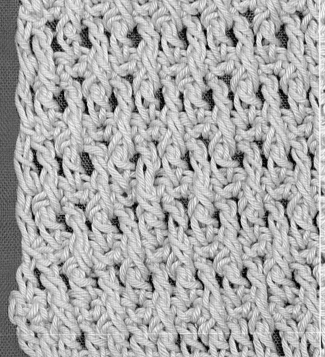

63

64

Textures

61 *Crosshatch*

Chain a multiple of 7 sts, plus 4; plus 3 for foundation row.

Foundation row (RS) Skip first 2 ch (counts as 1 dc), work 2 dc in next ch, *skip next 3 ch, sc in next ch, ch 3, dc in next 3 ch; rep from *, end skip next 3 ch, sc in last ch. Turn.

Row 1 Ch 3 (counts as 1 dc), work 2 dc in first sc, *skip next 3 dc, sc in first of next 3 ch, ch 3, dc in next 2 ch, dc in next sc; rep from *, end skip next 2 dc, sc in top of t-ch. Turn.

Rep row 1 for crosshatch.

63 *Sand Pattern*

Chain a multiple of 2 sts, plus 1; plus 2 for foundation row.

Front raised double crochet (FRDC) Yo, working from front to back to front, insert hook around post of stitch of 2 rows below, yo and draw up a lp, [yo and draw through 2 lps on hook] twice.

Note Do not work the sc directly behind the FRDC.

Foundation row (RS) Skip first 3 ch (counts as 1 dc), dc in next ch and each ch across. Turn.

Row 1 Ch 1 (counts as 1 sc), skip first st, sc in each st across, end sc in top of t-ch. Turn.

Row 2 Ch 3 (counts as 1 dc), skip first st, *FRDC around dc of 2 rows below, dc in next st; rep from * across. Turn.

Row 3 Rep row 1.

Row 4 Ch 3 (counts as 1 dc), skip first st, *dc in next st, FRDC around dc of 2 rows below; rep from *, end dc in last 2 sts. Turn.

Rep rows 1–4 for sand pat.

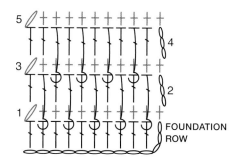

62 *Crosshatch—Tricolor*

With A, chain a multiple of 7 sts plus 4; plus 3 for foundation row.

Note When changing colors, draw new color through last 2 lps on hook to complete last st, then turn. Cut and join colors as needed.

Foundation row (RS) Work as for plain crosshatch, changing to B at end of row. Rep row 1 of crosshatch, working in stripe pat as follows: 1 row B, 1 row C and 1 row A.

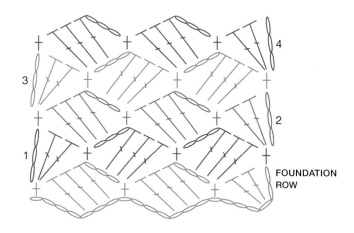

64 *Double Crochet Rib*

Chain a multiple of 2 sts; plus 2 for foundation row.

Front raised double crochet (FRDC) Yo, working from front to back to front, insert hook around post of stitch of row below, yo and draw up a lp, [yo and draw through 2 lps on hook] twice.

Back raised double crochet (BRDC) Yo, working from back to front to back, insert hook around post of stitch of row below, yo and draw up a lp, [yo and draw through 2 lps on hook] twice.

Foundation row (WS) Skip first 3 ch (counts as 1 dc), dc in next ch and each ch across. Turn.

Row 1 Ch 2 (counts as 1 dc), skip first st, *FRDC around post of next st, BRDC around post of next st; rep from *, end dc in top of t-ch. Turn.

Rep row 1 for dc rib.

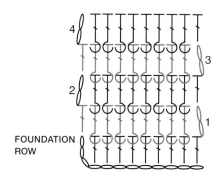

65

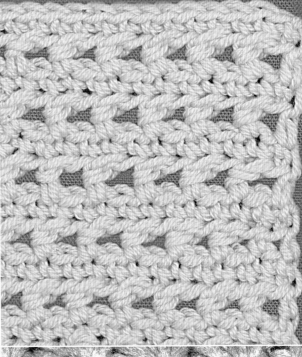

66

67

68

65 *Sand Pattern—Tricolor*

With A, chain a multiple of 2 sts, plus 1; plus 2 for foundation row.

Note When changing colors, draw new color through last 2 lps on hook to complete last st, then turn. Cut and join colors as needed.

Foundation row (RS) Work as for plain sand pat.

Row 1 Work as for sand pat, changing to B at end of row 1. Beg with row 2, continue to work as for sand pat, working in stripe pat as follows: 2 rows B, 2 rows C and 2 rows A.

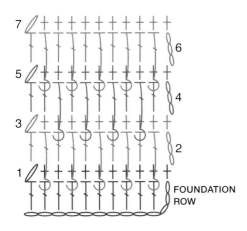

66 *Peephole Stitch*

Chain a multiple of 2 sts; plus 1 for foundation row.

Foundation row (WS) Hdc in 2nd ch from hook, *skip next ch, hdc in next ch, yo, insert hook to the right of hdc just made, yo and draw up a lp, yo and draw through 3 lps on hook; rep from *, end, hdc in last ch. Ch 1, turn.

Row 1 Working through front lps only, sc in each st across. Ch 1, turn.

Row 2 Hdc in first st, *skip next st, hdc in next st, yo, insert hook to the right of hdc just made, yo and draw through a lp, yo and draw through all 3 lps on hook; rep from *, end hdc in last st. Ch 1, turn.

Rep rows 1 and 2 for peephole st.

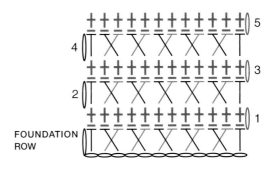

67 *Open Ridge*

Chain a multiple of 2 sts; plus 1 for foundation row.

Foundation row (RS) Sc in 2nd ch from hook and in each ch across. Ch 2, turn.

Row 1 Hdc in first st, *skip next st, hdc in next st, hdc in skipped st; rep from *, end hdc in last st. Ch 1, turn.

Row 2 Working through back lps only, sc in each st across. Ch 2, turn.

Rep rows 1 and 2 for open ridge.

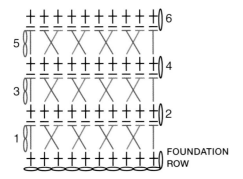

68 *Easy Peasy*

Chain a multiple of 2 sts, plus 1; plus 2 for foundation row.

Foundation row (RS) Work 2 sc in 3rd ch from hook, *skip next ch, work 2 sc in next ch; rep from *, end skip next ch, sc in last ch. Turn.

Row 1 Ch 2, *skip next st, work 2 sc in next st; rep from *, end skip last st, sc in 2nd ch of t-ch. Turn.

Rep row 1 for easy peasy.

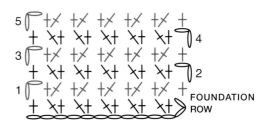

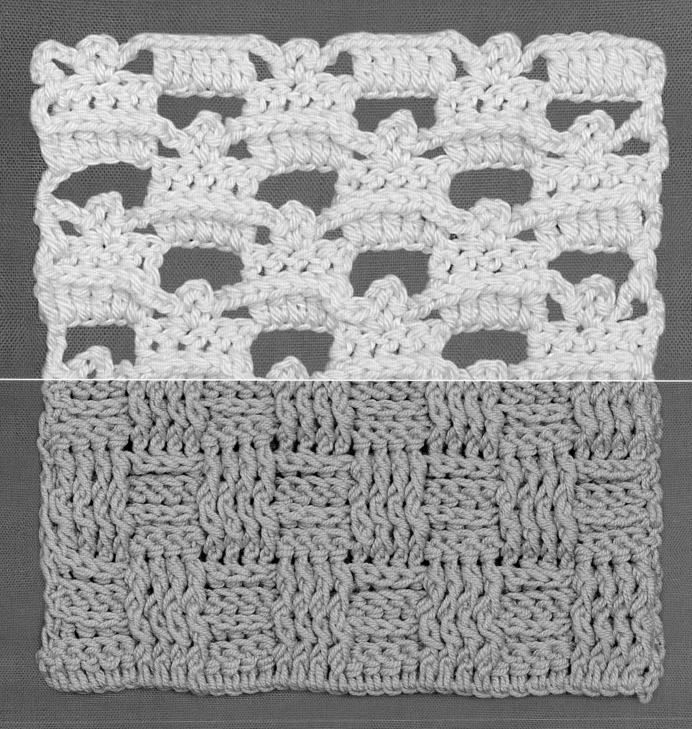

69

70

Chain a multiple of 10 sts, plus 3; plus 2 for foundation row.

Front raised double crochet (FRDC) Yo, working from front to back to front, insert hook around post of stitch of row below, yo and draw up a lp, [yo and draw through 2 lps on hook] twice.

Foundation row (RS) Skip first 3 ch (counts as 1 dc), *dc in next 5 ch, ch 3, skip next 2 ch, work (sc, ch 4, sc) in next ch, ch 3, skip next 2 ch; rep from *, end dc in last ch. Turn.

Row 1 Ch 8 (counts as 1 dc and ch 5), skip first st and next 3 ch-sps, *FRDC around each of next 5 dc sts, ch 5, skip next 3 ch-sps; rep from *, end FRDC around each of last 5 sts, dc in top of t-ch. Turn.

Row 2 Ch 6, skip first 3 sts, *work (sc, ch 4, sc) in next st, ch 3, skip next 2 sts, dc in each of next 5 ch**, ch 3, skip next 2 sts; rep from *, end last rep at **, then dc in next ch of t-ch. Turn.

Row 3 Ch 3 (counts as 1 dc), skip first st, *FRDC around each of next 5 sts, ch 5**, skip next 3 ch-sps; rep from *, end last rep at **, then skip next 2 ch-sps, dc in 3rd ch of ch-6t-ch. Turn.

Row 4 Ch 3 (counts as 1 dc), skip first st, *dc in each of next 5 ch, ch 3, skip next 2 sts, work (sc, ch 4, sc) in next st, ch 3, skip next 2 sts; rep from *, end dc in top of t-ch. Turn.

Rep rows 1–4 for picot archways.

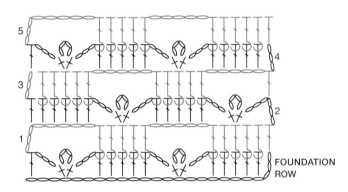

Chain a multiple of 8 sts, plus 2; plus 2 for foundation row.

Front raised double crochet (FRDC) Yo, working from front to back to front, insert hook around post of stitch of row below, yo and draw up a lp, [yo and draw through 2 lps on hook] twice.

Back raised double crochet (BRDC) Yo, working from back to front to back, insert hook around post of stitch of row below, yo and draw up a lp, [yo and draw through 2 lps on hook] twice.

Foundation row (WS) Skip first 3 ch (counts as 1 dc), dc in next ch and in each ch across. Turn.

Row 1 Ch 2 (counts as 1 dc), skip first st, *FRDC around each of next 4 sts, BRDC around each of next 4 sts; rep from *, end dc in top of -tch. Turn.

Rows 2–4 Rep row 1.

Row 5 Ch 2 (counts as 1 dc), skip first st, *BRDC around each of next 4 sts, FRDC around each of next 4 sts; rep from *, end dc in top of t-ch. Turn.

Rows 6–8 Rep row 5.

Rep rows 1–8 for basketweave.

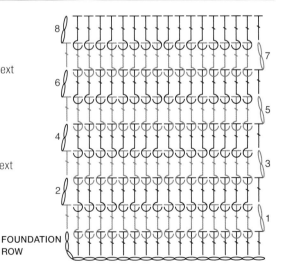

71

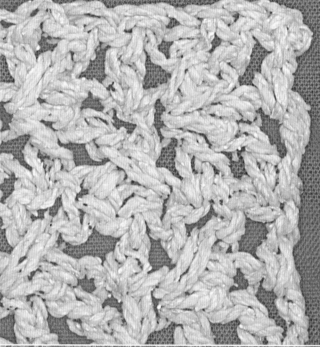

72

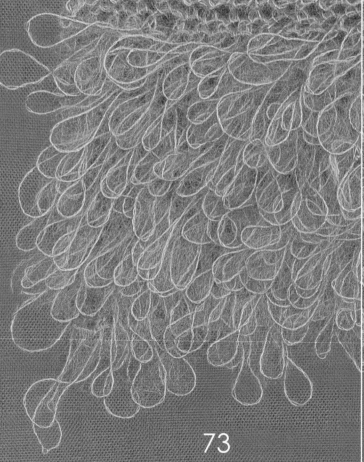

73

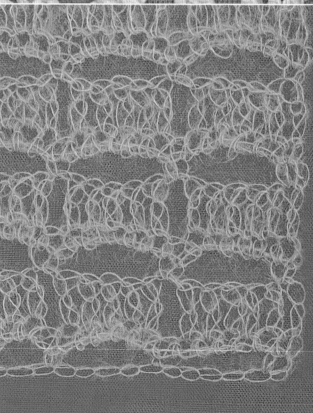

74

71 *Holey Zigzag*

Chain a multiple of 10 sts; plus 2 for foundation row.

Foundations row (RS) Skip first 2 ch (counts as 1 dc), dc in next 4 ch, *skip next 2 ch, dc in next 4 ch, ch 2, dc in next 4 ch; rep from *, end skip next 2 ch, dc in next 3 ch, work 2 dc in last ch. Turn.

Row 1 Ch 3 (counts as 1 dc), dc in first st, dc in next 3 sts, *skip next 2 sts, dc in next 3 sts, work (dc, ch 2, dc) in next ch-2 sp, dc in next 3 sts; rep from *, end skip next 2 sts, dc in next 3 sts, work 2 dc in top of t-ch. Turn.
Rep row 1 for holey zigzag.

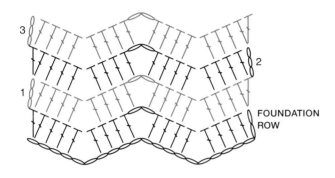

73 *Loopy Stitch*

Chain any number; plus 1 for foundation row.

Foundation row (RS) Sc in 2nd ch from hook and in each ch across. Ch 1, turn.

Row 1 (WS) *Yo hook, insert hook into next st, wrap yarn over left index finger, hook yarn coming from the ball and draw through st forming a 1"/2.5cm loop, drop loop from finger, then yo and draw through 3 lps on hook; rep from * across. Ch 1, turn.

Row 2 Sc in each st across. Ch 1, turn.
Rep rows 1 and 2 for loopy st.

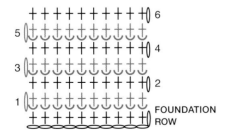

72 *Crisscross*

Chain a multiple of 4 sts, plus 1; plus 2 for foundation row.

Cross 2 double crochet (CR2dc) Skip 2 sts, dc in next st, ch 1, dc in first of 2 sts skipped working over last dc made.

Foundation row (RS) Skip first 3 ch (counts as 1 dc), *work CR2dc over next 3 ch, dc in next ch; rep from * across; end dc in last ch. Turn.

Row 1 Ch 3 (counts as 1 dc), dc in first st, skip next dc, *dc in next ch, work CR2dc over next 3 dc; rep from *, end dc in last ch, skip next dc, work 2 dc in top of t-ch. Turn.

Row 2 Ch 3 (counts as 1 dc), skip first st, *work CR2dc over next 3 dc, dc in next ch; rep from *, end work CR2dc over last 3 dc, dc in top of t-ch. Turn.
Rep rows 1 and 2 for crisscross.

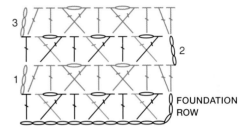

74 *Five Double Crochet Blocks*

Chain a multiple of 5 sts, plus 1; plus 1 for foundation row.

Foundation row (RS) Sc in 2nd ch from hook, *ch 5, skip next 4 ch, sc in next ch; rep from * across. Turn.

Row 1 Ch 1, sc in first sc, *work 5 sc in next ch-5 lp, sc in next sc; rep from * across. Turn.

Row 2 Ch 3 (counts as 1 dc), skip first sc, dc in next 5 sc, *ch 1, skip next sc, dc in next 5 sc; rep from * to last sc, end dc in last sc. Turn.

Row 3 Ch 1, sc in first dc, *ch 5, sc in next ch-sp; rep from *, end working last sc in 3rd ch of ch-3 at beg of row below. Turn.
Rep rows 1–3 for five dc blocks.

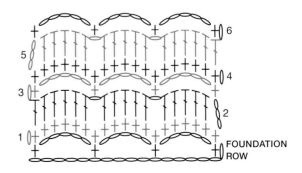

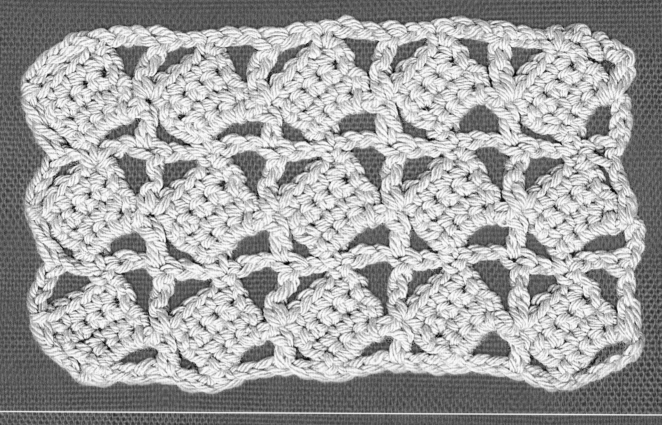

75

76

75 *Tipsi Blocks*

Chain a multiple of 6 sts; plus 6 for foundation row.

Foundation row (RS) Sc in 9th ch from hook (forms dc and ch-3 sp at beg of row), turn, ch 1, sc in sc, work 3 sc in ch-3 sp, [turn, ch 1, sc in each of the 4 sc] 3 times, skip next 2 ch on starting ch, dc in next ch, *ch 3, skip next 2 ch on starting ch, sc in next ch, turn, ch 1, sc in sc, work 3 sc in ch-3 sp, [turn, ch 1, sc in each of the 4 sc] 3 times, skip next 2 ch on starting ch, dc in next ch; rep from * across. Turn.

Row 1 Ch 6 (counts as 1 tr and ch 2), skip dc and 3 sc, sc in next sc, ch 2, tr in next dc, *ch 2, skip 3 sc, sc in next sc, ch 2, tr in next dc; rep from *, end last rep with tr in top of t-ch of row below. Turn.

Row 2 Ch 6 (count as 1 dc and ch 3), sc in first sc, turn, ch 1, sc in next sc, work 3 sc in ch-3 sp, [turn, ch 1, sc in each of the 4 sc] 3 times, dc in next tr, *ch 3, sc in next sc, turn, ch 1, sc in sc, work 3 sc in ch-3 sp, [turn, ch 1, sc in each of the 4 sc] 3 times, dc in next tr; rep from *, end last rep with tr in 4th ch of ch-6 t-ch of row below. Turn.

Rep rows 1 and 2 for tipsi blocks.

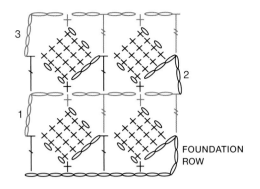

76 *3-D Zigzag*

With A, chain a multiple of 4 sts, plus 2; plus 1 for foundation row.

Foundation row (RS) Sc in 2nd ch from hook and in each ch across. Turn.

Row 1 Ch 3 (count as 1 dc), skip first sc, dc in each sc to end changing to B. Turn.

Row 2 Ch 1, sc in first 4 dc, ch 1, skip next dc, *sc in next 3 dc, ch 1, skip next dc; rep from * to last dc, end sc in 3rd ch of t-ch of row below. Turn.

Row 3 Ch 3, skip first sc, dc in each ch and sc across changing to A. Turn.

Row 4 Ch 1, sc in first dc, *dtr in next skipped dc of 3 rows below, skip next dc on 3rd row, sc in next 3 dc; rep from * to last dc, end sc in 3rd ch of t-ch of row below. Turn.

Row 5 Ch 3, skip first sc, dc in each sc and dtr across changing to B. Turn.

Row 6 Ch 1, sc in first dc, *ch 1, skip next dc, sc in next 3 dc; rep from * to last dc, end sc in 3rd ch of t-ch of row below. Turn.

Row 7 Ch 3, skip first sc, dc in each sc and ch across changing to A. Turn.

Row 8 Ch 1, sc in first 4 dc, dtr in first skipped dc of 3 rows below, skip next dc, *sc in next 3 dc, dtr in next skipped dc of 3 rows below, skip next dc; rep from * to last dc, end sc in 3rd ch of t-ch of row below. Turn.

Row 9 Ch 3, skip first sc, dc in each dtr and sc across changing to B. Turn.

Rep rows 2 to 9 for 3-D zigzag.

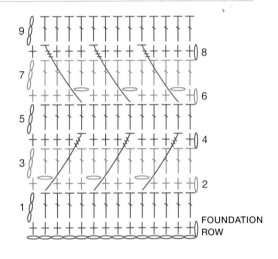

77

With A, chain a multiple of 7 sts, plus 1; plus 3 for
foundation row.

Make picot (MP) Ch 3, sl st in top of last dc made.

Make crown (MCR) Work (3 dc, MP, ch 1, dc, MP, 2 dc) in ch (or ch-sp).

Picot V stitch (PV-st) Work (dc, MP, dc) in ch-1 sp.

Note When changing colors, draw new color through last 2 lps on hook to complete last st, then turn. Cut and join colors as needed.

Foundation row (RS) Skip first 3 ch (counts as 1 dc), dc in next ch, MP, work 2 more dc in same ch as last dc, *skip next 6 ch, MCR in next ch; rep from * to last 7 ch, end skip next 6 ch, work (3dc, MP, dc) in last ch changing to B.

Row 1 Ch 3 (counts as 1 dc), dc in first st, *ch 3, work PV-st in ch-1 sp in center of next crown; rep from *, end ch 3, work 2 dc in top of t-ch changing to A. Turn.

Row 2 Ch 2 (counts as 1 hdc), skip first 2 sts, *MCR in next ch-3 sp, skip next PV-st; rep from *, end MCR in last sp, hdc in top of t-ch changing to B. Turn.

Row 3 Ch 4 (count as 1 dc and ch 1), *PV-st in ch-1 sp in center of next crown, ch 3; rep from *, end PV-st in ch-1 sp in center of last crown, ch 1, dc in top of t-ch changing to A. Turn.

Row 4 Ch 3 (counts as 1 dc), skip first st, work (dc, MP, 2 dc) in first ch-1 sp, *skip next PV-st, MCR in next ch-3 sp; rep from *, end skip last PV-st, work 3 dc in 4th ch t-ch of row below, MP, dc in next ch of t-ch changing to B. Turn.

Rep rows 1–4 for picot crown st.

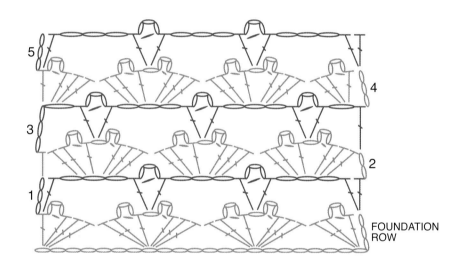

78

79

80

81

Spikes

78 *Alternating Stitch*

Chain a multiple of 2 sts; plus 2 for foundation row.

Spike single crochet (SSC) Insert hook below next st of one row down, yo, draw up a lp that is the same height as the working row, yo and draw through both lps on hook.

Foundation row (RS) Skip first 2 ch (counts as 1 sc), sc in each remaining ch across. Turn.

Row 1 Ch 1 (counts as 1 sc), skip first st, *sc in next st, work SSC over next st; rep from *, end sc in top of t-ch. Turn.

Rep row 1 for alternating st.

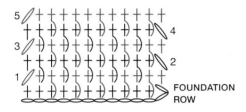

80 *Five-Spike Marguerite*

Chain a multiple of 2 sts, plus 1; plus 1 for foundation row.

Marguerite cluster with 5 spike loops (M5C) Pick up spike lps (ie: yo and draw through) inserting hook as follows: into lp which closed the previous M5C, under 2 threads of last spike lp of same M5C, into same place that last spike lp of same M5C was worked, into each of next 2 sts (6 lps on hook), yo and draw through all lps on hook.

Foundation row (WS) Sc in 2nd ch from hook and in each ch across. Turn.

Row 1 Ch 3, work M5C inserting hook into 2nd and 3rd ch from hook and then first 3 sts to pick up 5 spike lps, *ch 1, work M5C; rep from * across, skip t-ch. Turn.

Row 2 Ch 1, sc in lp which closed last M5C, *sc in next ch, sc in lp which closed next M5C; rep from *, end sc in next 2 ch of t-ch. Turn.

Rep rows 1 and 2 for five-spike Marguerite.

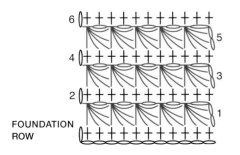

79 *Checkerboard*

With A, chain a multiple of 6 sts, plus 3; plus 2 for foundation row.

Spike double crochet (SDC) Work dc over ch-sp by inserting hook into top of next row below (or foundation chain).

Note When changing colors, draw new color through last 2 lps on hook to complete last st, then turn. Cut and join colors as needed.

Foundation row (RS) Skip first 3 ch (counts as 1 dc), dc in next 2 ch, *ch 3, skip next 3 ch, dc in next 3 ch; rep from * across changing to B. Turn.

Row 1 *Ch 3, skip next 3 sts, work SDC over next 3 sts; rep from * to last 3 sts, end ch 2, skip 2 sts, sl st into top of t-ch changing to C. Turn.

Row 2 Ch 3 (counts as 1 SDC), skip next st, work SDC over next 2 sts, *ch 3, skip next 3 sts, work SDC over next 3 sts; rep from * across changing to A. Turn.

Rep rows 1 and 2 for checkerboard, working in stripe pat as follows: 1 row A, 1 row B and 1 row C.

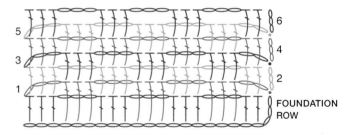

81 *Alternating Stitch—Tricolor*

With A, chain a multiple of 2 sts; plus 2 for foundation row.

Note When changing colors, draw new color through last 2 lps on hook to complete last st, then turn. Cut and join colors as needed.

Foundation row (RS) Work as for alternating st, changing to B at end of row.

Rep row 1 of alternating st, working in stripe pat as follows: 1 row B, 1 row C and 1 row A.

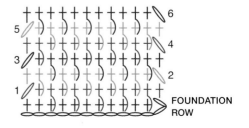

82

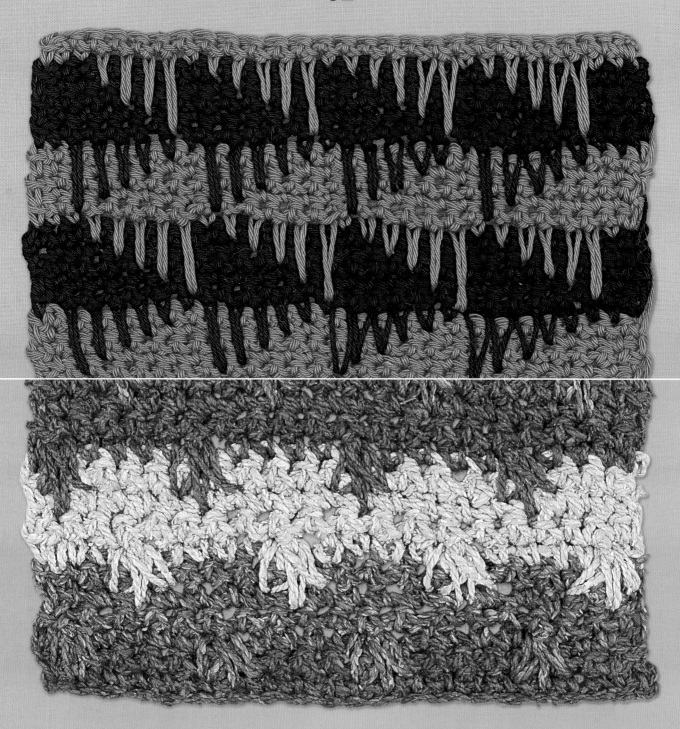

83

82 *Arrowhead*

With A, chain a multiple of 6 sts, plus 2; plus 1 for foundation row.

Spike single Crochet (SSC) Insert hook below next st of one or more rows below (will be indicated as: SSC1, SSC2, etc), yo, draw up a lp that is the same height as the working row, yo and draw through both lps on hook.

Note When changing colors, draw new color through last 2 lps on hook to complete last st, then turn. Cut and join colors as needed.

Foundation row (RS) Sc in 2nd ch from hook and in each ch across. Turn.

Row 1 Ch 1, sc in each st across. Turn.

Rows 2–5 Rep row 1, changing to B at end of row 5. Turn.

Row 6 Ch 1, sc in first st, *sc in next st, SSC1 over next st, SSC2 over next st, SSC3 over next st, SSC4 over next st, SSC5 over next st; rep from *, end sc in last st, skip t-ch. Turn.

Rows 7–11 Rep row 1, changing to A at end of row 11. Turn.

Row 12 Ch 1, sc in first st, *SSC5 over next st, SSC4 over next st, SSC3 over next st, SSC2 over next st, SSC1 over next st, sc in next st; rep from *, end sc in last st changing to A, skip t-ch. Turn.

Rep rows 1–12 for arrowhead.

83 *Crow's Foot Stripe*

With A, chain a multiple of 5 sts, plus 3; plus 1 for foundation row.

Spike cluster (SCL) Over next st pick up 3 spike lps by inserting hook as follows: one st to right of next st and one row down; directly below and 2 rows down; one st to left and one down (4 lps on hook). Now insert hook into top of next st itself, yo, draw through a lp, yo and draw through all 5 lps on hook.

Stripe pattern Continuing stripe pat, work 4 rows each in B, C and A throughout.

Note When changing colors, draw new color through last 2 lps on hook to complete last st, then turn. Cut and join colors as needed.

Foundation row (RS) Sc in 2nd ch from hook and in each ch across. Ch 1, turn.

Row 1 Sc in each st across. Ch 1, turn.

Row 2 Sc in first 3 sts, *SCL over next st, sc in next 4 sts; rep from * across. Ch 1, turn.

Rows 3–5 Sc in each st across. Ch 1, turn.

Row 6 Sc in first st, *SCL over next st, sc in next 4 sts; rep from *, end SCL over next st, sc in last st. Ch 1, turn.

Rows 7–9 Rep row 3.

Rep rows 2 to 9 for crow's foot stripe.

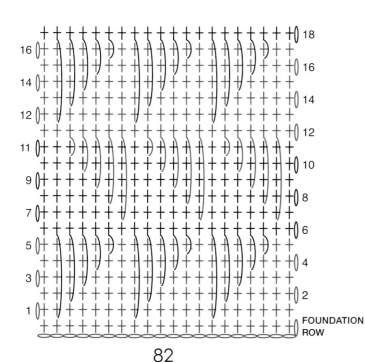

82

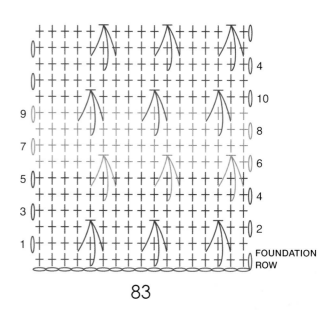

83

85

84 *Cluster Stripe*

With A, chain a multiple of 8 sts, plus 5; plus 1 for foundation row.

Spike cluster (SCL) Over next st pick up 5 spike lps by inserting hook as follows: 2 sts to right of next st and one row down; one st to right and 2 rows down; directly below and 3 rows down; one st to left and 2 rows down; 2 sts to left and one row down (6 lps on hook). Then insert hook into top of next st itself, yo, draw through a lp, yo and draw through all 7 lps on hook.

Stripe pattern Work 4 rows each in A, B and C throughout.

Note When changing colors, draw new color through last 2 lps on hook to complete last st, then turn. Cut and join colors as needed.

Foundation row (RS) Sc in 2nd ch from hook and in each ch across. Turn.

Rows 1– 3 Ch 1, sc in each st across, skip t-ch. Turn.

Row 4 Ch 1, sc in first 4 sts, *SCL over next st, sc in

next 7 sts; rep from *, end sc in last st, skip t-ch. Turn.

Rows 5–7 Rep row 1. Turn.

Row 8 Ch 1, sc in first 8 sts, *SCL over next st, sc in next 7 sts; rep from * to last 5 sts, end SCL over next st, sc in last 4 sts, skip t-ch. Turn.

Rep rows 1–8 for cluster stripe.

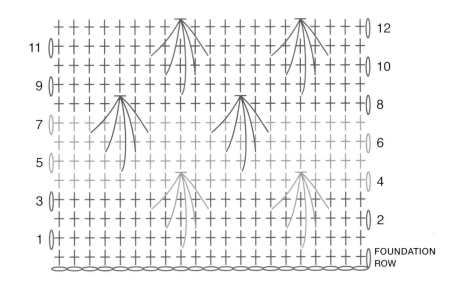

85 *Diagonal Spike*

Chain a multiple of 4 sts, plus 2; plus 2 for foundation row.

Spike double crochet (SDC) Yo, insert hook in same ch (or st) that first dc of 3 dc group just made was worked. Yo and draw up a lp to same height as

working row, taking care not to crush 3 dc group, [yo, draw through 2 lps on hook] twice.

Foundation row (RS) Skip first 3 ch (counts as 1 dc), *dc in next 3 ch, work SDC, skip next st; rep from *, end dc in last ch. Turn.

Row 1 Ch 3 (counts as 1 dc), skip first st, *dc in next 3 sts, work SDC, skip next st; rep from *, end dc in top of t-ch. Turn.

Rep row 1 for diagonal spike.

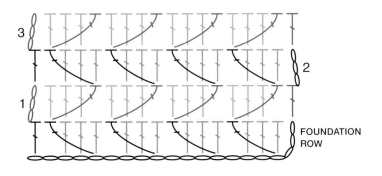

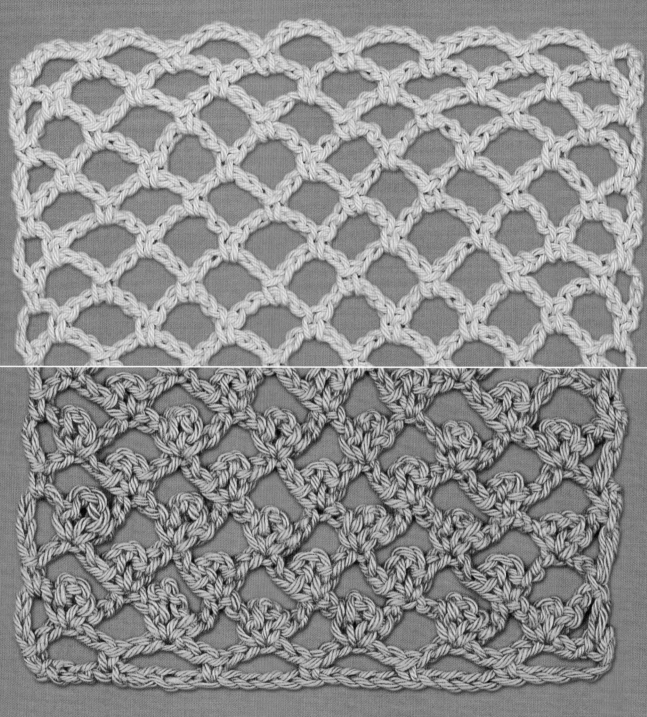

86

87

Lace

86 *Trellis Stitch*

Chain a multiple of 4 sts, plus 3; plus 3 for foundation row.

Foundation row (RS) Sc in 6th ch from hook, *ch 5, skip next 3 ch, sc in next ch; rep from * across. Turn.

Row 1 *Ch 5, sc in next ch-5 lp; rep from * across. Turn.

Rep row 1 for trellis st.

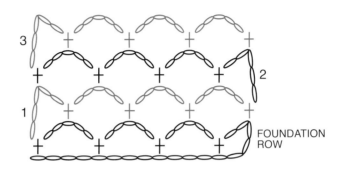

87 *Trellis Stitch—Picot*

Chain a multiple of 5 sts, plus 1; plus 1 for foundation row.

Foundation row (RS) Sc in 2nd ch from hook, *ch 5, skip next 4 ch, sc in next ch; rep from * across. Turn.

Row 1 *Ch 5, work (sc, ch 3, sc—picot) in 3rd ch of next ch-5 lp; rep from *, end ch 2, dc in last sc, skip t-ch. Turn.

Row 2 Ch 1, sc in first st, *ch 5, skip picot, picot in 3rd ch of next ch-5 lp; rep from *, end ch 5, skip last picot, sc in t-ch lp. Turn.

Rep rows 1 and 2 for picot trellis st.

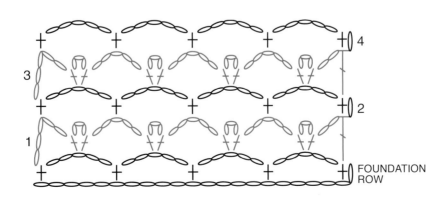

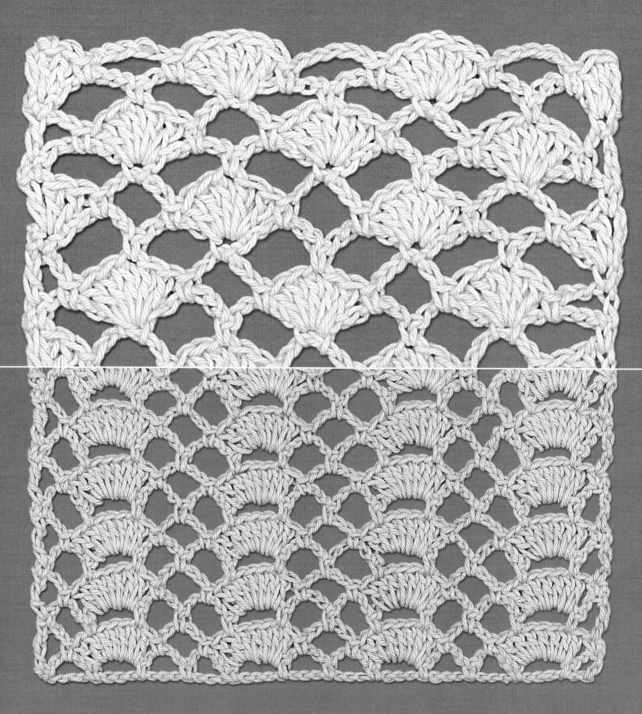

89

Chain a multiple of 12 sts, plus 1; plus 2 for foundation row.

Foundation row (RS) Work 2 dc in 3rd ch from hook, *skip next 2 ch, sc in next ch, ch 5, skip next 5 ch, sc in next ch, skip next 2 ch, work 5 dc (shell) in next ch; rep from *, end last rep with 3 dc in last ch. Turn.

Row 1 Ch 1, sc in first st, *ch 5, sc in next ch-5 lp, ch 5, sc in 3rd dc of next shell; rep from *, end last rep with sc in top of t-ch. Turn.

Row 2 *Ch 5, sc in next ch-5 lp, work 5 dc (shell) in next sc, sc in next ch 5 lp; rep from *, end ch 2, dc in last sc, skip t-ch. Turn.

Row 3 Ch 1, sc in first dc, *ch 5, sc in 3rd dc of next shell, ch 5, sc in next ch-5 lp; rep from * across. Turn.

Row 4 Ch 3 (counts as 1 dc), work 2 dc in first st, *sc in next ch-5 lp, ch 5, sc in next ch-5 lp, work 5 dc (shell) in next sc; rep from *, end last rep with 3 dc in last sc, skip t-ch. Turn.

Rep rows 1–4 for shell trellis st.

89 *Trellis Stitch—Fan*

Chain a multiple of 12 sts, plus 11; plus 1 for foundation row.

Foundation row (WS) Sc in 2nd ch from hook, *ch 5, skip next 3 ch, sc in next ch; rep from * to last 2 ch, end ch 2, skip next ch, dc in last ch. Turn.

Row 1 Ch 1, sc in first st, skip ch-2 sp, *work 7 dc (fan) in next ch-5 lp, sc in next ch-5 lp**, ch 5, sc in next ch-5 lp; rep from *, end last rep at **, then ch 2, tr in last sc, skip t-ch. Turn.

Row 2 Ch 1, sc in first st, *ch 5, sc in 2nd dc of next fan, ch 5, sc in 6th dc of same fan**, ch 5, sc in next ch-5 lp; rep from *, end last rep at **, then ch 2, tr in last sc, skip t-ch. Turn.

Rep rows 1 and 2 for fan trellis st.

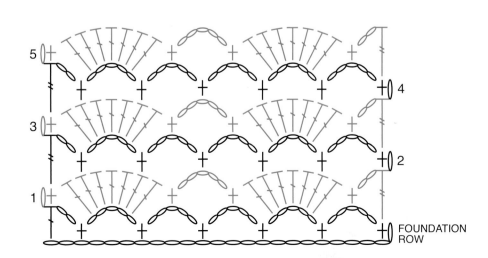

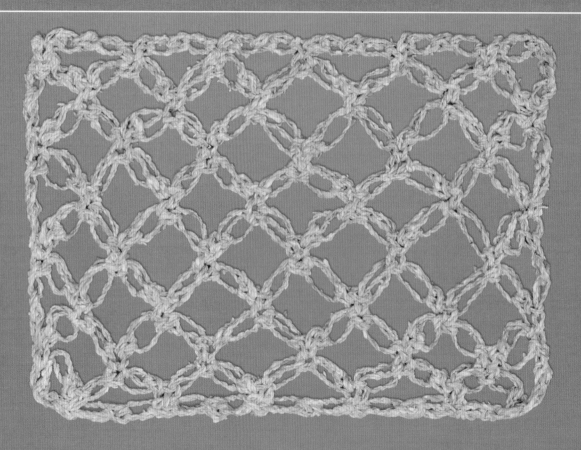

91

Make any number of flower units.

Foundation row (RS) Ch 7, *sl st in 4th ch from hook, ch 3, in ring just formed, work a base flower unit of (2 dc, ch 3, sl st, ch 3, 2 dc) **, ch 10; rep from *, end last rep at ** when fabric is required width, keep same side facing and turn to be able to work along underside of base flower units.

Row 1 (RS) *Ch 3, sl st in ch-ring at center of flower, ch 3, work (2 dc, ch 3, sl st—center petal completed, ch 3, 2 dc) in same ring, skip 2 ch of base chain which connects units, sl st in next ch, ch 7, skip 2 ch, sl st in next ch; rep from * in next and each base flower unit across. Turn.

Note Check that each base flower unit is not twisted before you work into it.

Row 2 Ch 11, sl st in 4th ch from hook, ch 3, work 2 dc in ring just formed, ch 3, sl st in top of ch-3 of center petal of last flower made in row below (see diagram), *ch 10, sl st in 4th ch from hook, ch 3, work 2 dc in ring just formed, sl st in 4th of next ch-7 lp of row below, ch 3, work (sl st, ch 3, 2 dc) in same ch-ring as last 2 dc, ch 3, sl st in top of ch-3 of center petal of next flower made in row below; rep from * across. Turn.

Row 3 Ch 9, skip 2 ch, sl st in next ch, *ch 3, sl st in ch-ring at center of flower, ch 3, work (2 dc, ch 3, sl st, ch 3, 2 dc) in same ring, skip 2 ch, sl st in next ch, ch 7, skip (3 ch, sl st and next 2 ch), sl st in next ch (i.e., before start of next petal); rep from *, end ch 3, sl st in ch-ring at center of last flower, ch 3, work 2 dc in same ring. Turn.

Row 4 *Ch 10, sl st in 4th ch from hook, ch 3, work 2 dc in ring just formed, sl st in 4th ch of next lp of row below, ch 3, work (sl st, ch 3, 2 dc) in same ch-ring as last 2 dc**, ch 3, sl st in top of ch-3 of center petal of next flower of row below; rep from *, end last rep at **. Turn.

Rep rows 1–4 for flower trellis st.

When fabric is required length, finish after 4th (RS) row (see asterisk on diagram), then continue down left side to complete edge flowers as follows: *Ch 3, work (sl st, ch 3, 2 dc, ch 3, sl st, ch 3, 2 dc) in ch-ring at center of edge flower, skip 3 ch, sl st in next ch**, ch 6, sl st in last ch before center petal of next edge flower (see diagram); rep from *, end last rep at ** after last edge flower.

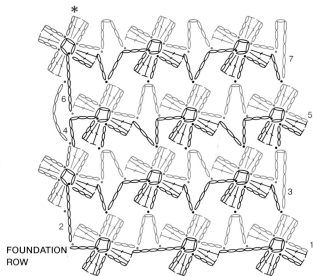

FOUNDATION ROW

A Solomon's knot is a long chain stitch that is locked in place with a sc st that is worked into its back lp. To make a Solomon's knot, make a slipknot and place on hook. Ch 1, *lengthen the lp on the hook to the stated length. Yo, draw through the lp on hook, keeping single thread of the long chain separate from the 2 front threads. Insert hook under the single back thread, yo, draw up a lp, yo and draw through both lps on the hook; rep from * for each Solomon's knot.

Edge Solomon's knot (ESK) These form the foundation "chain" and edges of the fabric and are two thirds the length of MSK's.

Main Solomon's knot (MSK) These form the main fabric and are half as long again as ESK's.

Multiple of 2 Solomon's knots, plus 1; plus 2 Solomon's knots for foundation "chain."

Foundation row (RS) Ch 2, sc in 2nd ch from hook, now make a multiple of 2 ESK's (approx ¾"/2cm long), ending with 1 MSK (approx 1¼"/3cm long).

Row 1 Sc in sc between 3rd and 4th lps from hook, *work 2 MSK, skip 2 lps, sc in next sc; rep from * across. Turn.

Row 2 Work 2 ESK and 1 MSK, sc in sc between 4th and 5th lps from hook, *work 2 MSK, skip 2 lps, sc in next sc; rep from *, end in top of ESK. Turn.

Rep row 2 for Solomon's knot.

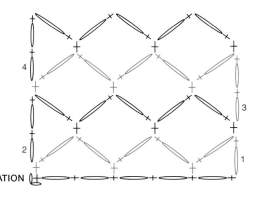

FOUNDATION ROW

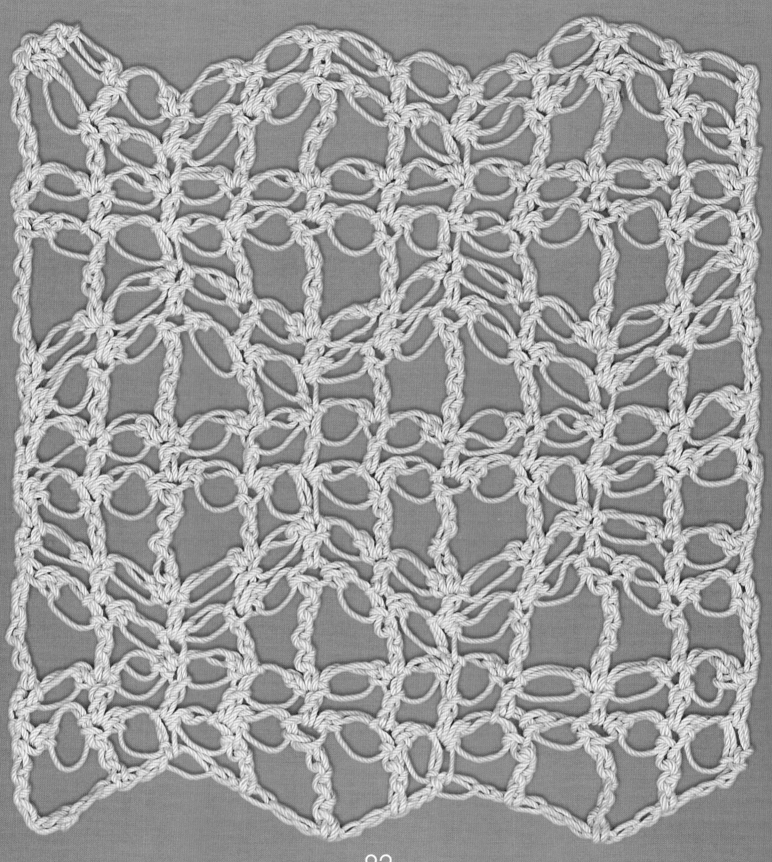

92

Chain a multiple of 16 sts, plus 1; plus 1 for foundation row.

Solomon's knot (SK) Make lp approx ⅝"/1.5cm long.

Foundation row (RS) Sc in 2nd ch from hook, *work SK, skip next 3 ch, tr in next ch, work SK, skip next 3 ch, ttr in next ch, work SK, skip next 3 ch, tr in next ch, work SK, skip next 3 ch, sc in next ch; rep from * across. Turn.

Row 1 Ch 3, sc in 2nd ch from hook, *work SK, skip next SK, dc in next st; rep from * across. Turn.

Row 2 Ch 6, sc in 2nd ch from hook, *work SK, skip next SK, tr in next st, work SK, skip next SK, sc in next st, work SK, skip next SK, tr in next st, work SK, skip next SK, ttr in next st; rep from * across. Turn.

Rows 3 and 5 Rep row 1.

Row 4 Rep row 2.

Row 6 Ch 1, sc in first st, *work SK, skip next SK, tr in next st, work SK, skip next SK, ttr in next st, work SK, skip next SK, tr in next st, work SK, skip next SK, sc in next st; rep from * across. Turn.

Row 7 Rep row 1.

Row 8 Rep row 6.

Rep rows 1–8 for butterfly wings.

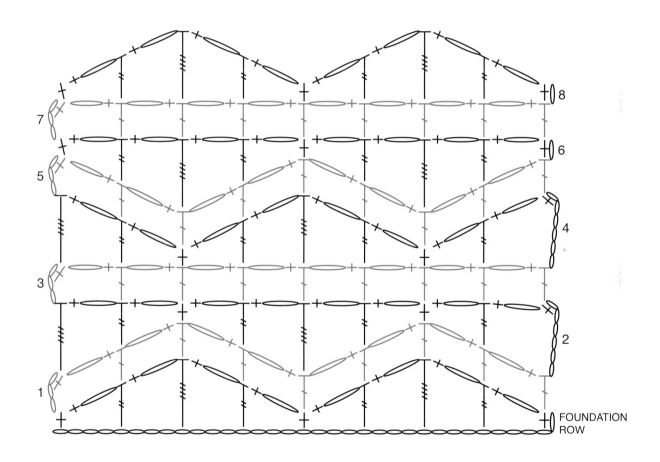

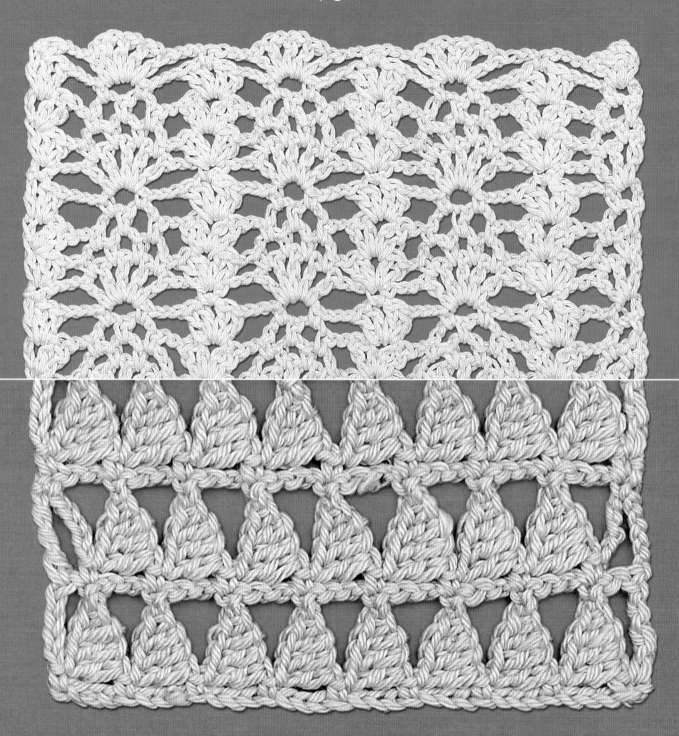

93

94

Chain a multiple of 12 sts, plus 7; plus 1 for foundation row.

Double V stitch (DV st) Work (2 dc, ch 1, 2 dc) in same st (or sp).

Foundation row (RS) Sc in 2nd ch from hook, *ch 3, skip next 5 ch, dc in next ch, then work [ch 1, dc] 4 times in same ch as last dc, ch 3, skip next 5 ch, sc in next ch; rep from *, end ch 3, skip next 5 ch, dc in last ch, then work [ch 1, dc] twice in same ch as last dc. Turn.

Row 1 [Ch 3, sc in next ch-sp] twice, *ch 1, skip next 3 ch, work DV st in next sc, ch 1, skip next 3 ch, sc in next ch-sp, [ch 3, sc in next ch-sp] 3 times; rep from *, end ch 1, skip next 3 ch, work 3 dc in last sc, skip t-ch. Turn.

Row 2 Ch 3 (counts as 1 dc), work 2 dc in first st, *ch 2, skip next ch, sc in next ch-3 sp**, [ch 3, sc in next ch-3 sp] twice, ch 2, skip next ch, work DV st in next ch-sp; rep from *, end last rep at **, then ch 3, sc in top of t-ch. Turn.

Row 3 Ch 4, sc in next ch-3 sp, *ch 3, skip next 2 ch, work DV st in next ch-sp, ch 3, skip next 2 ch, sc in next ch-3 sp, ch 3, sc in next ch-3 sp; rep from *, end ch 3, skip last 2 ch and dcs, work 3 dc in top of t-ch. Turn.

Row 4 Ch 1, sc in first st, *ch 3, skip next 3 ch, dc in next ch-3 sp, then work [ch 1, dc] 4 times in same ch-3 sp as last dc, ch 3, skip next 3 ch, sc in next ch-sp; rep from *, end ch 3, skip last 3 ch, work dc in t-ch, then work [ch 1, dc] twice in t-ch. Turn. Rep rows 1–4 for strawberry lace.

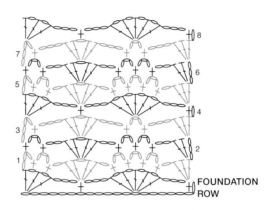

FOUNDATION ROW

Chain a multiple of 4 sts, plus 1; plus 1 for foundation row.

Triangle st Ch 6, sc in 3rd ch from hook, dc in next 3 ch.

Foundation row (RS) Sc in 2nd ch from hook, *work triangle st, skip next 3 ch, sc in next ch; rep from * across. Turn.

Row 1 Ch 6 (counts as 1 dtr and ch 1), *sc in ch at tip of next triangle st, ch 3; rep from *, end sc in ch at tip of last triangle st, ch 1, dtr into last sc, skip t-ch. Turn.

Row 2 Ch 10, skip next ch, sc in next sc, *work triangle st, skip next 3 ch, sc in next sc; rep from *, end ch 5, skip next ch, dtr in next ch of t-ch. Turn.

Row 3 Ch 1, sc in first st, *ch 3, sc in ch at tip of next triangle st; rep from * end last rep in center of ch-10 t-ch. Turn.

Row 4 Ch 1, sc in first st, *work triangle st, skip next 3 ch, sc in next sc; rep from *, end skip t-ch. Turn. Rep rows 1–4 for triangle st.

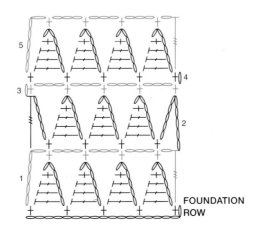

FOUNDATION ROW

95

Chain a multiple of 15 sts, plus 1; plus 2 for foundation row.

Double V stitch (DV st) Work (2 dc, ch 1, 2 dc) in next ch (or sp).

Foundation row (RS) Skip first 2 ch (counts as 1 dc), work 2 dc in next ch, *ch 7, skip next 5 ch, sc in next ch, ch 3, skip next 2 ch, sc in next ch, ch 7, skip next 5 ch**, work DV st in next ch; rep from *, end last rep at **, then work 3 dc in last ch. Turn.

Row 1 Ch 3 (counts as 1 dc), work 2 dc in first st, *ch 3, sc in ch-7 lp, ch 5, skip next 3 ch, sc in next ch-7 lp, ch 3**, work DV st in sp at center of next DV st; rep from * end last rep at **, then work 3 dc in top of t-ch. Turn.

Row 2 Ch 3 (counts as 1 dc), work 2 dc in first st, *skip next 3 ch, work 11 tr in next ch-5 lp, skip next 3 ch**, work DV st in next sp; rep from *, end last rep at **, then work 3 dc in top of t-ch. Turn.

Row 3 Ch 3 (counts as 1 dc), work 2 dc in first st, *ch 2, skip next 2 dc, sc in next tr, [ch 3, skip next tr, sc in next tr] 5 times, ch 2, skip next 2 dc**, work DV st in next sp; rep from *, end last rep at **, then work 3 dc in top of t-ch. Turn.

Row 4 Ch 3 (counts as 1 dc), work 2 dc in first st, *ch 3, skip next 2 ch, sc in next ch-3 sp, [ch 3, sc in next ch-3 sp] 4 times, ch 3, skip next 2 ch **, work DV st in next sp; rep from *, end last rep at **, then work 3 dc in top of t-ch. Turn.

Row 5 Ch 3 (counts as 1 dc), work 2 dc in first st, *ch 4, skip next 3 ch, sc in next ch-3 sp, [ch 3, sc in next ch-3 sp] 3 times, ch 4, skip next 3 ch**, work DV st in next sp; rep from *, end last rep at **, then work 3 dc in top of t-ch. Turn.

Row 6 Ch 3 (counts as 1 dc), work 2 dc in first st, *ch 5, skip next 4 ch, sc in next ch-3 sp, [ch 3, sc in next ch-3 sp] twice, ch 5, skip next 4 ch**, work DV st in next sp; rep from *, end last rep at **, then work 3 dc in top of t-ch. Turn.

Row 7 Ch 3 (counts as 1 dc), work 2 dc in first st, *ch 7, skip next 5 ch, sc in next ch-3 sp, ch 3, sc in next ch-3 sp, ch 7, skip next 5 ch**, work DV st in next sp; rep from *, end last rep at **, then work 3 dc in top of t-ch. Turn.

Rep rows 1–7 for pineapple st.

FOUNDATION ROW

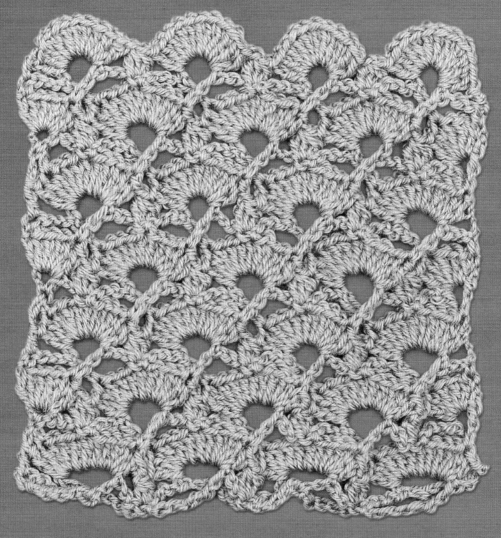

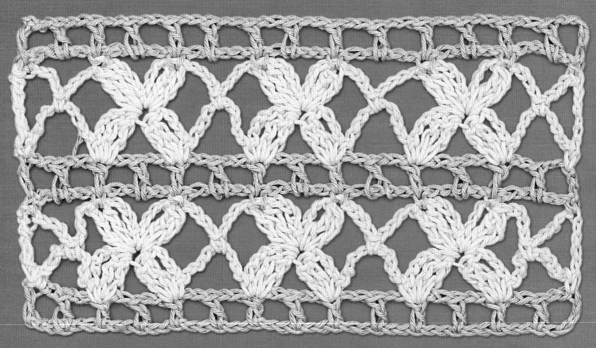

Chain a multiple of 10 sts, plus 1; plus 1 for foundation row.

Half double crochet 3 together (hdc3tog) [Yo, insert hook in st (or sp), yo and draw up a lp] 3 times, yo and draw through all 7 lps on hook.

Foundation row (WS) Sc in 2nd ch from hook, *ch 3, work 2 crossed dc as follows: skip 5 ch, dc in next ch, ch 5, inserting hook behind dc just made, work dc in 4th of the 5 ch just skipped, ch 3, skip 3 next ch, sc in next ch; rep from * across. Turn.

Row 1 Ch 3 (counts as 1 dc), skip first st, *skip next ch-3 sp, work 11 dc in next ch-5 lp (fan), skip next

ch-3 sp, work hdc3tog in next sc, ch 1; rep from *, end skip next ch-3 sp, work 11 dc in next ch-5 lp (fan), skip next ch-3 sp, dc in last sc, skip t-ch. Turn.

Row 2 Ch 2, skip first 2 dc, hdc in next dc, ch 4, hdc in top of hdc just made, *ch 3, skip 3 dc, sc in next dc, ch 3**, work 2 crossed dc as follows: dc in 2nd dc of next fan, ch 5, going behind dc just made, work dc in 10th dc of previous fan; rep from *, end last rep at **, then work dc in top of t-ch, ch 2, going behind dc just made, work dc in 10th dc of previous fan. Turn.

Row 3 Ch 3 (counts as 1 dc), skip first st, work 5 dc

in next ch-2 sp (half fan), *skip next ch-3 sp, work hdc3tog in next sc, ch 1, skip next ch-3 sp**, work 11 dc in next ch-5 lp; rep from *, end last rep at **, then work 6 dc in top of t-ch (half fan). Turn.

Row 4 Ch 1, sc in first st, ch 3, dc in 2nd dc of next fan, ch 5, going behind dc just made, work dc in 5th dc of half fan, *ch 3, skip next 3 dc, ** sc in next dc, ch 3, dc in 2nd dc of next fan, ch 5, going behind dc just made work dc in 10th dc of previous fan; rep from *, end last rep at ** in top of t-ch. Turn.

Rep rows 1–4 for fan st.

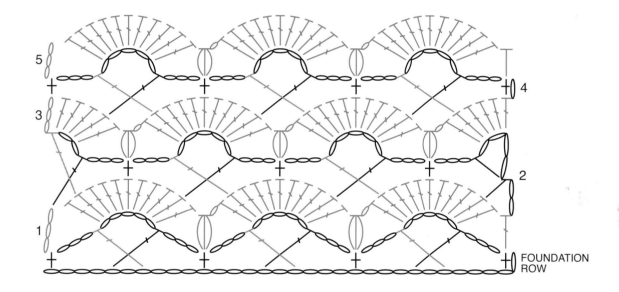

With A, chain a multiple of 12 st; plus 11 for foundation row.

Treble 2 together (tr2tog) [Yo, insert hook in next st, yo and draw up a lp, (yo, draw through 2 lps on hook) twice] twice, yo and draw through all 3 lps on hook.

Note When changing colors, draw new color through last 2 lps on hook to complete last st, then turn. Cut and join colors as needed.

Foundation row (RS) Dc in 8th ch from hook (counts as 1 dc, ch 2, skip 2 ch), *ch 2, skip next 2 ch, dc in next ch; rep from * across, changing to B. Turn.

Row 1 Ch 1, sc in first dc, *ch 9, skip next dc, work (sc, ch 4, tr2tog) in next dc, skip next dc, work (tr2tog, ch 4, sc) in next dc; rep from * to last 2 sps, end ch 9, skip last dc, sc in 3rd ch of t-ch of row below. Turn.

Row 2 Ch 10 (counts as 1 ttr and ch 4), sc in first ch-9 lp, *ch 4, work (tr2tog, ch 4, sl st, ch 4, tr2tog) in top of next tr2tog, ch 4, sc in next ch-9 lp; rep from *, end ch 4, 1 ttr into last sc changing to A.

Turn.

Row 3 Ch 1, sc in first ttr, *ch 5, sc in top of next tr2tog; rep from *, end working last sc in 6th ch of ch-10 t-ch of row below. Turn.

Row 4 Ch 5 (counts as 1 dc and ch 2), dc in next ch-5 lp, ch 2, dc in next sc, *ch 2, dc in next ch-5 lp, ch 2, dc in next sc; rep from * to end changing to B. Turn.

Rep rows 1–4 for flower stripe.

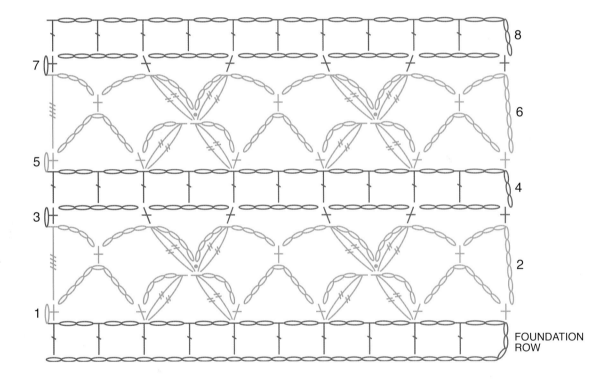

Motifs

Chapter 3

98

99

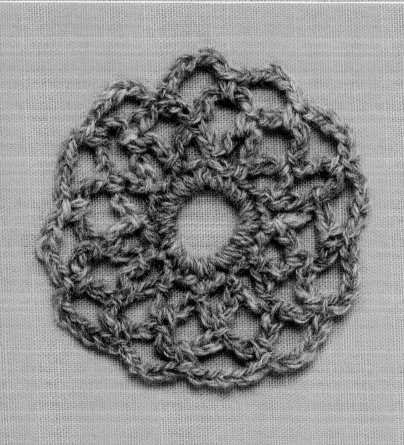

100

101

Motifs

Chapter 3

98

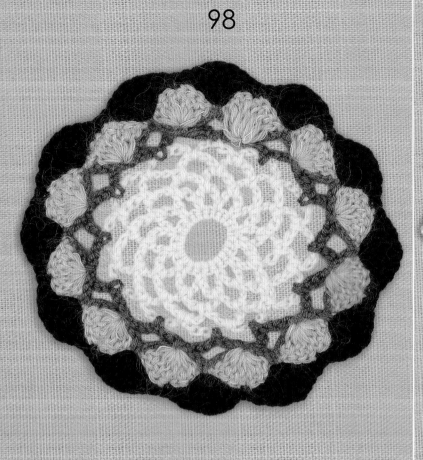

99

100

101

Circles

98 *Mandala*

To make an adjustable ring, with A, make a slipknot 10"/25.5cm from free end of yarn. Place slipknot on hook, then wrap free end of yarn twice around your first and second fingers on your left hand. Then work with yarn coming from ball as follows:

Rnd 1 (RS) Work 24 sc in ring, pull free end of yarn to close circle, then join rnd with a sl st in first sc.

Rnd 2 *Ch 5, sk next st, sl st in next st; rep from * around 10 times more, end ch 5, join rnd with a sl st in base of first ch-5—12 ch-5 lps.

Rnds 3–5 Sl st in first 3 ch of first ch-5 lp, *ch 5, sl st in next ch-5 lp; rep from * around 10 times more, end ch 5, join rnd with a sl st in 3rd sl st at beg of rnd—12 ch-5 lps. When rnd 5 is completed, fasten off.

Rnd 6 With RS facing, join yarn B with a sl st in any ch-5 lp, *ch 7, sl st in next ch-5 lp; rep from * around 10 times more, end ch 7, join rnd with a sl st in joining sl st—12 ch-7 lps.

Rnd 7 Sl st in first 4 ch of first ch-7 lp, *ch 7, sl st in next ch-7 lp; rep from * around 10 times more, end ch 7, join rnd with a sl st in 4th sl st at beg of rnd—12 ch-7 lps. Fasten off.

Rnd 8 With RS facing, join yarn C with a sl st in any ch-7 lp, *work 7 dc in next sl st, sl st in next ch-7 lp; rep from * around 10 times more, end work 7 dc in next sl st, join rnd with a sl st in joining sl st—12 shells. Fasten off.

Rnd 9 With RS facing, join yarn D with a sl st in 4th dc of any shell, *work 7 dc in next sl st, sl st in 4th dc of next shell; rep from * around 10 times more, end work 7 dc in next sl st, join rnd with a sl st in joining sl st—12 shells. Fasten off.

99 Flemish Motif

Chain 8. Join chain with a sl st, forming a ring.

Rnd 1 (RS) Ch 1, work 16 sc in ring, join rnd with a sl st in first sc.

Rnd 2 Ch 12 (count as 1 tr and ch 8), skip first 2 sc, *tr in next sc, ch 8, skip next sc; rep from * around 6 times more, join rnd with a sl st in 4th ch of beg ch-12—8 ch-8 lps.

Rnd 3 Ch 1, *in next ch-8 lp work (sc, hdc, dc, 3 tr, ch 4, insert hook down through top of tr just made and work a sl st to make picot, 2 tr, dc, hdc, sc); rep from * 7 times more, join rnd with a sl st in first sc. Fasten off.

100 Rose Window

To make an adjustable ring, make a slipknot 10"/25.5cm from free end of yarn. Place slipknot on hook, then wrap free end of yarn twice around your first and second fingers on your left hand. Then work with yarn coming from ball as follows:

Rnd 1 (RS) Work 24 sc in ring, pull free end of yarn to close circle, then join rnd with a sl st in first sc.

Rnd 2 *Ch 5, sk next st, sl st in next st; rep from * around 10 times more, end ch 5, join rnd with a sl st in base of first ch-5—12 ch-5 lps.

Rnds 3 and 4 Sl st in first 3 ch of first ch-5 lp, *ch 5, sc in next ch-5 lp; rep from * around 10 times more, end ch 5, join rnd with a sl st in 3rd sl st at beg of rnd—12 ch-5 lps. When rnd 4 is completed, fasten off.

99

100

Chain 8. Join chain with a sl st, forming a ring.

Double V stitch (DV st) Work (2 dc, ch 2, 2 dc) in same picot or sp.

Rnd 1 (RS) Ch 8, sl st in 6th ch from hook (counts as 1 dc and picot), *work 4 dc in ring, ch 5, sl st in top of last dc worked (picot made); rep from * around 6 times more, end work 3 dc in ring, join rnd with a sl st in 3rd ch of beg ch-8—8 picots.

Rnd 2 Sl st in first 2 ch of first picot, ch 3 (counts as 1 dc), work (dc, ch 2, 2 dc) into same picot, *ch 4, work DV st in next picot; rep from * around 6 times more, end ch 4, join rnd with a sl st in top of beg ch-3.

Rnd 3 Sl st in next dc and first ch, ch 3 (counts as 1 dc), work (dc, ch 2, 2 dc) in same ch-2 sp, *ch 6, skip next ch-4 sp, DV st in next ch-2 sp; rep from * around 6 times more, end ch 6, skip last ch-4 sp, join rnd with a sl st in top of beg ch-3.

Rnd 4 Sl st in next dc and first ch, ch 3 (counts as 1 dc), work (dc, ch 2, 2 dc) in same ch-2 sp, *ch 8, skip next ch-6 sp, DV st into next ch-2 sp; rep from * around 6 more times, end ch 8, skip last ch-6 lp, join rnd with a sl st in top of beg ch-3.

Rnd 5 Sl st in next dc and first ch, ch 3 (counts as 1 dc), work 4 dc in same ch-2 sp, *sc in next 8 ch, work 5 dc in next ch-2 sp; rep from * around 6 times more, end sc in last 8 ch, join rnd with a sl st in top of beg ch-3. Fasten off.

102

103

102 Picot Circle

Chain 2.

Rnd 1 (RS) Work 8 sc in 2nd ch from hook, join rnd with a sl st in first sc.

Rnd 2 Ch 1, work 2 sc in each st around, join rnd with a sl st in first sc—16 sc.

Rnd 3 Ch 1, work 2 sc in first st, *sc in next st, work 2 sc in next st; rep from * around to last st, end sc in last st, join rnd with a sl st in first sc—24 sc.

Rnd 4 Ch 1, sc in first st, *work 2 sc in next st, sc in next 2 sts; rep from * around to last 2 sts, end work 2 sc in next st, sc in last st, join rnd with a sl st in first sc—32 sc.

Rnd 5 Ch 1, work 2 sc in first st, *sc in next 3 sts, work 2 sc in next st; rep from * around to last 3 sts, end sc in last 3 sts, join rnd with a sl st in first sc—40 sc.

Rnd 6 Ch 1, work 2 sc in first st, sc in next 19 sts, work 2 sc in next st, sc in last 19 sts, join rnd with a sl st in first sc—42 sc. Turn.

Rnd 7 (WS) Ch 3, sl st in same sp as joining, sl st in next 3 sts, *ch 3, sl st into same st as last sl st, sl st in next 3 sts; rep from * around—14 picots. Fasten off.

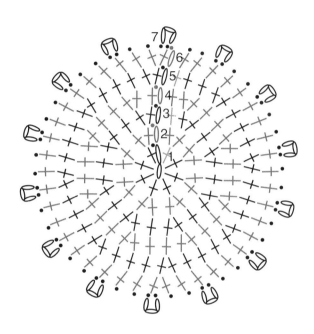

103 Tiny Circle

Chain 12. Join chain with a sl st forming a ring.

Rnd 1 (RS) Ch 1, work 24 sc in ring, join rnd with a sl st in first sc.

Rnd 2 *Ch 5, skip next st, sc in next st; rep from * around, join rnd with a sl st in first sc of rnd 1—12 ch-5 sps. Fasten off.

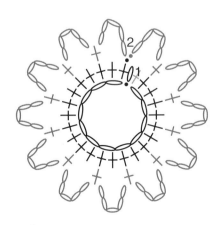

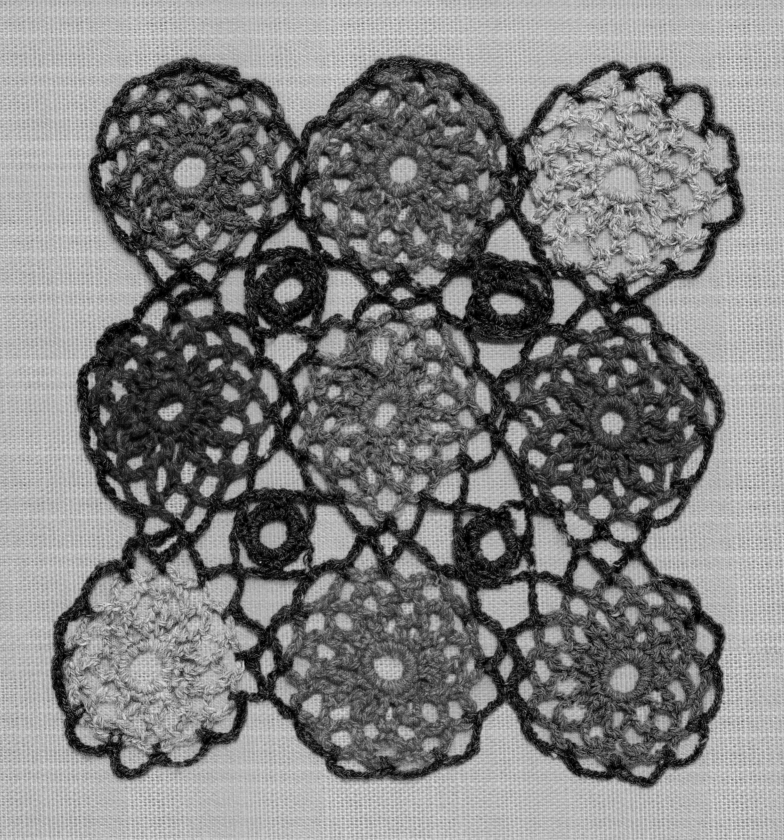

104

Note Join all rose window motifs tog first, then join each filler motif separately. Refer to photo for suggested placement and color scheme.

First motif

With A, work rnds 1–4 as for rose window (see page 104). Fasten off.

Rnd 5 (RS) With RS facing, join background color with a sl st in any ch-5 sp, ch 1, sc in same ch-5 sp, *ch 5, sc in next ch-5 lp; rep from * around, end ch 5, join rnd with a sl st in first sc. Fasten off.

Second motif

With B, work rnds 1–4 as for rose window. Fasten off.

Joining

Rnd 5 (RS) With RS facing, join background color with a sl st in any ch-5 sp, ch 1, sc in same ch-5 sp, ch 5, sc in next ch-5 lp, place second motif on top of first motif WS tog, to join motifs work as foll: Ch 2, sl st in ch-5 sp of first motif, ch 2, sc in next ch-5 sp of second motif, ch 2, sl st in next ch-5 sp of first motif, ch 2, sc in next ch-5 sp of second motif. Cont to work second motif as foll: *Ch 5, sc in next ch-5 lp; rep from * around, end ch 5, join rnd with a sl st in first sc. Fasten off. To form a square or rectangle, cont to make an even number of rose window motifs

and join tog on rnd 5, joining motifs at two points where they touch.

Filler motif With background color, work rnd 1 as for rose window—24 sc.

Joining

Rnd 2 Ch 1, sc in same place as joining, *ch 4, sc in center of free ch-5 lp of rose window motif, ch 4, skip next 5 sts of filler motif, sc in next st; rep from * around twice more, end ch 4, sc in center of free ch-5 lp of last rose window motif, ch 4, skip next 5 sts of filler motif, join rnd with a sl st in first sc. Fasten off.

105

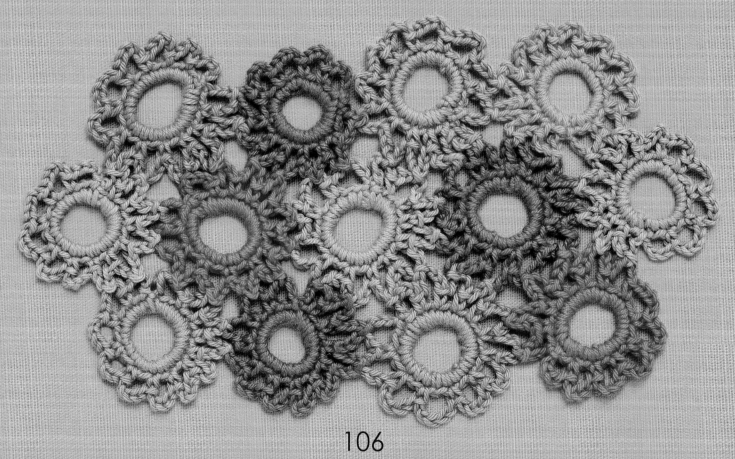

106

107

108

Make an even number of picot circles to form a square or rectangle.

Joining

Join circles to form strips by sewing 2 picots to 2 picots, then join strips together by sewing 3 picots to 3 picots as shown.

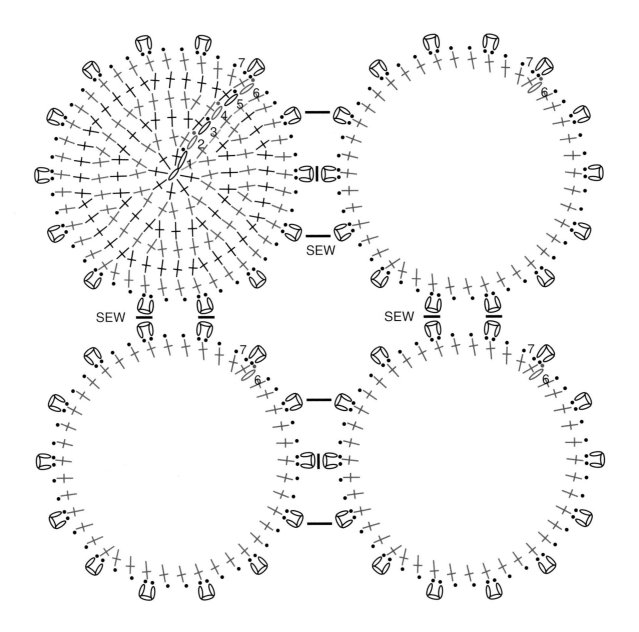

With A, chain 12. Join chain with a sl st, forming a ring.

First motif

Rnd 1 (RS) Ch 1, work 24 sc in ring, join rnd with a sl st in first sc.

Rnd 2 *Ch 5, skip next st, sc in next st; rep from * around, join rnd with a sl st in first sc of rnd 1—12 ch-5 sps. Fasten off.

With B, chain 12. Join ch with a sl st, forming a ring.

Second motif

Rnd 1 (RS) Work as for first motif.

Joining

Rnd 2 Ch 5, skip next st, sc in next st, place second motif on top of first motif WS tog, to join work as foll: [Ch 2, sl st in ch-5 sp of first motif, ch 2, sc in next st of second motif] twice. Cont to work second motif as foll: *Ch 5, skip next st, sc in next st; rep from * around, join rnd with a sl st in first sc of rnd. Fasten off. Referring to photo for suggested placement and color scheme, cont to make and join motifs tog on rnd 2, joining motifs at two points where they touch.

Chain 4. Join chain with a sl st forming a ring.

Rnd 1 (RS) Ch 4 (counts as 1 dc and ch 1), [dc in ring, ch 1] 7 times, join rnd with a sl st in 3rd ch of beg ch-4—8 ch-1 sps.

Rnd 2 Ch 1, sc in same place as joining, [ch 3, skip next ch-1 sp, sc in next dc] 7 times, end ch 3, skip last ch-1 sp, join rnd with a sl st in first sc.

Rnd 3 Sl st in first 2 ch, ch 1, sc in same place as last sl st, [ch 6, sc in next ch-3 sp] 7 times, end ch 6, join rnd with a sl st in first sc.

Rnd 4 Sl st in first 3 ch, ch 1, sc in same place as last sl st, [ch 6, sc in next ch-6 sp] 7 times, end ch 6, join rnd with a sl st in first sc.

Rnd 5 Ch 1, sc in same place as joining, [work (2 dc, ch 4, 2 dc) in next ch-6 lp, sc in next sc] 7 times, end work (2 dc, ch 4, 2 dc) in last ch-6 lp, join rnd with a sl st in first sc.

Rnd 6 Sl st in first 2 dc and next 2 ch, ch 1, sc in same place as last sl st, [ch 8, sc in next ch-4 lp] 7 times, end ch 8, join rnd with a sl st in first sc.

Rnd 7 Ch 1, [work (sc, hdc, 2 dc, tr, 2 dc, hdc, sc) in next ch-8 lp (shell made)] 8 times, join rnd with a sl st in first sc.

Rnd 8 Sl st in first 4 sts, ch 1, sc in same place as last sl st, [ch 11, sc in center tr st of next shell] 7 times, end ch 11, join rnd with a sl st in first sc.

Rnd 9 Ch 1, [work (2 sc, 2 hdc, 2 dc, 4 tr, 2 dc, 2 hdc, 2 sc) in next ch-11 lp] 8 times, join rnd with a sl st in first sc. Fasten off.

With A, chain 4. Join chain with a sl st forming a ring.

Rnd 1 (RS) Ch 4 (counts as 1 dc and ch 1), [dc in ring, ch 1] 7 times, join rnd with a sl st in 3rd ch of beg ch-4—8 ch-1 sps.

Rnd 2 Ch 1, sc in same place as joining, [ch 3, skip next ch-1 sp, sc in next dc] 7 times, end ch 3, skip last ch-1 sp, join rnd with a sl st in first sc.

Rnd 3 Sl st in first 2 ch, ch 1, sc in same place as last sl st, [ch 6, sc in next ch-3 sp] 7 times, end ch 6, join rnd with a sl st in first sc. Fasten off.

Rnd 4 With RS facing, join B with a sl st in 3rd ch of any ch-6 lp, ch 1, sc in same place as joining, [ch 6, sc in next ch-6 sp] 7 times, end ch 6, join rnd with a sl st in first sc.

Rnd 5 Ch 1, sc in same place as joining, [work (2 dc, ch 4, 2 dc) in next ch-6 lp, sc in next sc] 7 times, end work (2 dc, ch 4, 2 dc) in last ch-6 lp, join rnd with a sl st in first sc. Fasten off.

Rnd 6 With RS facing, join C with a sl st in 2nd ch of any ch-4 lp, ch 1, sc in same place as joining, [ch 8, sc in next ch-4 lp] 7 times, end ch 8, join rnd with a sl st in first sc.

Rnd 7 Ch 1, [work (sc, hdc, 2 dc, tr, 2 dc, hdc, sc) in next ch-8 lp (shell made)] 8 times, join rnd with a sl st in first sc. Fasten off.

Rnd 8 With RS facing, join D with a sl st in center st of any shell, ch 1, sc in same place as joining, [ch 11, sc in center st of next shell] 7 times, end ch 11, join rnd with a sl st in first sc.

Rnd 9 Ch 1, [work (2 sc, 2 hdc, 2 dc, 4 tr, 2 dc, 2 hdc, 2 sc) in next ch-11 lp] 8 times, join rnd with a sl st in first sc. Fasten off.

109

110

111

112

With A, chain 4. Join chain with a sl st forming a ring.

Rnd 1 (RS) Ch 4 (counts as 1 dc and ch 1), [dc in ring, ch 1] 7 times, join rnd with a sl st in 3rd ch of beg ch-4—8 ch-1 sps.

Rnd 2 Ch 1, sc in same place as joining, [ch 3, skip next ch-1 sp, sc in next dc] 7 times, end ch 3, skip last ch-1 sp, join rnd with a sl st in first sc.

Rnd 3 Sl st in first 2 ch, ch 1, sc in same place as last sl st, [ch 6, sc in next ch-3 sp] 7 times, end ch 6, join rnd with a sl st in first sc. Fasten off.

Rnd 4 With RS facing, join B with a sl st in 3rd ch of any ch-6 lp, ch 1, sc in same place as joining, [ch 6, sc in next ch-6 sp] 7 times, end ch 6, join rnd with a sl st in first sc.

Rnd 5 Ch 1, sc in same place as joining, [work (2 dc, ch 4, 2 dc) in next ch-6 lp, sc in next sc] 7 times, end work (2 dc, ch 4, 2 dc) in last ch-6 lp, join rnd with a sl st in first sc. Fasten off.

Rnd 6 With RS facing, join C with a sl st in 2nd ch of any ch-4 lp, ch 1, sc in same place as joining, [ch 8, sc in next ch-4 lp] 7 times, end ch 8, join rnd with a sl st in first sc.

Rnd 7 Ch 1, [work (sc, hdc, 2 dc, tr, 2 dc, hdc, sc) in next ch-8 lp (shell made)] 8 times, join rnd with a sl st in first sc. Fasten off.

Rnd 8 With RS facing, join D with a sl st in center st of any shell, ch 1, sc in same place as joining, [ch 11, sc in center st of next shell] 7 times, end ch 11, join rnd with a sl st in first sc.

Rnd 9 Ch 1, [work (2 sc, 2 hdc, 2 dc, 4 tr, 2 dc, 2 hdc, 2 sc) in next ch-11 lp] 8 times, join rnd with a sl st in first sc. Fasten off.

109

110

111

112

109 *Lace Circle*

Chain 6. Join chain with a sl st, forming a ring.

Double crochet 2 together (dc2tog) [Yo, insert hook in st, yo and draw up a lp, yo, draw through 2 lps on hook] twice, yo and draw through all 3 lps on hook.

Double crochet 3 together (dc3tog) [Yo, insert hook in st, yo and draw up a lp, yo, draw through 2 lps on hook] 3 times, yo and draw through all 4 lps on hook.

Half double crochet 4 together (hdc4tog) In same ch-2 sp work [yo, insert hook in ch-2 sp, yo and draw up a lp] 4 times, yo and draw through all 9 lps on hook.

Half double crochet 5 together (hdc5tog) In same ch-2 sp work [yo, insert hook in ch-2 sp, yo and draw up a lp] 5 times, yo and draw through all 11 lps on hook.

Rnd 1 (RS) Ch 6 (counts as 1 tr and ch 2), [tr in ring, ch 2] 7 times, join rnd with a sl st in 4th ch of beg ch-6—8 ch-2 sps.

Rnd 2 Ch 2, work hdc4tog in next ch-2 sp (counts as hdc5tog), [ch 7, work hdc5tog in next ch-2 sp] 7 times, end ch 7, join rnd with a sl st in first hdc.

Rnd 3 Sl st in first 3 ch, ch 1, work 3 sc in same ch-7 sp, [ch 9, work 3 sc in next ch-7 sp] 7 times, end ch 9, join rnd with a sc in first sc.

Rnd 4 Ch 3, skip next sc, dc2tog over center sc and next ch (counts as dc3tog), *ch 2, skip next ch, dc in next ch, ch 2, skip next ch, work (dc, ch 3, dc) in next ch, ch 2, skip next ch, dc in next ch, ch 2, skip next ch**, work dc3tog over (next ch, center sc and next ch); rep from * around 6 times more, then from * to ** once, join rnd with a sl st in top beg ch-3. Fasten off.

110 *Asteroid*

Chain 8. Join chain with a sl st, forming a ring.

Rnd 1 (RS) Ch 1, [sc in ring, ch 3, tr in ring, ch 3] 8 times, join rnd with a sl st in first sc.

Rnd 2 Sl st in first 3 ch and first tr, [ch 15, dc in 12th ch from hook, ch 3, sl st to top of next tr] 8 times.

Rnd 3 Sl st in next 4 ch, ch 3 (count as 1dc), *work (hdc, 7 sc, hdc) in next ch-8 lp, dc in next dc, skip last 3 ch of same segment and first 3 ch of next segment**, dc in next ch, (i.e. opposite side of same ch as dc of rnd 2); rep from * around 6 times more, then from * to ** once, join rnd with a sl st in top of beg ch-3.

Rnd 4 Ch 1, sc inserting hook under sl st which joined rnd 3, *ch 3, skip next hdc and sc, sc in next sc, ch 3, skip next sc, work (sc, ch 4, sc) in next sc, ch 3, skip next sc, sc in next sc, ch 3, skip next sc, hdc and dc**, sc between next 2 dc, skip next dc; rep from * around 6 times more, then from * to ** once, join rnd with a sl st in first sc. Fasten off.

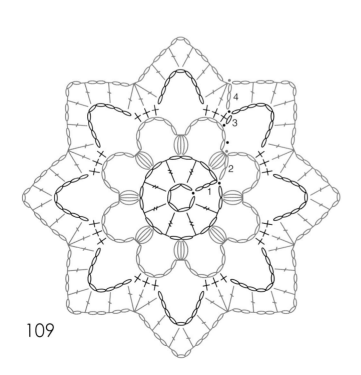

109

110

With A, chain 8. Join chain with a sl st, forming a ring.

Double crochet 2 together (dc2tog) In same sp work [yo, insert hook in sp, yo and draw up a lp, yo, draw through 2 lps on hook] twice, yo and draw through all 3 lps on hook.

Cluster (CL) Work (dc2tog, ch 3, dc2tog) in a st to form a cluster.

Note When changing colors, draw new color through when you sl st to join rnd..

Rnd 1 (RS) Ch 3 (count as 1 dc), work 31 dc in ring, join rnd with a sl st in top of beg ch-3, changing to B—32 dc. Fasten off.

Rnd 2 Ch 3, dc in same place as joining (counts as dc2tog), ch 3, work dc2tog in same place as last dc2tog (first cluster made), *ch 7, skip next 3 sts, work (dc2tog, ch 3, dc2tog) in next st (cluster made);

rep from * around 6 times more, end ch 7, skip next 3 sts, join rnd with a sl st in top of first cluster.

Rnd 3 Sl st in first ch of first ch-3 sp, ch 3, dc in same ch-3 sp (counts as 2dctog), ch 3, work dc2tog in same ch-3 sp, *ch 7, skip next ch-7 lp, work (dc2tog, ch 3, dc2tog) in next ch-3 sp; rep from * around 6 times more, end ch 7, skip next ch-7 lp, join rnd with a sl st in top of first cluster.

Rnd 4 Sl st in first ch of first ch-3 sp, ch 3, dc in same ch-3 sp (counts as dc2tog), ch 3, work dc2tog in same ch-3 sp, *ch 4, sc under ch-7 lp of rnd 2 to enclose ch-7 lp of rnd 3, ch 4**, work (dc2tog, ch 3, dc2tog) in next ch-3 sp; rep from * around 6 times more, then from * to ** once, join rnd with a sl st in top of first cluster, changing to C.

Rnd 5 Sl st in first ch of first ch-3 sp, ch 3, dc in

same ch-3 sp (counts as dc2tog), ch 3, work dc2tog into same ch-3 sp, *ch 15, sl st in 12th ch from hook, ch 3, sl st in top of previous cluster, working right to left work 6 dc in ch-12 ring, skip next 4 ch, sl st in next sc, work 8 dc in ring, skip next 4 ch (inner half of Sylvan Circle completed) **, work (dc2tog, ch 3, dc2tog) in next ch-3; rep from * around 6 times more, then from * to ** once, join rnd with a sl st in top of first cluster.

Rnd 6 *Ch 1, work (dc2tog, ch 6, sl st in 5th ch from hook, ch 1, dc2tog) into next ch-3 sp, ch 1, sl st in top of next cluster, work 16 dc in next ch-12 ring (outer half of Sylvan Circle completed), sl st in top of next cluster; rep from * around 7 times more. Fasten off.

Chain 5.

Double treble crochet 2 together (dtr2tog) In same ch-3 sp work [yo twice, insert hook in sp, yo and draw up a lp, (yo, draw through 2 lps on hook) twice] twice, yo and draw through all 3 lps on hook.

Rnd 1 (RS) Work 19 tr in 5th ch from hook, join rnd with a sl st in top of 5 ch.

Rnd 2 Ch 8 (count as 1 dtr and ch 3), [dtr in next tr, ch 3] 19 times, join rnd with a sl st in 5th ch of beg ch-8—20 ch-3 sps.

Rnd 3 Sl st in in first ch-3 sp, ch 5 (counts as 1 dtr), dtr in same ch-3 sp as sl st, ch 6 [dtr2tog in next ch-3 sp, ch 6] 19 times, join rnd with a sl st in first dtr.

Rnd 4 Sl st in first 3 ch of first ch-6 lp, ch 1, sc in same ch-6 lp as last sl st, [ch 8, sc in next ch-6 lp] 19 times, end ch 4, join rnd with a tr in first sc (counts as last ch-8 lp).

Rnd 5 Ch 1, sc under tr just made, ch 9, [sc in next ch-8 lp, ch 9] 19 times, join rnd with a sl st in first sc. Fasten off.

113

114

Hexagons

113 *Double Crochet Cluster—Solid*

Chain 6. Join chain with a sl st, forming a ring.

Double crochet 2 together (dc2tog) [Yo, insert hook in sp, yo and draw up a lp, yo, draw through 2 lps on hook] twice, yo and draw through all 3 lps on hook.

Double crochet 3 together (dc3tog) [Yo, insert hook in sp, yo and draw up a lp, yo, draw through 2 lps on hook] 3 times, yo and draw through all 4 lps on hook.

Rnd 1 (RS) Ch 3 (counts as 1 dc), dc2tog into ring (with beg ch-3 counts as dc3tog), *ch 3, work dc3tog in ring; rep from * around 4 times more, end ch 1, join rnd with a hdc in top of first cluster—6 clusters.

Rnd 2 Ch 3 (counts as 1 dc), dc2tog in sp formed by hdc (with beg ch-3 counts as dc3tog), *ch 3, work (dc3tog, ch 3, dc3tog) into next ch-3 sp; rep from * around 4 times more, end ch 3, dc3tog in last sp, ch 1, join rnd with a hdc in top of first cluster—12 clusters.

Rnd 3 Ch 3 (counts as 1 dc), dc2tog in sp formed by hdc (with beg ch-3 counts as dc3tog), *ch 3, work (dc3tog, ch 3, dc3tog) into next ch-3 sp **, ch 3, dc3tog into next ch-3 sp; rep from * around 4 times more, then rep from * to ** once, end ch 1, join rnd

with a hdc in top of first cluster—18 clusters.

Rnd 4 Ch 3 (counts as 1 dc), dc in sp formed by hdc, *work 3 dc in next ch-3 sp, work (3 dc, ch 3, 3 dc) in next ch-3 sp**, work 3 dc in next ch-3 sp; rep from * around 4 times more times, then from * to ** once, end dc in beg sp, join rnd with a sl st in top of beg ch-3.

Rnd 5 Ch 1, sc in same sp as joining, sc in each dc and ch around, join rnd with a sl st in first sc. Fasten off.

114 *Double Crochet Cluster—Bicolor*

With A, chain 6. Join chain with a sl st, forming a ring.

Double crochet 2 together (dc2tog) [Yo, insert hook in sp, yo and draw up a lp, yo, draw through 2 lps on hook] twice, yo and draw through all 3 lps on hook.

Double crochet 3 together (dc3tog) [Yo, insert hook in sp, yo and draw up a lp, yo, draw through 2 lps on hook] 3 times, yo and draw through all 4 lps on hook.

Rnd 1 (RS) Ch 3 (counts as 1 dc), dc2tog into ring (with beg ch-3 counts as dc3tog), *ch 3, work dc3tog in ring; rep from * around 4 times more, end ch 1, join rnd with a hdc in top of first cluster—6 clusters. Fasten off.

Rnd 2 From RS, join B with a sl st in sp formed by

hdc, ch 3 (counts as 1 dc), dc2tog in same sp (with beg ch-3 counts as dc3tog), *ch 3, work (dc3tog, ch 3, dc3tog) into next ch-3 sp; rep from * around 4 times more, end ch 3, dc3tog in last sp, ch 1, join rnd with a hdc in top of first cluster—12 clusters. Fasten off.

Rnd 3 From RS, join A with a sl st in sp formed by hdc, ch 3 (counts as 1 dc), dc2tog in same sp (with beg ch-3 counts as dc3tog), *ch 3, work (dc3tog, ch 3, dc3tog) into next ch-3 sp **, ch 3, dc3tog into next ch-3 sp; rep from * around 4 times more, then rep from * to ** once, end ch 1, join rnd with a hdc

in top of first cluster—18 clusters. Fasten off.

Rnd 4 From RS, join B with a sl st in sp formed by hdc, ch 3 (counts as 1 dc), dc in same sp, *work 3 dc in next ch-3 sp, work (3 dc, ch 3, 3 dc) in next ch-3 sp**, work 3 dc in next ch-3 sp; rep from * around 4 times more, then from * to ** once, end dc in beg sp, join rnd with a sl st in top of beg ch-3. Fasten off.

Rnd 5 From RS, join A with a sl st in any st, ch 1, sc in same sp as joining, sc in each dc and ch around, join rnd with a sl st in first sc. Fasten off.

113 and 114

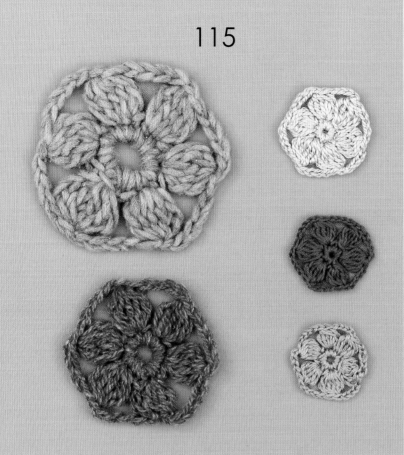

115

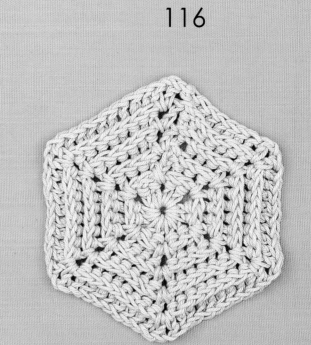

116

117

118

115 Bobble

Chain 6. Join chain with a sl st, forming a ring.

Bobble In same sc work [yo, insert hook in sc, yo and draw up a lp, yo, draw through 2 lps on hook] 5 times, yo and draw through all 6 lps on hook.

Rnd 1 (RS) Ch 1, work 12 sc in ring, join rnd with a sl st in first sc.

Rnd 2 Ch 3 (counts as 1 dc), in same st as joining work [yo, insert hook in sc, yo and draw up a lp, yo, draw through 2 lps on hook] 4 times, yo and draw through all 5 lps on hook (with beg ch 3 counts as first bobble), *ch 5, skip next st, work bobble in next st; rep from * around 4 times more, end ch 5, join rnd with a sl st in top of first bobble. Fasten off.

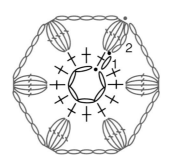

116 3-D—Solid

Chain 4. Join chain with a sl st, forming a ring.

Back raised double crochet (BRDC) Yo, working from back to front to back, insert hook around post of stitch of rnd below, yo and draw up a lp, [yo and draw through 2 lps on hook] twice.

V-st Work (dc, ch 1, dc) in same sp.

Rnd 1 (RS) Ch 3 (counts as 1 dc), dc in ring, *ch 1, work 2 dc in ring; rep from * around 4 times more, end ch 1, join rnd with a sl st in top of beg ch-3— 6 ch-1 sps.

Rnd 2 Sl st in first dc and first ch, ch 3 (counts as 1 dc), *BRDC around each of next 2 dc**, V-st in next ch-1 sp; rep from * 4 times more, then from * to ** once, end dc in last ch-1 sp, ch 1, join rnd with a sl st in top of beg ch-3.

Rnd 3 Ch 3 (counts as 1 dc), BRDC around each dc and work a V-st in each ch-1 sp around, join rnd with a sl st in top of beg ch-3—6 groups of 6 dc.

Rnd 4 Rep rnd 3—6 groups of 8 dc.

Rnd 5 Rep rnd 3—6 groups of 10 dc. Fasten off.

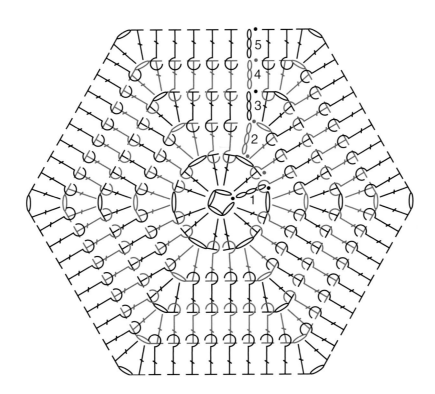

With A, chain 4. Join chain with a sl st, forming a ring.

Back raised double crochet (BRDC) Yo, working from back to front to back, insert hook around post of stitch of rnd below, yo and draw up a lp, [yo and draw through 2 lps on hook] twice.

V-st Work (dc, ch 1, dc) in same sp.

Note When changing colors, draw new color through when you sl st to join rnd.

Rnd 1 (RS) Ch 3 (counts as 1 dc), dc in ring, *ch 1, work 2 dc in ring; rep from * around 4 times more, end ch 1, join rnd with a sl st in top of beg ch-3—6 ch-1 sps.

Rnd 2 Sl st in first dc and first ch, ch 3 (counts as 1 dc), *BRDC around each of next 2 dc**, V-st in next ch-1 sp; rep from * 4 times more, then from * to ** once, end dc in last ch-1 sp, ch 1, join rnd with a sl st

in top of beg ch-3 changing to B.

Rnd 3 Ch 3 (counts as 1 dc), BRDC around each dc and work a V-st in each ch-1 sp around, join rnd with a sl st in top of beg ch-3 changing to C—6 groups of 6 dc.

Rnd 4 Rep rnd 3, changing to D—6 groups of 8 dc.

Rnd 5 Rep rnd 3—6 groups of 10 dc. Fasten off.

118 *Oblong*

Chain 12. Join chain with a sl st, forming a ring.

Rnd 1 (RS) Ch 1, work 24 sc in ring, join rnd with a sl st in first sc.

Rnd 2 Ch 12 (counts as 1 tr and ch 8), skip first sc, sc in next sc, turn, *ch 3 (counts as 1 dc), dc in first 7 ch of arch, turn, ch 3, skip first dc, dc in next 6 dc, dc in top of ch-3 **; (first oblong made), † skip next sc

on ring, tr in next sc, ch 8, skip next sc, sc in next sc, turn and work from * to ** for next oblong. Rep from † 4 times more, join rnd with a sl st in 4th ch of beg ch-12.

Rnd 3 Sl st in top of ch-3 at corner of first oblong, ch 1, sc in top of ch-3, ch 13, (sc in 3rd ch of ch-3 at top of next oblong, ch 13] 5 times, join rnd with a sl st in

first sc.

Rnd 4 Ch 6 (counts as 1 dc and ch 3), dc in same st as joining, [ch 1, skip next ch, dc in next ch] 6 times, ch 1, *work (dc, ch 3, dc) in next sc, [ch 1, skip next ch, dc in next ch] 6 times, ch 1; rep from * around 4 times more, join rnd with a sl st in 3rd ch of beg ch-6. Fasten off.

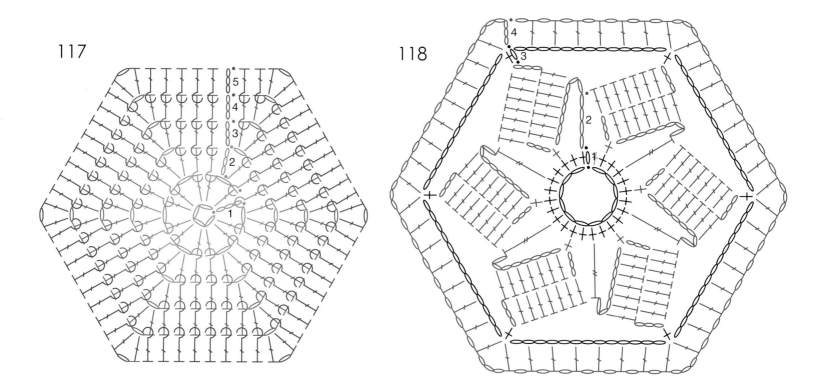

117

118

119

Chain 17.

Single crochet 2 together (sc2tog) [Insert hook in st, yo and draw up a lp] twice, yo and draw through all 3 lps on hook.

Center of star

Row 1 (RS) Sc in 2nd ch from hook and in each ch across—16 sts. Ch 1, turn.

Row 2 Sc in first st, work 2 sc in next st, sc in 12 next sts, work 2 sc in next st, sc in last st—18 sts. Ch 1, turn.

Row 3 and all RS rows Sc in each st across. Ch 1, turn.

Row 4 Sc in first st, work 2 sc in next st, sc in each st to last 3 sts, end work 2 sc in next st, sc in last st—20 sts. Ch 1, turn.

Rows 6, 8, 10, 12 and 14 Rep row 4. When row 14 is completed—30 sts. Ch 1, turn.

Row 16 Sc in first st, sc2tog, sc in each st to last 3 sts, end sc2tog, sc in last st—28 sts. Ch 1, turn.

Rows 18, 20, 22, 24, 26 and 28 Rep row 16. When row 28 is completed—16 sts. Do not ch, turn.

Star points

Rnd 1 (RS) Ch 3 (counts as 1 dc), skip first st, dc in next 15 sts, ch 3, [work 16 dc evenly spaced across next side edge, ch 3] twice, turn to bottom edge, working in bottom lps of beg ch, dc in next 16 lps, ch 3, [work 16 dc evenly spaced across next side edge, ch 3] twice, join rnd with a sl st in top of beg ch-3—6 ch-3 sps.

Rnd 2 Sl st in first st, ch 3 (counts as 1 dc), dc in next 13 sts, *ch 3, work (dc, ch 3, dc) in next ch-3 sp, ch 3, skip next dc, dc in next 14 sts; rep from * working around 4 sides, end ch 3, work (dc, ch 3, dc) in next ch-3 sp, ch 3, join rnd with a sl st in top of beg ch-3.

Rnd 3 Sl st in first st, ch 3 (counts as 1 dc), dc in next 11 sts, *ch 3, sc in next ch-3 sp, ch 3, work (sc, ch 3, sc) in next ch-3 sp, ch 3, sc in next ch-3 sp, ch 3, skip

next dc, dc in next 12 sts; rep from * working around 4 sides, end ch 3, sc in next ch-3 sp, ch 3, work (sc, ch 3, sc) in next ch-3 sp, ch 3, sc in next ch-3 sp, ch 3, join rnd with a sl st in top of beg ch-3.

Rnd 4 Sl st in first st, ch 3 (counts as 1 dc), dc in next 9 sts, *[ch 3, sc in next ch-3 sp] 5 times, ch 3, skip next dc, dc in next 10 sts; rep from * working around 4 sides, end [ch 3, sc in next ch-3 sp] 5 times, ch 3, skip next dc, join rnd with a sl st in top of beg ch-3.

Rnd 5 Sl st in first st, ch 3 (counts as 1 dc), dc in next 7 sts, *[ch 3, sc in next ch-3 sp] twice, ch 3, sc in next ch-3 sp, sc in next sc, sc in next ch-3 sp, [ch 3, sc in next ch-3 sp] twice, ch 3, skip next dc, dc in next 8 sts; rep from * working around 4 sides, end [ch 3, sc in next ch-3 sp] twice, ch 3, sc in next ch-3 sp, sc in next sc, sc in next ch-3 sp, [ch 3, sc in next ch-3 sp] twice, ch 3, skip next dc, join rnd with a sl st in top of beg ch-3.

Rnd 6 Sl st in first st, ch 3 (counts as 1 dc), dc in next 5 sts, *[ch 3, sc in next ch-3 sp] twice, ch 3, sc in next ch-3 sp, sc in next 3 sc, sc in next ch-3 sp, [ch 3, sc in next ch-3 sp] twice, ch 3, skip next dc, dc in next 6 sts; rep from * working around 4 sides, end [ch 3, sc in next ch-3 sp] twice, ch 3, sc in next ch-3 sp, sc in next 3 sc, sc in next ch-3 sp, [ch 3, sc in next ch-3sp], twice ch 3, skip next dc, join rnd with a sl st in top of beg ch-3.

Rnd 7 Sl st in first st, ch 3 (counts as 1 dc), dc in next 3 sts, *[ch 3, sc in next ch-3 sp] twice, ch 3, sc in next ch-3 sp, sc in next 5 sc, sc in next ch-3 sp, [ch 3, sc in next ch-3 sp] twice, ch 3, skip next dc, dc in next 4 sts; rep from * working around 4 sides, end [ch 3, sc in next ch-3 sp] twice, ch 3, sc in next ch-3 sp, sc in next 5 sc, sc in next ch-3 sp, [ch 3, sc in next ch-3 sp] twice, ch 3, skip next dc, join rnd with a sl st in top of beg ch-3.

Rnd 8 Sl st in first st, ch 3 (counts as 1 dc), dc in next st, *[ch 3, sc in next ch-3 sp] 3 times, ch 3, skip next sc, sc in next 5 sc, [ch 3, sc in next ch-3 sp] 3 times, ch 3, skip next dc, dc in next 2 sts; rep from * working around 4 sides, end [ch 3, sc in next ch-3 sp] 3 times, ch 3, sc in next ch-3 sp, skip next sc, sc in next 5 sc, skip next sc, [ch 3, sc in next ch-3 sp] 3 times, ch 3, join rnd with a sl st in top of beg ch-3.

Rnd 9 Sl st in sp between first 2 dc, ch 6 (counts as 1 dc and ch 3), dc in same sp, *[ch 3, sc in next ch-3 sp] 4 times, ch 3, skip next sc, sc in next 3 sc, [ch 3, sc in next ch-3 sp] 4 times, ch 3, work (dc, ch 3, dc) in sp between next 2 dc; rep from * working around 4 sides, end [ch 3, sc in next ch-3 sp] 4 times, ch 3, skip next sc, sc in next 3 sc, [ch 3, sc in next ch-3 sp] 4 times, ch 3, join rnd with a sl st in 3rd ch of beg ch-6.

Rnd 10 Sl st in first ch-3 sp, ch 6 (counts as 1 dc and ch 3), dc in same sp, *[ch 3, sc in next ch-3 sp] 5 times, ch 3, skip next sc, sc in next sc, [ch 3, sc in next ch-3 sp] 5 times, ch 3, work (dc, ch 3, dc) in next ch-3 sp; rep from * working around 4 sides, end [ch 3, sc in next ch-3 sp] 5 times, ch 3, skip next sc, sc in next sc, [ch 3, sc in next ch-3 sp] 5 times, ch 3, join rnd with a sl st in 3rd ch of beg ch-6.

Rnd 11 Sl st in first ch-3 sp, ch 6 (counts as 1 dc and ch 3), dc in same sp, *[ch 3, sc in next ch-3 sp] 12 times, ch 3, work (dc, ch 3, dc) in next ch-3 sp; rep from * working around 4 sides, end [ch 3, sc in next ch-3 sp] 12 times, ch 3, join rnd with a sl st in 3rd ch of beg ch-6.

Rnd 12 Sl st in first 2 ch of first ch-3 sp, ch 3, sl st in same sp as last sl st (picot made), *sl st in next (ch, st and 2 ch), ch 3, sl st in same sp as last sl st; rep from * working around 4 sides, end sl st in last 3 sts, join rnd with a sl st in first sl st. Fasten off.

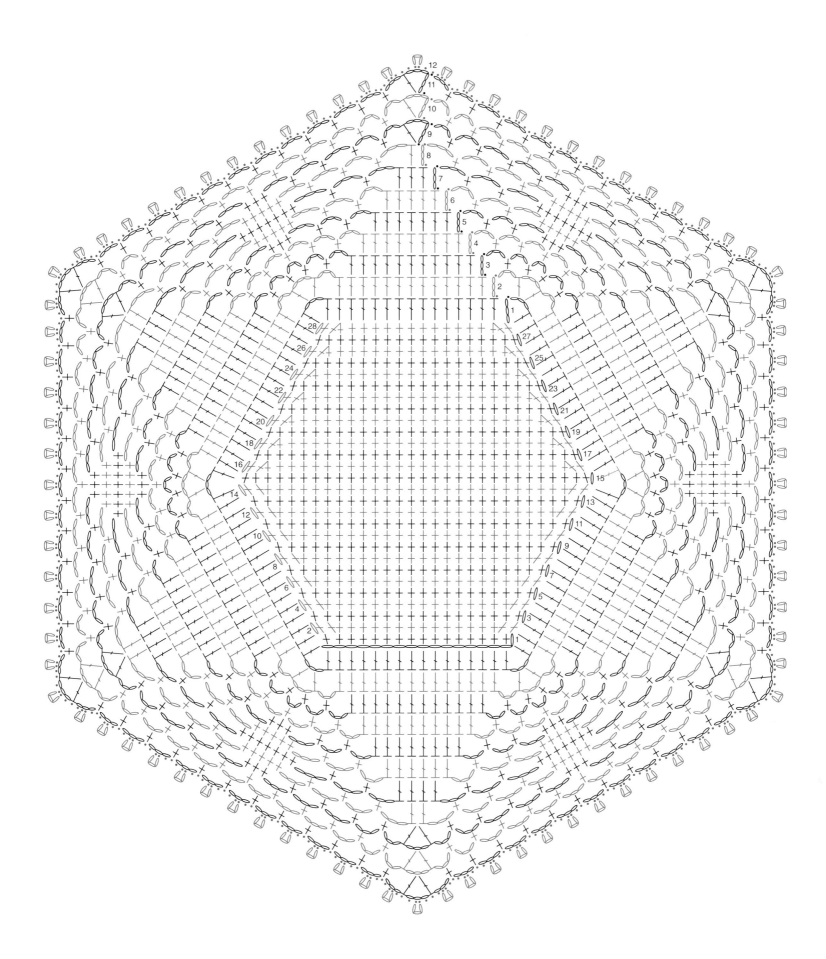

120

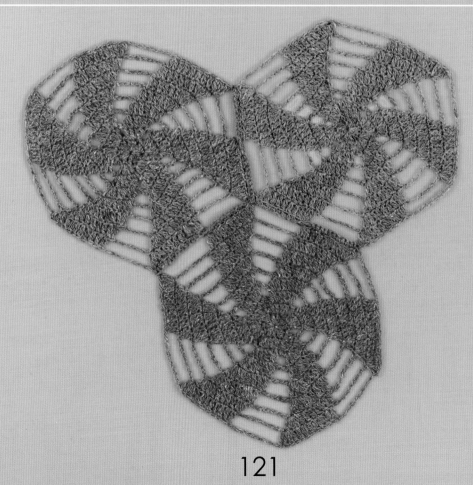

121

120 *Wheel*

Chain 4. Join chain with a sl st, forming a ring.

Double crochet 2 together (dc2tog) [Yo, insert hook in next dc, yo and draw up a lp, yo, draw through 2 lps on hook] twice, yo and draw through all 3 lps on hook.

Rnd 1 (RS) Ch 3 (count as 1 dc), dc in ring, *ch 2, work 2 dc in ring; rep from * around 4 more times, ch 2, join rnd with a sl st in top of beg ch-3.

Rnd 2 Ch 3 (count as 1dc), work 2 dc in same sp as joining, dc in next dc, *ch 3, skip next 2 ch, work 3 dc in next dc, dc in next dc; rep from * around 4 more times, end ch 3, skip last 2 ch, join rnd with a sl st in top of beg ch-3—6 segments of 4 dc and 3 ch.

Rnd 3 Ch 3 (counts as 1 dc), work 2 dc in same sp as joining, dc in next dc, dc2tog all next 2 dc, *ch 4, skip next 3 ch, work 3 dc in next dc, dc in next dc, dc2tog

over next 2 dc; rep from * around 4 more times, end ch 4, skip last 3 ch, join rnd with a sl st in top of beg ch-3.

Rnd 4 Ch 3 (counts as 1 dc), work 2 dc in same sp as joining, dc in next 2 dc, dc2tog over next 2 dc, *ch 5, skip next 4 ch, work 3 dc in next dc, dc in next 2 dc, dc2tog all next 2 dc; rep from * around 4 more times, end ch 5, skip last 4 ch, join rnd with a sl st in top of beg ch-3.

Rnd 5 Ch 3 (counts as 1 dc), work 2 dc in same sp as joining, dc in next 3 dc, dc2tog over next 2 dc, *ch 6, skip next 5 ch, work 3 dc in next dc, dc in next 3 dc, dc2tog all next 2 dc; rep from * around 4 more times, end ch 6, skip last 5 ch, join rnd with a sl st in top of beg ch-3.

Rnd 6 Ch 3 (counts as 1 dc), work 2 dc in same sp as joining, dc in next 4 dc, dc2tog all next 2 dc, *ch 7,

skip next 6 ch, work 3 dc in next dc, dc in next 4 dc, dc2tog all next 2 dc; rep from * around 4 more times, end ch 7, skip last 6 ch, join rnd with a sl st in top of beg ch-3.

Rnd 7 Ch 3 (counts as 1 dc), work 2 dc in same sp as joining, dc in next 5 dc, dc2tog all next 2 dc, *ch 8, skip next 7 ch, work 3 dc in next dc, dc in next 5 dc, dc2tog all next 2 dc; rep from * around 4 more times, end ch 8, skip last 7 ch, join rnd with a sl st in top of beg ch-3.

Rnd 8 Ch 3 (counts as 1 dc), work 2 dc in same sp as joining, dc in next 6 dc, dc2tog all next 2 dc, *ch 9, skip next 8 ch, work 3 dc in next dc, dc in next 6 dc, dc2tog all next 2 dc; rep from * around 4 more times, end ch 9, skip last 8 ch, join rnd with a sl st in top of beg ch-3. Fasten off.

121 *Wheels—Connected*

Make 3 wheels using A, B and C.

Joining

Place 2 motifs together, WS facing and edges even.

With RS facing, sc motifs together, working 1 sc in each dc and ch across edge using the contrasting color. Referring to photo, continue to join motifs together.

120
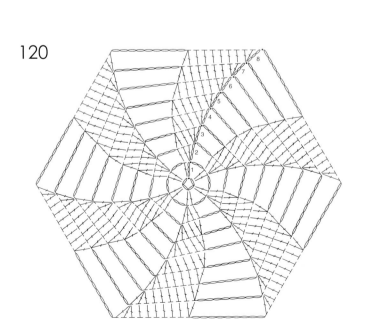

121
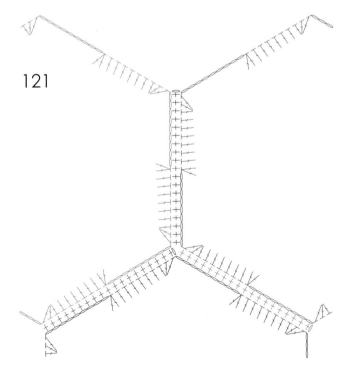

123

122 Starfish

Chain 9. Join chain with a sl st forming a ring.

Rnd 1 (RS) Ch 1, work 18 sc in ring, join rnd with a sl st in first sc.

Rnd 2 Ch 9, sc in 4th ch from hook, hdc in next 2 ch, dc in next 3 ch, skip first 3 sc on ring, sl st in next sc, *ch 9, sc in 4th ch from hook, hdc in next 2 ch, dc in next 3 ch, skip next 2 sc on ring, sl st in next sc; rep from * around 4 more times, join rnd with a sl st in sl st of rnd 2. Fasten off.

123 Flower

Chain 6. Join chain with a sl st forming a ring.

Rnd 1 (RS) Ch 4 (counts as 1 dc and ch 1), *dc in ring, ch 1; rep from * around 10 times more, join rnd with a sl st in 3rd ch of beg ch-4—12 ch-1 sps.

Rnd 2 Ch 3 (counts as 1 dc), work 2 dc in first ch-1 sp, dc in next dc, ch 2, *skip next ch-1 sp, dc in next dc, work 2 dc in next ch-1 sp, dc in next dc, ch 2; rep from * around 4 more times, join rnd with a sl st in top of beg ch-3—6 ch-2 sps.

Rnd 3 Ch 3 (counts as 1 dc), dc in same sp as joining, dc in next 2 dc, work 2 dc in next dc, ch 2, *work 2 dc in next dc, dc in next 2 dc, 2 dc in next dc, ch 2; rep from * around 4 times more, join rnd with a sl st in top of beg ch-3.

Rnd 4 Ch 3 (counts as 1 dc), dc in same sp as joining, dc in next 4 dc, work 2 dc in next dc, ch 2, *work 2 dc in next dc, dc in next 4 dc, 2 dc in next dc, ch 2; rep from * around 4 times more, join rnd with a sl st in top of beg ch-3.

Rnd 5 Ch 3 (counts as 1 dc), dc in next 7 dc, *ch 3, sc in next ch-2 sp, ch 3, dc in next 8 dc; rep from * around 4 times more, end ch 3, sc in last ch-2 sp, ch 3, join rnd with a sl st in top of beg ch-3.

Rnd 6 Sl st in first dc, ch 3 (counts as 1 dc), dc in next 5 dc, *ch 3, [sc in next ch-3 sp, ch 3] twice, skip next dc, dc in next 6 dc; rep from * around 4 times more, end ch 3, [sc in next ch-3 sp, ch 3] twice, join rnd with a sl st in top of beg ch-3.

Rnd 7 Sl st in first dc, ch 3 (counts as 1 dc), dc in next 3 dc, *ch 3, [sc in next ch-3 sp, ch 3] 3 times, skip next dc, dc in next 4 dc; rep from * around 4 times more, end ch 3, [sc in next ch-3 sp, ch 3] 3 times, join rnd with a sl st in top of beg ch-3.

Rnd 8 Sl st between 2nd and 3rd dc of group, ch 3 (counts as 1 dc), dc in same sp as sl st, *ch 3, [sc in next ch-3 sp, ch 3] 4 times, work 2 dc between 2nd and 3rd dc of group; rep from * around 4 times more, end ch 3, [sc in next ch-3 sp, ch 3] 4 times, join rnd with a sl st in top of beg ch-3.

Rnd 9 Sl st in first dc and ch-3 sp, ch 3 (counts as 1 dc), work 3 dc in same ch-3 sp, [work 4 dc in next ch-3 sp] 4 times, *ch 3, skip next 2 dc, [work 4 dc in next ch-3 sp] 5 times; rep from * around 4 times more, end ch 3, join rnd with a sl st in top of beg ch-3. Fasten off.

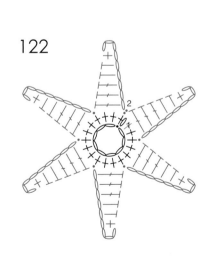

122

123

124

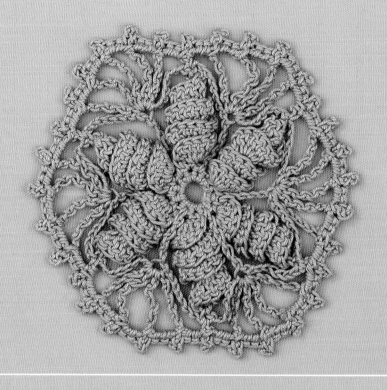

125

124

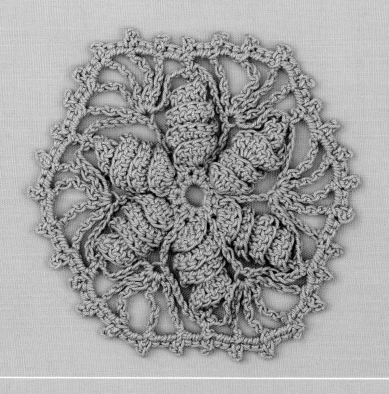

125

124 *Curly Wurly*

Chain 6. Join chain with a sl st, forming a ring.

Make curlique (MCR) Ch 12, work 5 dc in 4th ch from hook, work 5 dc in next and each rem ch to end, then sl st in same place as ch 12.

Make picot (MP) Ch 3, insert hook down through top of sc just made, then work sl st to close.

Rnd 1 (RS) Ch 1, work 12 sc in ring, join rnd with a sl st in first sc—12 sc.

Rnd 2 *MCR, sl st in next 2 sc; rep from * around 4 times more, end MCR, sl st in last sc—6 curliques.

Rnd 3 Ch 14 (counts as 1 ttr and ch 8), *sc in tip of next curlique, ch 8**, ttr in sc of first rnd between curlicues, ch 8; rep from * around 4 more times, then from * to ** once, join rnd with a sl st in 6th ch of beg ch-14.

Rnd 4 Ch 8 (counts as 1 ttr and ch 2), work [ttr, ch 2] 4 times in same place as ch-8, *skip next 8 ch, sc in next sc, ch 2, skip next 8 ch**, work [ttr, ch 2] 5 times in next ttr; rep from * around 4 times more, then from * to ** once, join rnd with a sl st in 6th ch of beg ch-8.

Rnd 5 Ch 1, *work 3 sc in next ch-2 sp, MP; rep from * in each ch-2 sp around, join rnd with a sl st in first sc. Fasten off.

125 *Picot*

Chain 12. Join chain with a sl st, forming a ring.

Make picot (MP) Ch 3, sl st in top of st just made.

Rnd 1 (RS) Ch 1, work 24 sc in ring, join rnd with a sl st in first sc—24 sc.

Rnd 2 Ch 1, sc in same sp as joining, *sc in next st, MP **, sc in next st; rep from * around 10 times more, then from * to ** once, join rnd with a sl st in first sc—12 picots.

Rnd 3 Ch 8 (counts as 1 tr and ch 4), skip picot, *tr in next sc between picots, ch 4; rep from * around 10 times more, join rnd with a sl st in 4th ch of beg ch-8.

Rnd 4 Ch 1, *work 5 sc in next ch-4 sp; rep from * around 11 times more, join rnd with a sl st in first sc.

Rnd 5 Ch 1, *sc in back lp of next 5 sc, ch 15, skip next 5 sc; rep from * around 5 times more, join rnd with a sl st in first sc—6 ch-15 lps.

Rnd 6 Ch 1, *sc in back lp of next 5 sc, work 15 sc in next ch-15 lp; rep from * around 5 times more, join rnd with a sl st in first sc.

Rnd 7 Sl st into back lp of next st, ch 1, sc in same sp as joining, sc in back lp of next 2 sc, *skip next sc, [sc in next 3 sc, MP] 4 times, sc in next 3 sc, skip next sc**, sc in back lp of next 3 sc; rep from * around 4 times more, then work from * to ** once, join rnd with a sl st in first sc. Fasten off.

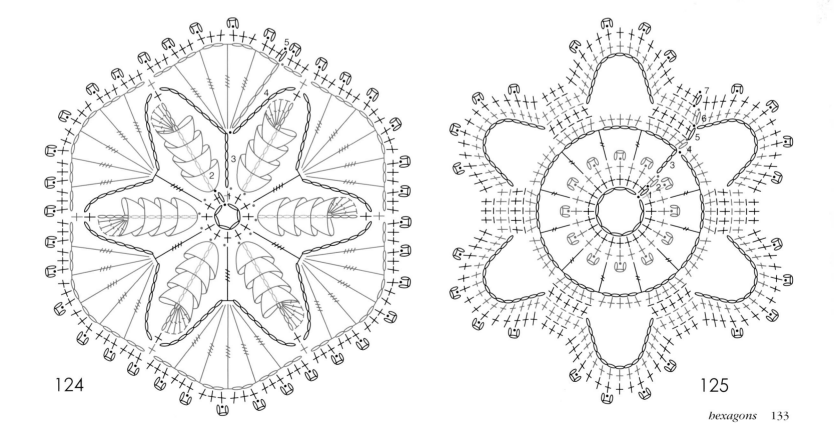

124

125

126

127

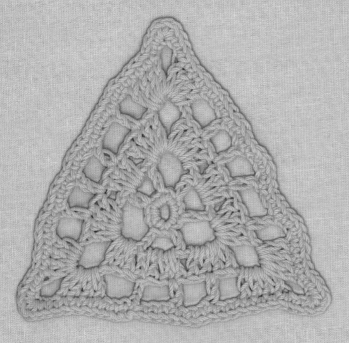

128

129

126

127

128

129

Triangles

126 *Single Crochet Triangle*

Chain 2.

Row 1 (RS) Sc in 2nd ch from hook—1 sc. Ch 1, turn.

Row 2 Work 3 sc in st—3 sc. Ch 1, turn.

Row 3 Work 2 sc in first st, sc in next st, work 2 sc in last st—5 sc. Ch 1, turn.

Row 4 Sc in each st across. Ch 1, turn.

Row 5 Work 2 sc in first st, sc in each st to next to last st, work 2 sc in last st. Ch 1, turn.

Row 6 Sc in each st across. Ch 1, turn.

Rep rows 5 and 6 until desired size is reached. Fasten off.

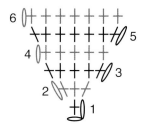

127 *Half Double Crochet Triangle*

To make an adjustable ring, make a slipknot 10"/25.5cm from free end of yarn. Place slipknot on hook, then wrap free end of yarn twice around your first and second fingers on your left hand. Then work with yarn coming from ball as follows:

Rnd 1 (RS) Work 12 sc in ring, pull free end of yarn to close circle, then join rnd with a sl st in first sc—12 sc.

Rnd 2 Ch 10 (counts as 1 dc and ch 7), skip first 2 sts, *dc in next st, ch 3, skip next st, dc in next st, ch 7, skip next st; rep from * around once more, end, dc in next st, ch 3, skip last st, join rnd with a sl st in 3rd ch of beg ch-10—3 ch-7 lps.

Rnd 3 Ch 2 (counts as 1 hdc), work (3 hdc, ch 7, 4 hdc) in first ch-7 lp, *work 3 hdc in next ch-3 lp, work (4 hdc, ch 7, 4 hdc) in next ch-7 lp; rep from * around once more, end work 3 hdc in last ch-3 lp, join rnd with a sl st in top of beg ch-2—3 ch-7 corners.

Rnd 4 Ch 2 (counts as 1 hdc), hdc in first 3 sts, *work (2 hdc, ch 5, 2 hdc) in next ch-7 lp, hdc in next 11 sts; rep from * around once more, end work (2 hdc, ch 5, 2 hdc) in last ch-7 lp, hdc in last 7 sts, join rnd with a sl st in top of beg ch-2.

Rnd 5 Ch 2 (counts as 1 hdc), hdc in first 5 sts, *work (2 hdc, ch 5, 2 hdc) in next ch-5 lp, hdc in next 15 sts; rep from * around once more, end work (2 hdc, ch 5, 2 hdc) in last ch-5 lp, hdc in last 9 sts, join rnd with a sl st in top of beg ch-2. Fasten off.

To make an adjustable ring, make a slipknot 10"/25.5cm from free end of yarn. Place slipknot on hook, then wrap free end of yarn twice around your first and second fingers on your left hand. Then work with yarn coming from ball as follows:

Rnd 1 (RS) Work 12 sc in ring, pull free end of yarn to close circle, then join rnd with a sl st in first sc—12 sc.

Rnd 2 Ch 10 (counts as 1 dc and ch 7), skip first 2 sts, *dc in next st, ch 3, skip next st, dc in next st, ch 7, skip next st; rep from * around once more, end, dc in next st, ch 3, skip last st, join rnd with a sl st in 3rd ch of beg ch-10—3 ch-7 lps.

Rnd 3 Ch 3 (counts as 1 dc), work (3 dc, ch 7, 4 dc) in first ch-7 lp, *work 3 dc in next ch-3 lp, work (4 dc, ch 7, 4 dc) in next ch-7 lp; rep from * around once more, end work 3 dc in last ch-3 lp, join rnd with a sl st in top of beg ch-3—3 ch-7 corners.

Rnd 4 Ch 6 (counts as 1 dc and ch 3), *work (4 dc, ch 5, 4 dc) in next ch-7 lp, [ch 3, skip next 2 sts, dc in next st] 3 times, ch 3; rep from * around once more, end work (4 dc, ch 5, 4 dc) in last ch-7 lp, [ch 3, skip next 2 sts, dc in next st] twice, ch 3, join rnd with a sl st in 3rd ch of beg ch-6—3 ch-5 corners.

Rnd 5 Ch 1, sc in first 3 ch, sc in first 4 sts, sc in next 2 ch, work 4 sc in next ch, sc in next 2 ch, *sc in next 4 sts, [sc in next 3 ch, sc in next st] 3 times, sc in next 3 ch, sc in next 4 sts, sc in next 2 ch, work 4 sc in next ch, sc in next 2 ch; rep from * around once more, end sc in next 4 sts, [sc in next 3 ch, sc in next st] twice, sc in last 3 ch, join rnd with a sl st in first sc. Fasten off.

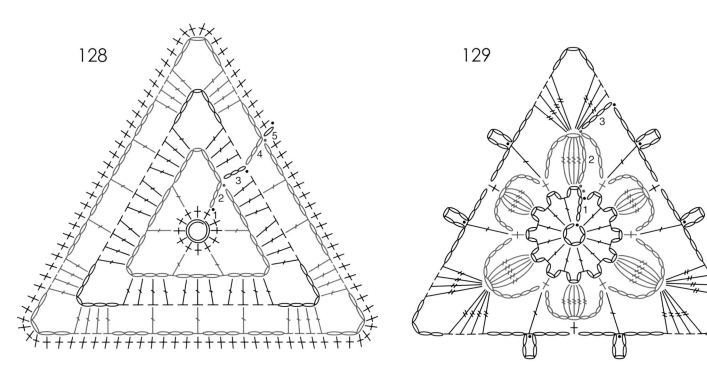

128

129

129 *Popcorn*

Chain 6. Join chain with a sl st, forming a ring.

Popcorn Work 5 tr in same ch-sp, drop lp from hook. Working from front to back, insert hook into both lps of first tr, pick up dropped lp and draw through tr, then ch 1 to secure popcorn.

Make picot (MP) Ch 5, sl st in top of dc just made.

Rnd 1 (RS) Ch 6 (counts as 1 dc and ch 3), *dc in ring, ch 3; rep from * around 10 times more, join rnd with a sl st in 3rd ch of beg ch-6—12 ch-3 sps.

Rnd 2 Sl st in first 2 ch of beg ch-3 sp, ch 4 (counts as 1 tr), work 4 tr in beg ch-3 sp, drop lp from hook, working from front to back, insert hook into top of beg ch-4, pick up dropped lp and draw through ch, then ch 1 to secure popcorn (beg popcorn made), ch 5, sc in next ch-3 sp, *ch 5, skip first ch of next ch-3 sp, work popcorn in next ch, ch 5, sc in next ch-3 sp; rep from * around 4 times more, end ch 5, join rnd with a sl st in top of beg popcorn—6 popcorns.

Rnd 3 Ch 4 (counts as 1 tr), work (3 tr, ch 5, 4 tr) in top of first popcorn, ch 3, dc in next sc, MP, ch 3, sc in top of next popcorn, ch 3, dc in next sc, MP, ch 3, *work (4 tr, ch 5, 4 tr) in top of next popcorn, ch 3, dc in next sc, MP, ch 3, sc in top of next popcorn, ch 3, dc in next sc, MP, ch 3; rep from * around once more, join rnd with a sl st in top of beg ch-4—3 ch-5 corners and 6 picots. Fasten off.

130

With A, chain 6. Join chain with a sl st, forming a ring.

Popcorn Work 5 tr in same ch-sp, drop lp from hook. Working from front to back, insert hook into both lps of first tr, pick up dropped lp and draw through tr, then ch 1 to secure popcorn.

Rnd 1 (RS) Ch 6 (counts as 1 dc and ch 3), *dc in ring, ch 3; rep from * around 10 times more, join rnd with a sl st in 3rd ch of beg ch-6—12 ch-3 sps.

Rnd 2 Sl st in first 2 ch of beg ch-3 sp, ch 4 (counts as 1 tr), work 4 tr in beg ch-3 sp, drop lp from hook, working from front to back, insert hook into top of beg ch-4, pick up dropped lp and draw through ch, then ch 1 to secure popcorn (beg popcorn made), ch 5, sc in next ch-3 sp, *ch 5, skip first ch of next ch-3 sp, work popcorn in next ch, ch 5, sc in next ch-3 sp; rep from * around 4 times more, end ch 5, join rnd with a sl st in top of beg popcorn—6 popcorns.

Rnd 3 Ch 4 (counts as 1 tr), work (3 tr, ch 5, 4 tr) in top of first popcorn, ch 3, dc in next sc, ch 3, sc in top of next popcorn, ch 3, dc in next sc, ch 3, *work (4 tr, ch 5, 4 tr) in top of next popcorn, ch 3, dc in next sc, ch 3, sc in top of next popcorn, ch 3, dc in next sc, ch 3; rep from * around once more, join rnd with a sl st in top of beg ch-4—3 ch-5 corners.

Rnd 4 Ch 1, sc in first 3 tr, sc in next 2 ch, *work (sc, ch 2, sc) in next ch, sc in next 2 ch, sc in next 4 tr, sc in next 3 ch, sc in next dc, sc in next 3 ch, sc in next sc, sc in next 3 ch, sc in next dc, sc in next 3 ch, sc in next 4 tr, sc in next 2 ch; rep from * around once more, end work (sc, ch 2, sc) in next ch, sc in next 2 ch, sc in next 4 tr, sc in next 3 ch, sc in next dc, sc in next 3 ch, sc in next sc, sc in next 3 ch, sc in next dc, sc in last 3 ch, join rnd with a sl st in first sc—3 ch-2 corners. Fasten off. Make 2 more motifs using B and C.

Joining

Place 2 motifs together, WS facing and edges even. With RS facing, sc motifs together using the contrasting colors.

grannies

Chapter 4

132

Grannies—*Basic*

131 *Diagonal Increase Square*

This square is made by working increases in the center st of each row.

Chain 2.

Row 1 (RS) Work 3 sc in 2nd ch from hook—3 sc. Ch 1, turn.

Row 2 Sc in first st, work 3 sc in center st, sc in last st. Ch 1, turn.

Row 3 Sc in first 2 sts, work 3 sc in center st, sc in last 2 sts. Ch 1, turn.

Row 4 Sc in first 3 sts, work 3 sc in center st, sc in last 3 sts. Ch 1, turn.

Row 5 Sc in first 4 sts, work 3 sc in center st, sc in last 4 sts. Ch 1, turn. Working in this manner, cont to work 3 sc in center st of of each row until square is the required or desired size. When last row is completed, do not ch and turn; fasten off.

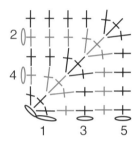

132 *Four Increase Square*

This square is made by working increases in each corner of each round.

To make an adjustable ring, make a slipknot 10"/25.5cm from free end of yarn. Place slipknot on hook, then wrap free end of yarn twice around your first and second fingers on your left hand. Then work with yarn coming from ball as follows:

Rnd 1 (RS) Work 12 sc in ring, pull free end of yarn to close circle, then join rnd with a sl st in first sc—12 sc.

Rnd 2 Ch 1, sc in first st, *work 3 sc in next st (corner made), sc in next 2 sts; rep from * around twice, end work 3 sc in next st (last corner made), sc in last st, join rnd with a sl st in first st—4 corners made.

Rnd 3 Ch 1, sc in first 2 sts, *work 3 sc in next st, sc in next 4 sts; rep from * around twice, end work 3 sc in next st, sc in last 2 sts, join rnd with a sl st in first st.

Rnd 4 Ch 1, sc in first 3 sts, *work 3 sc in next st, sc in next 6 sts; rep from * around twice, end work 3 sc in next st, sc in last 3 sts, join rnd with a sl st in first st.

Rnd 5 Ch 1, sc in first 4 sts, *work 3 sc in next st, sc in next 8 sts; rep from * around twice, end work 3 sc in next st, sc in last 4 sts, join rnd with a sl st in first st. Working in this manner, cont to work 2 more sc along each side every rnd until square is the required or desired size. Fasten off.

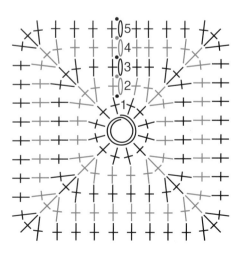

133

134

133 *Traditional Granny*

Chain 4. Join chain with a sl st, forming a ring.

Rnd 1 (RS) Ch 5 (counts as 1 dc and ch 2), [3 dc in ring, ch 2] 3 times, work 2 dc in ring, join rnd with a sl st in 3rd ch of beg ch-5.

Rnd 2 Sl st in first ch of first ch-2 sp, ch 5 (counts as 1 dc and ch 2), work 3 dc in same ch-2 sp, *ch 1, skip next 3 dc, work (3 dc, ch 2, 3 dc) in next ch-2 sp (corner made); rep from * around twice more, end ch 1, skip next 2 dc, work 2 dc in same sp as 5 ch at beg of round, join rnd with a sl st in 3rd ch of beg ch-5.

Rnd 3 Sl st in first ch of first ch-2 sp, ch 5 (counts as 1 dc and ch 2), work 3 dc in same ch-2 sp, *ch 1, skip next 3 dc, work 3 dc in next ch-1 sp, ch 1, skip next 3 dc**, work (3 dc, ch 2, 3 dc) in next ch-2 sp; rep from * around twice more, then from * to ** once, end ch1, work 2 dc in first ch-2 sp, join rnd with a sl st in 3rd ch of beg ch-5.

Rnd 4 Sl st in first ch of first ch-2 sp, ch 5 (counts as 1 dc and ch 2), work 3 dc in same ch-2 sp, *[ch 1, skip next 3 dc, work 3 dc in next ch-1 sp] twice, ch 1, skip next 3 dc**, work (3 dc, ch 2, 3 dc) in next ch-2 sp; rep from * around twice more, then from * to ** once, end ch1, work 2 dc in first ch-2 sp, join rnd with a sl st in 3rd ch of beg ch-5.

Rnd 5 Sl st in first ch of first ch-2 sp, ch 5 (counts as 1 dc and ch 2), work 3 dc in same ch-2 sp, *[ch 1, skip next 3 dc, work 3 dc in next ch-1 sp] 3 times, ch 1, skip next 3 dc**, work (3 dc, ch 2, 3 dc) in next ch-2 sp; rep from * around twice more, then from * to ** once, end ch1, work 2 dc in first ch-2 sp, join rnd with a sl st in 3rd ch of beg ch-5.

Rnd 6 Sl st in first ch of first ch-2 sp, ch 5 (counts as 1 dc and ch 2), work 3 dc in same ch-2 sp, *[ch 1, skip next 3 dc, work 3 dc in next ch-1 sp] 4 times, ch 1, skip next 3 dc**, work (3 dc, ch 2, 3 dc) in next ch-2 sp; rep from * around twice more, then from * to ** once, end ch1, work 2 dc in first ch-2 sp, join rnd with a sl st in 3rd ch of beg ch-5. Fasten off.

134 *Traditional Granny—Tricolor*

Note When changing colors, draw new color through when you sl st to join rnd.

Work as for traditional granny in color sequence as follows:

Rnd 1 A. **Rnd 2** B. **Rnd 3** C. **Rnd 4** A. **Rnd 5** B. **Rnd 6** C.

136

135 *Double Crochet Granny*

Chain 6. Join chain with a sl st, forming a ring.

Rnd 1 (RS) Ch 5 (counts and 1 dc and ch 2), [3 dc in ring, ch 2] 3 times, work 2 dc in ring, join rnd with a sl st in 3rd ch of beg ch-5—4 groups of 3 dc made.

Rnd 2 Sl st in first ch of first ch-2 sp, ch 7 (counts as 1 dc and ch 4), *work 2 dc in next ch-2 sp, dc in each dc across side of square**, work 2 dc in next ch-2 sp, ch 4; rep from * around twice more, then from * to ** once, end 2 dc in first ch-2 sp, join rnd with a sl st in 3rd ch of beg ch-7—4 groups of 7 dc made.

Rnd 3 Sl st in first ch of first ch-4 sp, ch 7 (counts as 1 dc and ch 4), *work 2 dc in next ch-4 sp, dc in each dc across side of square**, work 2 dc in next ch-4 sp, ch 4; rep from * around twice more, then from * to ** once, end 2 dc in first ch-4 sp, join rnd with a sl st in 3rd ch of beg ch-7—4 groups of 11 dc made.

Rnd 4 Rep rnd 3—4 groups of 15 dc made. Fasten off.

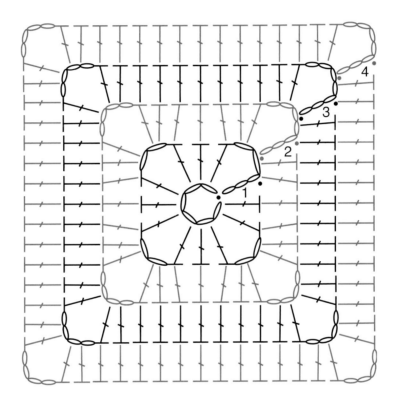

136 *Double Crochet Granny—Multicolor*

With A, chain 6. Join chain with a sl st, forming a ring.

Note When changing colors, draw new color through when you sl st to join rnd.

Work as for double crochet granny in color sequence as follows:

Rnd 1 A. **Rnd 2** B. **Rnd 3** C. **Rnd 4** D.

137

To make an adjustable ring, use A to make a slipknot 10"/25.5cm from free end of yarn. Place slipknot on hook, then wrap free end of yarn twice around your first and second fingers on your left hand. Then work with yarn coming from ball as follows:

Rnd 1 (RS) Ch 3 (counts as 1 dc), work 2 dc in ring, ch 2, *work 3 dc in ring, ch 2; rep from * around twice more, pull free end of yarn to close circle, then join rnd with a sl st in 3rd ch of beg ch-3—4 ch-2 sps. Fasten off.

Rnd 2 With RS facing, join B with a sl st in any corner ch-2 sp, ch 4 (counts as 1 sc and ch 3), sc in same ch-2 sp, ch 3, *work (sc, ch 3, sc) in next ch-2 sp, ch 3; rep from * around twice more, join rnd with a sl st in first ch of beg ch-4—4 corner ch-3 sps. Fasten off.

Rnd 3 With RS facing, join A with a sl st in any corner ch-3 sp, ch 3 (counts as 1 dc), work (2 dc, ch 3, 3 dc) in same ch-3 sp, ch 1, work 3 dc in next ch-3 sp, ch 1, *work (3 dc, ch 3, 3 dc) in next corner ch-3 sp, ch 1, work 3 dc in next ch-3 sp, ch 1; rep from * around twice more, join rnd with a sl st in top of beg ch-3. Fasten off.

Rnd 4 With RS facing, join B with a sl st in any corner ch-3 sp, ch 4 (counts as 1 sc and ch 3), * sc in next ch-3 sp, ch 3, [sc in next ch-1 sp, ch 3] twice, rep from * around three times more, join rnd with a sl st in first ch of beg ch-4. Fasten off.

Rnd 5 With RS facing, join A with a sl st in any corner ch-3 sp, ch 3 (counts as 1 dc), work (2 dc, ch 3, 3 dc) in same ch-3 sp, ch 1, [work 3 dc in next ch-3 sp, ch 1] 3 times, *work (3 dc, ch 3, 3 dc) in next corner ch-3 sp, ch 1, [work 3 dc in next ch-3 sp, ch 1] 3 times; rep from * around twice more, join rnd with a sl st in top of beg ch-3. Fasten off.

Rnd 6 With RS facing, join B with a sl st in any corner ch-3 sp, ch 4 (counts as 1 sc and ch 3), sc in same ch-3 sp, ch 3, [sc in next ch-1 sp, ch 3] 4 times, *work (sc, ch 3, sc) in next corner ch-3 sp, ch 3, [sc in next ch-1 sp, ch 3] 4 times; rep from * around twice more, join rnd with a sl st in first ch of beg ch-4. Fasten off.

Rnd 7 With RS facing, join A with a sl st in any corner ch-3 sp, ch 3 (counts as 1 dc), work (2 dc, ch 3, 3 dc) in same ch-3 sp, ch 1, [work 3 dc in next ch-3 sp, ch 1] 5 times, *work (3 dc, ch 3, 3 dc) in next corner ch-3 sp, ch 1, [work 3 dc in next ch-3 sp, ch 1] 5 times; rep from * around twice more, join rnd with a sl st in top of beg ch-3. Fasten off.

Rnd 8 With RS facing, join B with a sl st in any corner ch-3 sp, ch 4 (counts as 1 sc and ch 3), sc in same ch-3 sp, ch 3, [sc in next ch-1 sp, ch 3] 6 times, *work (sc, ch 3, sc) in next corner ch-3 sp, ch 3, [sc in next ch-1 sp, ch 3] 6 times; rep from * around twice more, join rnd with a sl st in first ch of beg ch-4. Fasten off.

Rnd 9 With RS facing, join A with a sl st in any corner ch-3 sp, ch 3 (counts as 1 dc), work (2 dc, ch 3, 3 dc) in same ch-3 sp, ch 1, [work 3 dc in next ch-3 sp, ch 1] 7 times, *work (3 dc, ch 3, 3 dc) in next corner ch-3 sp, ch 1, [work 3 dc in next ch-3 sp, ch 1] 7 times; rep from * around twice more, join rnd with a sl st in top of beg ch-3. Fasten off.

Rnd 10 With RS facing, join B with a sl st in any corner ch-3 sp, ch 4 (counts as 1 sc and ch 3), sc in same ch-3 sp, ch 3, [sc in next ch-1 sp, ch 3] 8 times, *work (sc, ch 3, sc) in next corner ch-3 sp, ch 3, [sc in next ch-1 sp, ch 3] 8 times; rep from * around twice more, join rnd with a sl st in first ch of beg ch-4.

Rnd 11 Ch 1, sc in same place as joining, sc in each st around, working 3 sc in each ch-3 sp along side edges and 5 sc in each corner ch-3 sp, join rnd with a sl st in first st. Fasten off.

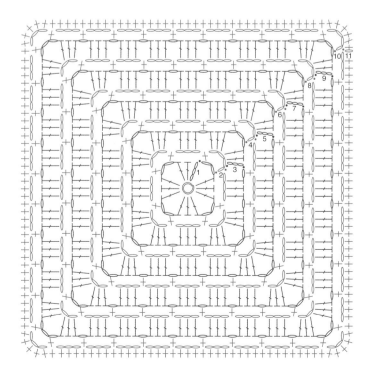

138

To make an adjustable ring, use A to make a slipknot 10"/25.5cm from free end of yarn. Place slipknot on hook, then wrap free end of yarn twice around your first and second fingers on your left hand. Then work with yarn coming from ball as follows:

Rnd 1 (RS) Ch 3 (counts as 1 dc), work 15 dc in ring, pull free end of yarn to close circle, then join rnd with a sl st in 3rd ch of beg ch-3—16 dc. Fasten off.

Rnd 2 With RS facing, join B with a sl st in any st, ch 5 (counts as 1 dc and ch 2), [dc in next st, ch 2] 15 times, join rnd with a sl st in 3rd ch of beg ch-5—16 ch-2 sps. Fasten off.

Rnd 3 With RS facing, join C with a sl st in any ch-2 sp, ch 3 (counts as 1 dc), work 2 dc in same ch-2 sp, ch 1, *work (3 dc, ch 1) into next ch-2 sp; rep from * around, join rnd with a sl st in top of beg ch-3. Fasten off.

Rnd 4 With RS facing, join D with a sl st in any ch-1 sp, ch4, sc in next ch-1 sp, [ch 3, sc in next ch-1 sp] twice, *ch 6, sc in next ch-1 sp, [ch 3, sc in next ch-1 sp] 3 times; rep from * around, end ch 6, join rnd with a sl st in second ch of first ch-4.

Rnd 5 Ch 3 (counts as 1 dc), work 2 dc in first ch-3 sp, [work 3 dc in next ch-3 sp] twice, *work (5 dc, ch 2, 5 dc) in next corner ch-6 lp, [work 3 dc in next ch-3 sp] 3 times; rep from * around, join rnd with a sl st in top of beg ch-3. Fasten off.

Rnd 6 With RS facing, join E with a sl st in center st along any side edge, ch 3 (counts as 1 dc), dc in each st around, working (dc, tr, dc) in each corner ch-2 sp, join rnd with a sl st in top of beg ch-3. Fasten off.

Rnd 7 With RS facing, join A with a sl st in center st along any side edge, ch 1, sc in each st around, working (sc, ch 1, sc) in each corner tr st, join rnd with a sl st in first st. Fasten off.

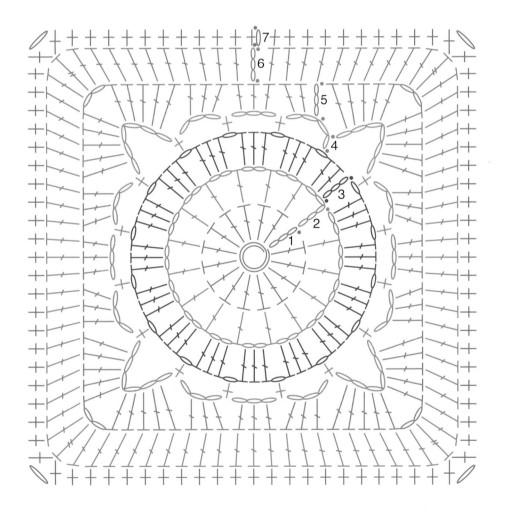

139

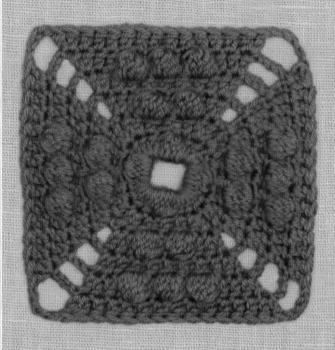

140

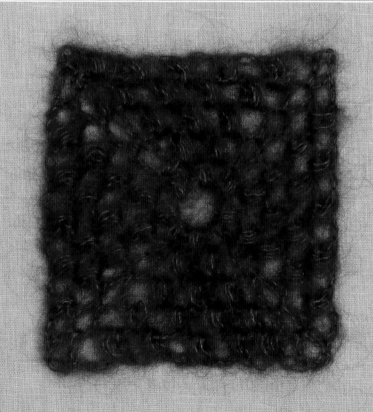

141

142

143

To make an adjustable ring, use A to make a slipknot 10"/25.5cm from free end of yarn. Place slipknot on hook, then wrap free end of yarn twice around your first and second fingers on your left hand. Then work with yarn coming from ball as follows:

Note When changing colors, draw new color through when you sl st to join rnd.

Rnd 1 (RS) Ch 1, work 15 sc in ring, pull free end of yarn to close circle, then join rnd with a sl st in first st.

Rnd 2 Ch 1, sc in first sc, ch 10, *skip 3 sc, sc in next st, ch 10; rep from * around 3 times more, end join rnd with a sl st in first ch of beg ch-11—4 ch-10 lps.

Rnd 3 Ch 1, sc in sc, *work 11 sc in next ch-10 lp, sc in next sc; rep from * around twice more, end work 11 sc in last ch-1 lp, join rnd with a sl st in first sc. Fasten off.

Rnd 4 With RS facing, join B with a sl st in 6th st of any 11-sc group, ch 1, sc in same place as joining, work (ch 1, sc) in same place as joining (first corner made), cont to sc in each st around working (sc, ch 1, sc) in each 6th st of every 11-sc group around, join rnd with a sl st in first sc. Fasten off.

Rnd 5 With RS facing, join C with a sl st in any corner ch-1 sp, ch 1, sc in same place as joining, work (ch 1, sc) in same place as joining, cont to sc in each st around working (sc, ch 1, sc) in each corner ch-1 sp, join rnd with a sl st in first sc. Fasten off.

Rnd 6 With D, rep rnd 5.

Rnd 7 With C, rep rnd 5.

Rnd 8 With B, rep rnd 5.

Rnd 9 With A, rep rnd 5.

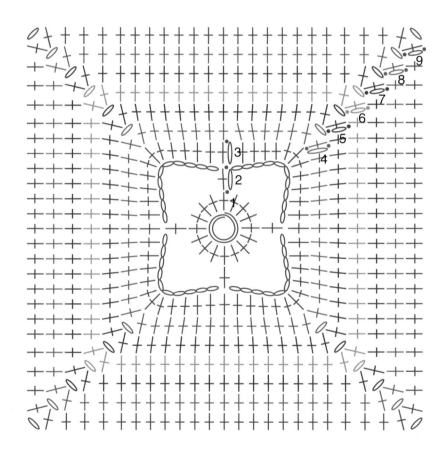

Chain 12. Join chain with a sl st, forming a ring.

Bobble (BL) [Yo, insert hook in ring (or st), yo, draw up a lp, yo and draw through 2 lps on hook] 6 times, yo and draw through 6 lps on hook, yo and draw through rem 2 lps on hook.

Rnd 1 (WS) Ch 3 (counts as 1 dc), dc in ring, *work BL in ring, work 4 dc in ring; rep from * around twice more, end work BL in ring, 2 dc in ring, join rnd with a sl st in top of beg ch-3.

Rnd 2 Ch 3 (counts as 1 dc), dc in same place as joining, *dc in next 3 sts, work 2 dc in next st, ch 1, work 2 dc in next st; rep from * around twice more, end dc in next 3 sts, work 2 dc in last st, ch 1, join rnd with a sl st in top of beg ch-3.

Rnd 3 Ch 3 (counts as 1 dc), dc in same place as joining, *[dc in next st, work BL in next st] twice, dc in next st, work 2 dc in next st, ch 2, work 2 dc in next st; rep from * around twice more, end [dc in next st, work BL in next st] twice, dc in next st, work 2 dc in next st, ch 2, join rnd with a sl st in top of beg ch-3.

Rnd 4 Ch 3 (counts as 1 dc), dc in same place as joining, *dc in next 7 sts, work 2 dc in next st, ch 3, work 2 dc in next st; rep from * around twice more, end dc in next 7 sts, work 2 dc in last st, ch 3, join rnd with a sl st in top of beg ch-3.

Rnd 5 Ch 3 (counts as 1 dc), dc in same place as joining, *dc in next 2 sts, [work BL in next st, dc in next st] 3 times, dc in next st, work 2 dc in next st, ch 4, work 2 dc in next st; rep from * around twice more, end dc in next 2 sts, [work BL in next st, dc in next st] 3 times, dc in next st, work 2 dc in last st, ch 4, join rnd with a sl st in top of beg ch-3.

Rnd 6 Ch 3 (counts as 1 dc), dc in same place as joining, *dc in next 11 sts, work 2 dc in next st, ch 4, work 2 dc in next st; rep from * around twice more, end dc in next 11 sts, work 2 dc in next st, ch 4, join rnd with a sl st in top of beg ch-3. Fasten off.

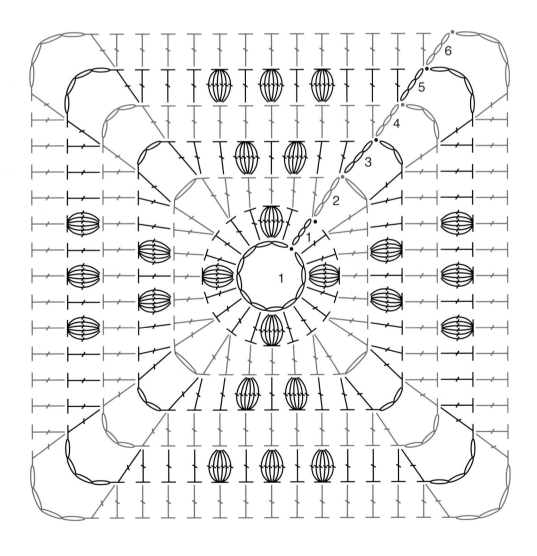

141 *Puff*

Chain 8. Join chain with a sl st, forming a ring.

Beg puff st (hdc4tog) In same sp work [yo, insert hook in sp, yo and draw up a lp] 4 times, yo and draw through all 9 lps on hook.

Puff stitch (hdc5tog) In same sp work [yo, insert hook in sp, yo and draw up a lp] 5 times, yo and draw through all 11 lps on hook.

V-st Work (dc, ch 2, dc) in same st.

Rnd 1 (RS) Ch 2 (counts as 1 hdc), work beg puff st in ring (counts as 1 puff st), ch 2, [puff st in ring, ch 2] 7 times, join rnd with a sl st in first puff st.

Rnd 2 Ch 5 (counts as 1 dc and ch 2), dc in same puff st, *ch 2, [puff st in next sp, ch 2] twice**, V-st in next puff st; rep from * around twice more, then from * to ** once, join rnd with a sl st in 3rd ch of beg ch-3.

Rnd 3 Sl st in first ch of first ch-2 sp, ch 5 (counts as 1 dc and ch 2), dc in same ch-2 sp, *ch 2, [puff st in next ch-2 sp, ch 2] 3 times**, V-st in next ch-2 corner sp; rep from * around twice more, then from * to ** once, join rnd with a sl st in 3rd ch of beg ch-5.

Rnd 4 Rep rnd 3, working 4 puff sts across each side of square.

Rnd 5 Rep rnd 3, working 5 puff sts across each side of square. Fasten off.

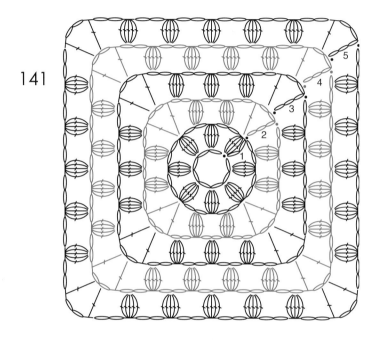

141

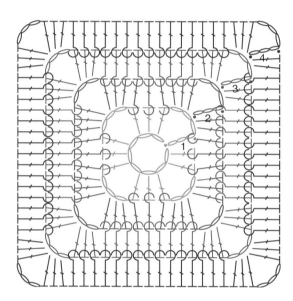

142

142 *3-D*

With A, chain 8. Join chain with a sl st, forming a ring.

Front raised dc (FRDC) Yo, working from front to back to front, insert hook around post of stitch of rnd below, yo and draw up a lp, [yo and draw through 2 lps on hook] twice.

Back raised dc (BRDC) Yo, working from back to front to back, insert hook around post of stitch of rnd below, yo and draw up a lp, [yo and draw through 2 lps on hook] twice.

Rnd 1 (RS) Ch 6 (counts as 1 dc and ch 3), [3 dc in ring, 3 ch] 3 times, work 2 dc in ring, join rnd with a sl st in 3rd ch of beg ch-6. Fasten off.

Rnd 2 With RS facing, join B with a sl st in any corner ch-3 sp, ch 6 (counts as ch 3 and 1 dc), work 3 dc in same ch-3 sp, *FRDC around each of next 3 sts**, work (3 dc, ch 3, 3 dc) in next corner ch-3 sp; rep from * around twice more, then work 2 FRDC around next 2 st, 1 FRDC in beg corner ch-3 sp, 2 dc in beg corner ch-3 sp, join rnd with a sl st in top of beg ch-3. Fasten off.

Rnd 3 With RS facing, join C with a sl st in any corner ch-3 sp, ch 6 (counts as 1 dc and ch 3, work 3 dc in same ch-3 sp, *BRDC around each of next 3 sts, FRDC around each of next 3 sts, BRDC around each of next 3 sts**, work (3 dc, ch 3, 3 dc) in next corner ch-3 sp; rep from * around twice more, then from * to ** once, end work 2 BRDC in beg corner ch-3 sp, join rnd with a sl st in 3rd ch of beg ch-6. Fasten off.

Rnd 4 With RS facing, join D with a sl st in any corner ch-3 sp, ch 6 (counts as ch3 and 1 dc), work 3 dc in same ch-3 sp, *[FRDC around each of next 3 sts, BRDC around each of next 3 sts] twice, FRDC around each of next 3 sts**, work (3 dc, ch 3, 3 dc) in next corner ch-3 sp; rep from * around twice more, then from * to ** once, with last BRDC worked in ch 3 of prev row ch-6 sp, 2 dc in corner 3-ch sp, join rnd with a sl st in top of beg ch-3. Fasten off.

Motif I

Work rnds 1–4 as for 3-D.

Rnd 5 With RS facing, join B with a sl st in any corner ch-3 sp, ch 1, sc in each st around, working 5 sc in each corner ch-3 sp, join rnd with a sl st in first sc. Fasten off.

Motif II

Work rnds 1–4 as for 3-D in color sequence as follows: **Rnd 1** D. **Rnd 2** C. **Rnd 3** B. **Rnd 4** A. Work rnd 5 as for motif 1, using B.

Joining

Place motifs I and II tog, WS facing. With RS facing you, join B with a sl st in back lp of motif in front. Ch 1, working in back lp of motif in front and in front lp of motif in back, sc across. Working in the same manner, cont to sc motifs tog to form strips, then sc strips tog.

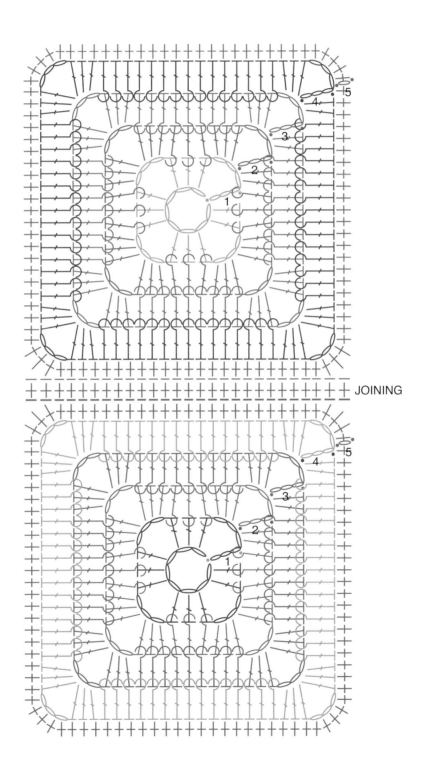

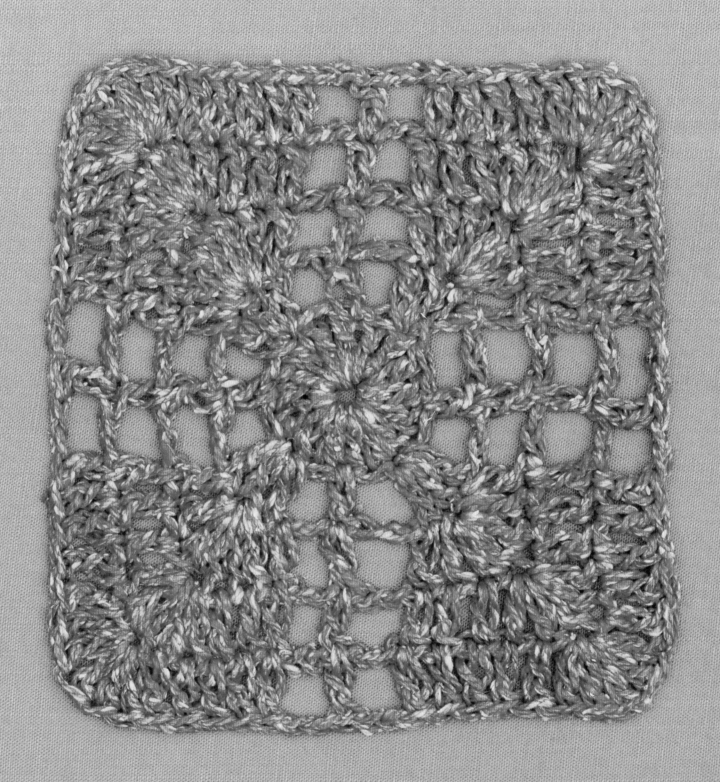

144

Grannies–*Lace*

144 *Peephole*

Chain 6. Join chain with a sl st, forming a ring.

Rnd 1 (RS) Ch 3 (counts as 1 dc), work 15 dc in ring, join rnd with a sl st in top of beg ch-3.

Rnd 2 Ch 3 (counts as 1 dc), work 2 dc in same place as joining, ch 2, skip next st, dc in next st, ch 2, skip next st, *work 3 dc in next st, ch 2, skip next st, dc in next st, ch 2, skip next st; rep from * around twice more, join rnd with a sl st in top of beg ch-3.

Rnd 3 Ch 3 (counts as 1 dc), work 5 dc in next st, *dc in next st, [ch 2, dc in next dc] twice, work 5 dc in next st; rep from * around twice more, end [dc in next dc, ch 2] twice, join rnd with a sl st in top of beg ch-3.

Rnd 4 Ch 3 (counts as 1 dc), dc in first 2 sts, work 5 dc in next st, *dc in next 3 sts, ch 2, dc in next st, ch 2, dc in next 3 sts, work 5 dc in next st; rep from * around twice more, end dc in next 3 sts, ch 2, dc in last st, ch 2, join rnd with a sl st in top of beg ch-3.

Rnd 5 Ch 3 (counts as 1 dc), dc in next 4 sts, work 5 dc in next st, *dc in next 5 sts, ch 2, dc in next st, ch 2, dc in next 5 sts, work 5 dc in next st; rep from * around twice more, end dc in next 5 sts, ch 2, dc in last st, ch 2, join rnd with a sl st in top of beg ch-3. Fasten off.

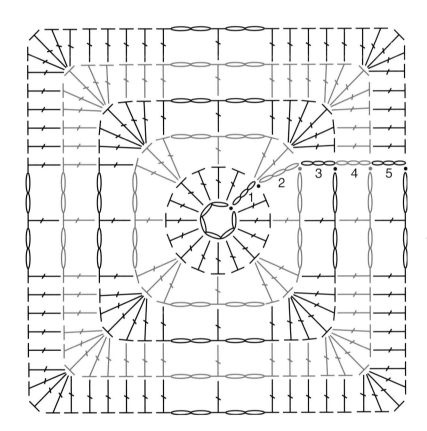

145

146

147

148

Chain 8. Join chain with a sl st, forming a ring.

Double crochet 2 together (dc2tog)—cluster Yo, insert hook in *same* ch-7 lp as last 2-dc group, yo and draw up a lp, yo, draw through 2 lps on hook; yo, insert hook in *next* ch-7 lp, yo and draw up a lp, yo, draw through 2 lps on hook, yo and draw through all 3 lps on hook.

Rnd 1 (RS) Ch 1, work 16 sc in ring, join rnd with a sl st in first st.

Rnd 2 Ch 1, sc in same place as joining, [ch 8, skip next 3 sts, sc in next st] 3 times, ch 7, skip last 3 sts, join rnd with a sl st in first sc.

Rnd 3 Sl st across to 3rd ch of first ch-8 lp, ch 3 (counts as 1 dc), dc in same ch-7 lp, *work (ch 3, 2 dc) in same ch-7 lp as last 2-dc group, ch 3, make cluster, ch 3, work 2 dc in same ch-7 lp as 2nd leg of cluster; rep from * around 3 times more, omitting work 2 dc in same ch-7 lp as 2nd leg of cluster, join rnd with a sl st in top of beg ch-3.

Rnd 4 Sl st in first dc and first ch of first ch-3 sp, ch 3 (counts as 1 dc), dc in same ch-3 sp, *work (ch 3, 2 dc) in same ch-3 sp as last 2-dc group, ch 3, skip next 2 dc, work 3 dc in next ch-3 sp, dc in next cluster, work 3 dc in next ch-3 sp, ch 3, skip next 2 dc, work 2 dc in next ch-3 sp; rep from * around 3 times more, omitting work 2 dc in next ch-3 sp at end of last rep, join rnd with a sl st in top of beg ch-3.

Rnd 5 Sl st in first dc and first ch of first ch-3 sp, ch 3 (counts as 1 dc), work 2 dc in same ch-3 sp, *work (ch 3, 3 dc) in same ch-3 sp as last 3-dc group, ch 6, skip next (2 dc, ch-3 sp and dc), dc in next 5 dc, ch 6, skip next (dc, ch-3 sp, 2 dc), work 3 dc in next ch-3 sp; rep from * around 3 times more, omitting work 3 dc in next ch-3 sp at end of last rep, join rnd with a sl st in top of beg ch-3.

Rnd 6 Ch 3 (counts as 1 dc), dc in next 2 dc, *work (3 dc, ch 5, 3 dc) in next ch-3 sp, dc in next 3 dc, ch 6, skip next (ch-6 lp and dc), dc in next 3 dc, ch 6, skip next (dc and ch-6 lp), dc in next 3 dc; rep from * around 3 times more, omitting dc in next 3 dc at end of last rep, join rnd with a sl st in top of beg ch-3. Fasten off.

146 *Spider*

Chain 6. Join chain with a sl st, forming a ring.

Double crochet 2 together (dc2tog)—cluster

In same ch-15 lp, [yo, insert hook in ch-15 lp, yo and draw up a lp, yo, draw through 2 lps on hook] twice, yo and draw through all 3 lps on hook.

Double crochet 3 together (dc3tog)—cluster

In same ch-15 lp, [yo, insert hook in ch-15 lp, yo and draw up a lp, yo, draw through 2 lps on hook] 3 times, yo and draw through all 4 lps on hook.

Rnd 1 (RS) Ch 1, [sc in ring, ch 15] 12 times, join rnd with a sl st in first sc.

Rnd 2 Sl st in first 7 ch of first ch-15 lp, ch 3, dc2tog in same ch-15 lp (counts as dc3tog), *ch 4, dc3tog in same ch-15 lp as last dc3tog, [ch 4, sc in next ch-15 lp] twice, ch 4, dc3tog in next ch-15 lp; rep from * around twice more, end ch 4, dc3tog in same ch-15 lp as last dc3tog, [ch 4, sc in next ch-15 lp] twice, ch 4, join rnd with a sl st in top of beg dc3tog.

Rnd 3 Sl st in first 2 ch of first ch-4 sp, ch 3, dc2tog in same ch-4 sp (counts as dc3tog), *ch 4, dc3tog in same ch-4 sp as last dc3tog, [ch 4, sc in next ch-4 sp, ch 4, dc3tog in next ch-4 sp] twice; rep from * around twice more, end ch 4, dc3tog in same ch-4 sp as last dc3tog, ch 4, sc in next ch-4 sp, ch 4, dc3tog in next ch-4 sp, ch 4, sc in next ch-4 sp, ch 4, join rnd with a sl st in top of beg dc3tog. Fasten off.

147 *Wheel*

Chain 8. Join chain with a sl st, forming a ring.

Rnd 1 (RS) Ch 1, work 12 sc in ring, join rnd with a sl st in first st.

Rnd 2 Ch 6 (counts as 1 tr and ch 2), skip first st, [tr in next st, ch 2] 11 times, join rnd with a sl st in 4th ch of beg ch-6.

Rnd 3 Sl st in first 2 ch of ch-2 sp, ch 5 (counts as 1 dc and ch 2), *[sc in next ch-2 sp, ch 2] twice, work (3 dc, ch 2, 3 dc) in next ch-2 sp, ch 2; rep from * around twice more, end [sc in next ch-2 sp, ch 2] twice, work (3 dc, ch 2, 2 dc) in last ch-4 sp, join rnd with a sl st in 3rd ch of beg ch-5.

Rnd 4 Ch 1, *[sc in next ch-2 sp, ch 2] 3 times, work (3 dc, ch 2, 3 dc) in corner ch-2 sp, ch 2; rep from * around 3 times more, join rnd with a sl st in first sc.

Rnd 5 Ch 1, sc in each st around, working 2 sc in each ch-2 sp along side edges and 3 sc in each corner ch-2 sp, join rnd with a sl st in first sc. Fasten off.

148 *Cranesbill Lace*

Chain 6. Join chain with a sl st forming a ring.

Beg cluster In same sp work, [yo, insert hook in sp, yo and draw up a lp, yo, draw through 2 lps on hook] twice, yo and draw through all 3 lps on hook.

Cluster In same sp, [yo, insert hook in sp, yo and draw up a lp, yo, draw through 4 lps on hook] 3 times, yo and draw through all 4 lps on hook.

Rnd 1 (RS) Ch 3 (counts as 1 dc), work beg cluster in ring (counts as 1 cluster), [ch 2, work cluster in ring] 7 times, ch 2, join rnd with a sl st in top of first cluster.

Rnd 2 Sl st in first 2 ch of first ch-3 sp, ch 1, sc in same ch-3 sp, [ch 5, sc in next ch-3 sp] 7 times, ch 2, join rnd with a dc in first sc.

Rnd 3 *Ch 5, work (cluster, ch 3, cluster) in next ch-5 lp**, ch 5, sc in next ch-5 sp; rep from * around twice more, then from * to ** once, end ch 2, to join

rnd, dc in dc that joined rnd 2.

Rnd 4 *Ch 5, sc in next ch-5 lp, ch 5, work (sc, ch 5, sc) in next corner ch-3 sp, ch 5, sc in next ch-5 lp; rep from * around 3 times more, ending last rep sc in dc that joined rnd 3 (instead of next ch-5 lp), join rnd with a sl st in first ch of beg ch-5. Fasten off.

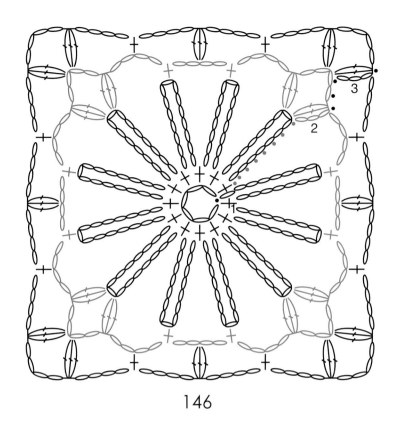

146

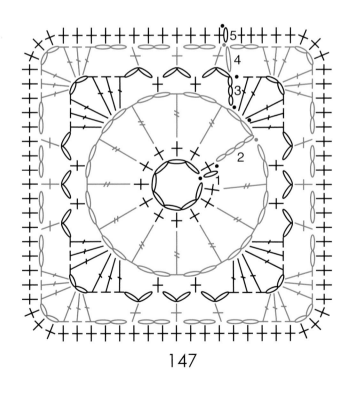

147

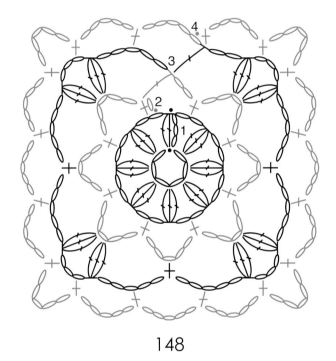

148

149

To make an adjustable ring, use A to make a slipknot 10"/25.5cm from free end of yarn. Place slipknot on hook, then wrap free end of yarn twice around your first and second fingers on your left hand. Then work with yarn coming from ball as follows:

Beg cluster In same sp work, [yo, insert hook in sp, yo and draw up a lp, yo, draw through 2 lps on hook] twice, yo and draw through all 3 lps on hook.

Cluster In same sp, [yo, insert hook in sp, yo and draw up a lp, yo, draw through 2 lps on hook] 3 times, yo and draw through all 4 lps on hook.

Rnd 1 (RS) Ch 4 (counts as 1 dc and ch 1), [dc in ring, ch 1] 11 times, ch 5, pull free end of yarn to close circle, then join rnd with a sl st in 3rd ch of beg ch-4—12 ch-1 sps. Fasten off.

Rnd 2 With RS facing, join B with a sl st in any ch-1 sp, ch 3 (counts as 1 dc), work beg cluster in same sp as joining, [ch 3, work cluster in next ch-1 sp] 11 times, ch 3, join rnd with a sl st in top of beg cluster.

Rnd 3 Sl st in first 2 ch of first ch-3 sp, ch 1, sc into same ch-3 sp, [ch 5, sc in next ch-3 sp] 11 times, ch 5, join rnd with a sl st with sl st into first sc. Fasten off.

Rnd 4 With RS facing, join C with a sl st in any ch-5 lp, ch 3 (counts as 1 dc), work 4 dc in same ch-5 lp, *ch 1, sc in next ch-5 lp, ch 5, sc in next ch-5 lp, ch 1**, work (5 dc, ch 3, 5 dc) in next ch-5 lp; rep from * around twice more, then from * to ** once, end work 5 dc in beg ch-5 lp, ch 3, join rnd with a sl st in top of beg ch-3. Fasten off.

Rnd 5 With RS facing, join A with a sl st in any corner ch-3 sp, ch 3 (counts as 1 dc), work (dc, ch 2, 2 dc) in same ch-3 sp, *dc in next 5 dc, ch 4, sc in next ch-5 sp, ch 4, skip next sc, dc in next 5 dc**, work (2 dc, ch 2, 2 dc) in next corner ch-3 sp; rep from * around twice more, then from * to ** once, join rnd with a sl st in top of beg ch-3.

Rnd 6 Ch 1, sc in same place as joining, sc in each st around, working 4 sc in each ch-4 sp, and 3 sc in each ch-2 space, join rnd with a sl st in first st. Fasten off.

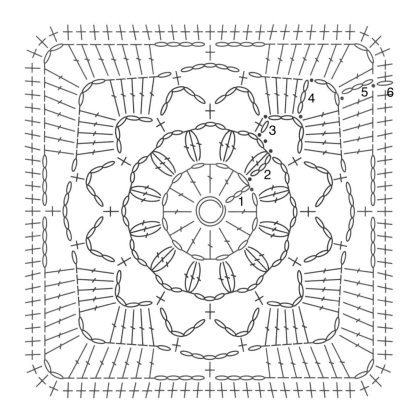

150

With A, chain 8. Join chain with a sl st, forming a ring.

Note Use three different colors for motifs I and motifs II.

Rnd 1 (RS) Ch 1, work 12 sc in ring, join rnd with a sl st in first st.

Rnd 2 Ch 6 (counts as 1 tr and ch 2), skip next st, [tr in next st, ch 2] 11 times, join rnd with a sl st in 4th ch of beg ch-6—12 ch-2 sps. Fasten off.

Rnd 3 With RS facing, join B with a sl st in any ch-2 sp, ch 5 (counts as 1 dc and ch 2), *[sc in next ch-2 sp, ch 2] twice, work (3 dc, ch 2, 3 dc) in next ch-2 sp, ch 2; rep from * around twice more, end [sc in next ch-2 sp, ch 2] twice, work (3 dc, ch 2, 2 dc) in last ch-4 sp, join rnd with a sl st in 3rd ch of beg ch-5. Fasten off.

Rnd 4 With RS facing, join C with a sl st in any ch-2 sp, ch 1, *[sc in next ch-2 sp, ch 2] 3 times, work (3 dc, ch 2, 3 dc) in next ch-2 sp, ch 2; rep from * around 3 more times. Join rnd with a sl st in top of beg ch-3.

Rnd 5 Ch 1, sc in each st around, working 2 sc in each ch-2 sp along side edges and 3 sc in each corner ch-2 sp, join rnd with a sl st in first sc. Fasten off.

Joining

Place motifs I and II tog, WS facing. With RS facing you, join desired color with a sl st in back lp of motif in front. Ch 1, working in back lp of motif in front and in front lp of motif in back, sc across. Working in the same manner, cont to sc two motifs tog to form strips, then sc strips tog.

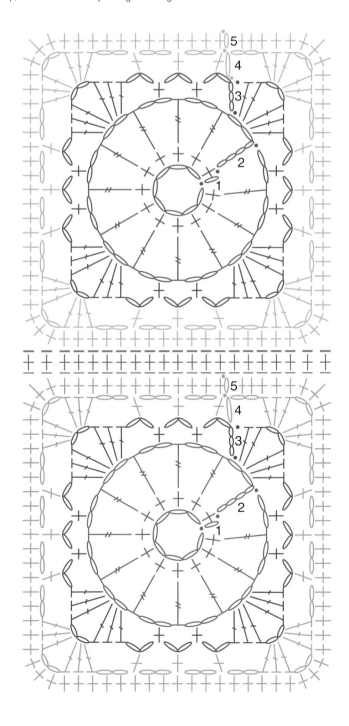

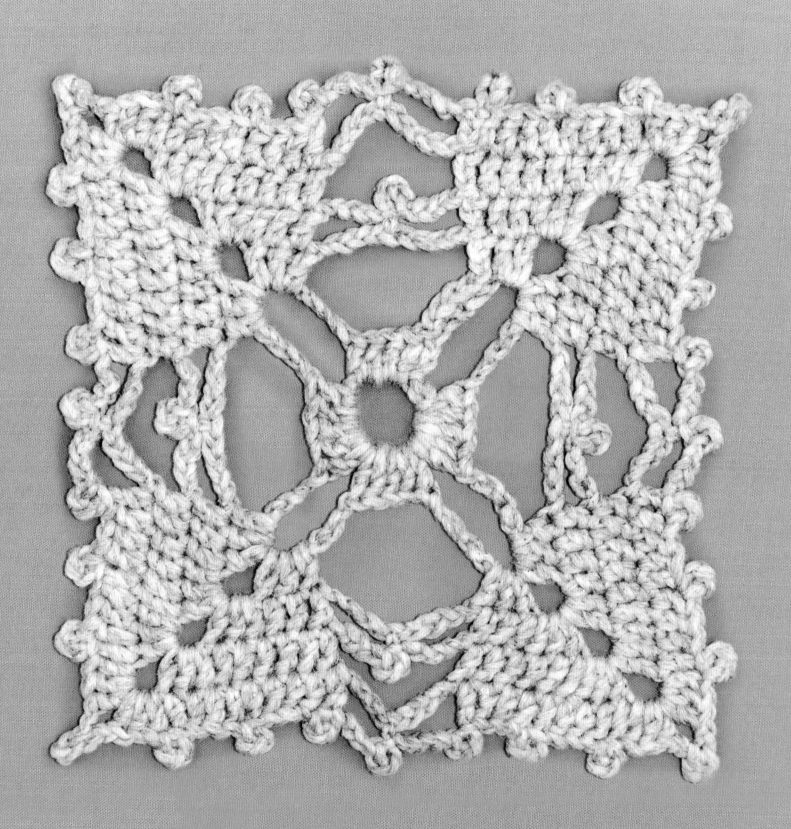

151

Chain 10. Join chain with a sl st, forming a ring.

Make picot (MP) Ch 3, sl st in top of last st.

Rnd 1 (RS) Ch 14 (counts as 1 dc and ch 11), [work 5 dc in ring, ch 11] 3 times, work 4 dc in ring, join rnd with a sl st in 3rd ch of beg ch-14.

Rnd 2 Sl st in first 5 ch of first ch-11 lp, ch 3 (counts as 1 dc), work (2 dc, ch 3, 3 dc) in same ch-11 lp, *ch 9, work (3 dc, ch 3, 3 dc) in next ch-11 lp; rep from * around twice more, end ch 9, join rnd with a sl st in top of beg ch-3.

Rnd 3 Ch 3 (counts as 1 dc), dc in first 2 dc, *work (3 dc, ch 3, 3 dc) in next ch-3 sp, dc in next 3 dc, ch 4, skip next 4 ch, sc in next ch, MP, ch 4, skip next 4 ch**, dc in next 3 dc; rep from * around twice, then from * to ** once, join rnd with a sl st in top of beg ch-3.

Rnd 4 Ch 3 (counts as 1 dc), dc in next 5 dc, *work (3 dc, ch 3, 3 dc) in next ch-3 sp, dc in next 6 dc, ch 9**, dc in next 6 dc; rep from * around twice more, then from * to ** once, join rnd with a sl st in top of beg ch-3.

Rnd 5 Ch 6, sl st in 4th ch from hook (counts as 1 dc and picot), *[dc in next 4 dc, MP] twice, work (3 dc, ch 5, sl st in 4th ch from hook, ch 1, 3 dc) in next ch-3 sp, dc in next dc, MP, [dc in next 4 dc, MP] twice, ch 4, skip next 4 ch, sc in next ch, MP, ch 4, skip next 4 ch**, dc in next dc, MP; rep from * around twice more, then from * to ** once, join rnd with a sl st in 3rd ch of beg ch-6. Fasten off.

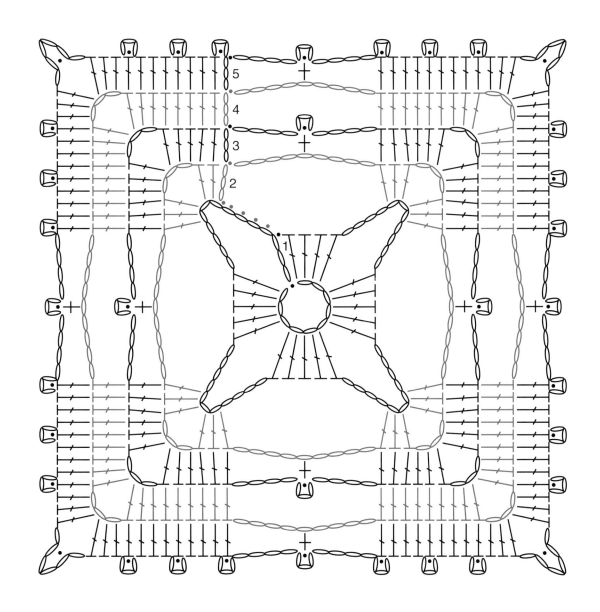

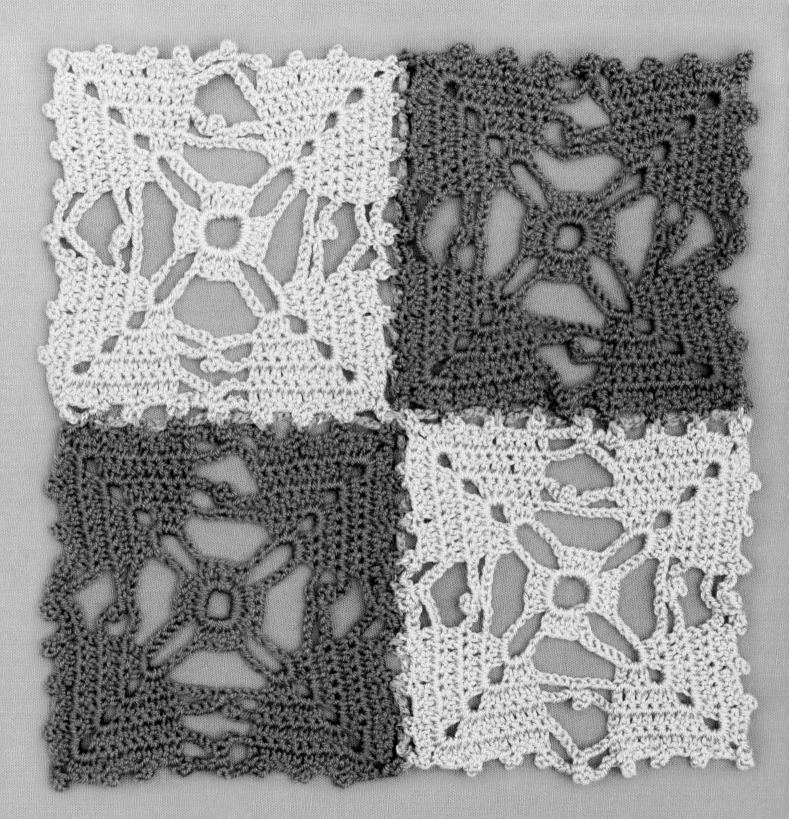

152

Work rnds 1–5 as for Crystal, using different colors for motif I and motif II.

Joining

Place motifs I and II tog, WS facing. With RS facing you, join a contrasting-color yarn with a sl st in corner picots of motif in front and motif in back, ch 1, sc in same picots, *ch 4, sc in next pair of picots; rep from * to end. Working in the same manner, cont to sc motifs tog to form strips, then sc strips tog.

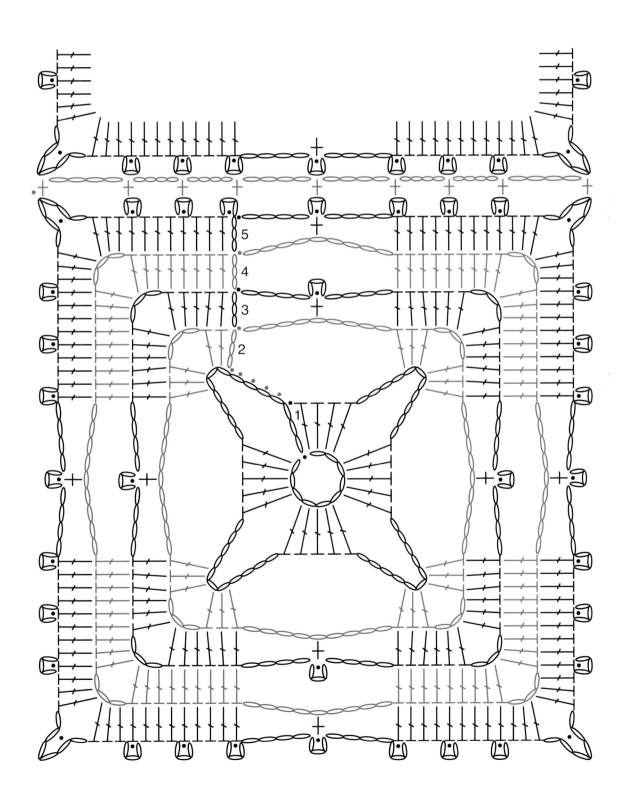

153

154

Chain 4. Join chain with a sl st, forming a ring.

V-st Work (3 dc, ch 2, 3 dc) in same ch-sp.

Rnd 1 (RS) Ch 4 (counts as 1 dc and ch 1), [dc in ring, ch 1] 7 times, join rnd with a sl st in 3rd ch of beg ch-4.

Rnd 2 Ch 4 (counts as 1 dc and ch 2), *work 3 dc in next ch-sp, ch 1**, work 3 dc in next ch-sp, ch 1; rep from * around twice more, then from * to ** once, end work 2 dc in next ch-sp, join rnd with a sl st in 3rd ch of beg ch-5.

Rnd 3 Sl st in first ch of first ch-sp, ch 5 (counts as 1 dc and ch 2), work 3 dc in same ch-sp, *ch 1, sc in next ch-sp, ch 1**, V-st in next ch-2 sp; rep from * around twice more, then from * to ** once, end work 2 dc in next ch-sp, join rnd with a sl st in 3rd ch of beg ch-5.

Rnd 4 Sl st in first ch of first ch-sp, ch 5 (counts as 1 dc and ch 2), work 3 dc in same ch-sp, *ch 1, skip next ch, work (dc, ch 2, dc) in next sc, ch 1, skip next ch**, V-st in next ch-2 sp; rep from * around twice more, then from * to ** once, end work 2 dc in next ch-sp, join rnd with a sl st in 3rd ch of beg ch-5.

Rnd 5 Sl st in first ch of first ch-sp, ch 5 (counts as 1 dc and ch 2), work 3 dc in same ch-sp, *ch 2, skip next ch, work 10 dc in next ch-2 sp, ch 2, skip next ch**, V-st in next ch-sp; rep from * around twice more, then from * to ** once, end work 2 dc in next ch-sp, join rnd with a sl st in 3rd ch of beg ch-5.

Rnd 6 Sl st in first ch of first ch-sp, ch 5 (counts as 1 dc and ch 2), work 3 dc in same ch-sp, *ch 2, skip next 2 ch, dc in next dc, [ch 1, dc in next dc] 9 times, ch 2, skip next 2 ch**, V-st in next ch-sp; rep from * around twice more, then from * to ** once, work 2 dc in next ch-sp, join rnd with a sl st in 3rd ch of beg ch-5.

Rnd 7 Sl st in first ch of first ch-sp, ch 5 (counts as 1 dc and ch 2), V-st in same ch-sp, *ch 2, skip next 2 ch, sc in next ch-sp, [ch 3, sc in next ch-sp] 8 times, ch 2, skip next 2 ch**, work (V-st, ch 2, 3 dc) in next ch-sp; rep from * around twice more, then from * to **

once, end work 2 dc in next ch-sp, join rnd with a sl st in 3rd ch of beg ch-5.

Rnd 8 Sl st in first ch of first ch-sp, ch 5 (counts as 1 dc and ch 2), skip next 3 dc, *V-st in next ch-sp, ch 2, skip next 2 ch, sc in next ch-3 sp, [ch 3, sc in next ch-sp] 7 times, ch 2, skip next 2 ch**, V-st in next ch-sp, ch 2; rep from * around twice more, then from * to ** once, end work (3 dc, ch 2, 2 dc) in next ch-sp, join rnd with a sl st in 3rd ch of beg ch-5.

Rnd 9 Sl st in first ch of first ch-sp, ch 5 (counts as 1 dc and and 2), work 3 dc in same ch-sp, *V-st in next ch-sp, ch 2, skip next 2 ch, sc in next ch-3 sp, [ch 3, sc in next ch-3 sp] 6 times, ch 2, skip next 2 ch, V-st in next ch-sp**, V-st in next ch-sp; rep from * around twice more, then from * to ** once, end work 2 dc in next ch-sp, join rnd with a sl st in 3rd ch of beg ch-5.

Rnd 10 Sl st in first ch of first ch-sp, ch 5 (counts as 1 dc and ch 2), V-st in same ch-sp, *ch 2, V-st in next ch-sp, ch 2, skip next 2 ch, sc in next ch-3 sp, [ch 3, sc in next ch-3 sp] 5 times, ch 2, skip next 2 ch, V-st in next ch-sp, ch 2**, work (V-st, ch 2, 3 dc) in next ch-sp; rep from * around twice more, then from * to ** once, end work 2 dc in next ch-sp, join rnd with a sl st in 3rd ch of beg ch-5.

Rnd 11 Sl st in first 2 ch of first ch-sp, ch 5 (counts as 1 dc and ch 2), skip next 3 dc, *[V-st in next ch-sp, ch 2, skip next 2 ch] twice, sc in next ch-3 sp, [ch 3, sc in next ch-3 sp] 4 times, [ch 2, skip next 2 ch, V-st in next ch-sp] twice**, ch 2; rep from * around twice more, then from * to ** once omitting 1 dc at end of last rep, join rnd with a sl st in 3rd ch of beg ch-5.

Rnd 12 Sl st in first ch of first ch-sp, ch 5 (counts as 1 dc and ch 2), work 3 dc in same ch-sp, *[V-st in next ch-sp, ch 2, skip next 2 ch] twice, sc in next ch-3 sp, [ch 3, sc in next ch-3 sp] 3 times, [ch 2, skip next 2 ch, V-st in next ch-sp] twice**, V-st in next 2 ch-sp; ch 2, V-st in next ch-sp; rep from * around twice more, then from * to ** once, end work work 2 dc in next ch-sp, join rnd with a sl st in 3rd ch of beg ch-5.

Rnd 13 Sl st in first ch of first ch-sp, ch 5 (counts as

1 dc and ch 2), V-st in same ch-sp, *ch 2, [V-st in next ch-sp, ch 2, skip next 2 ch] twice, sc in next ch-3 sp, [ch 3, sc in next ch-3 sp] twice, [ch 2, skip next 2 ch, V-st in next ch-sp] twice, ch 2**, work (V-st, ch 2, 3 dc) in next ch-sp; rep from * around twice more, then from * to ** once, end work 2 dc in next ch-sp, join rnd with a sl st in 3rd ch of beg ch-5.

Rnd 14 Sl st in first 2 ch of first ch-sp, ch 5 (counts as 1 dc and ch 2), skip next 3 dc, *[V-st in next ch-sp, ch 2, skip next 2 ch] 3 times, sc in next ch-3 sp, ch 3, sc in next ch-3 sp, [ch 2, skip next 2 ch, V-st in next ch-sp] 3 times**, ch 2; rep from * around twice more, then from * to ** once omitting 1 dc at end of last rep, join rnd with a sl st in 3rd ch of beg ch-5.

Rnd 15 Sl st in first ch of first ch-sp, ch 5 (counts as 1 dc and ch 2), 3 dc in same ch-sp, *[V-st in next ch-sp, ch 2, skip next 2 ch] twice, V-st in next ch-sp, ch 3, skip next 2 ch, sc in next ch-3 sp, ch 3, skip next 2 ch, V-st in next ch-sp, [ch 2, skip next 2 ch, V-st in next ch-sp] twice**, V-st in next ch-sp; rep from * around twice more, then from * to ** once, end work 2 dc in next ch-sp, join rnd with a sl st in 3rd ch of beg ch-5.

Rnd 16 Sl st in first ch of first ch-sp, ch 5 (counts as 1 dc and ch 2), V-st in same ch-sp, *ch 2, [V-st in next ch-sp, ch 2, skip next 2 ch] twice, V-st in next ch-sp, ch 2, skip next (3 ch, sc and 3 ch), [V-st in next ch-2 sp, ch 2, skip next 2 ch] twice, V-st in next ch-sp, ch 2**, work (V-st, ch 2, 3 dc) in next ch-sp; rep from * around twice more, then from * to ** once, end work 2 dc in next ch-sp, join rnd with a sl st in 3rd ch of beg ch-5.

Rnd 17 Sl st in first ch of first ch-sp, ch 5 (counts as 1 dc and ch 2), skip next 3 dc, *V-st in next ch-sp, [ch 2, skip next 2 ch, V-st in next ch-sp] 3 times, ch 2 V-st in next ch-sp, [ch 2, skip next 2 ch, V-st in next ch-sp] 3 times**, ch 2; rep from * around twice more, then from * to ** once omitting 1 dc at end of last rep, join rnd with a sl st in 3rd ch of beg ch-5. Fasten off.

Chain 16. Join chain with a sl st, forming a ring.

Double treble 2 together (dtr2tog) [Yo 3 times, insert hook in next st (or same place), yo and draw up a lp, (yo, draw through 2 lps on hook) 3 times] twice, yo and draw through all 3 lps on hook.

Double treble 3 together (dtr3tog) In same st work [yo 3 times, insert hook in st, yo and draw up a lp, (yo, draw through 2 lps on hook) 3 times] 3 times, yo and draw through all 4 lps on hook.

Quadruple treble (quadtr) Yo 4 times, insert hook in st, yo and draw up a lp, [yo and draw through 2 lps on hook] 5 times.

Quintuple treble (quintr) Yo 5 times, insert hook in st, yo and draw up a lp, [yo and draw through 2 lps on hook] 6 times.

Make picot (MP) Ch 5, sc in 5th ch from hook.

Rnd 1 (RS) Ch 1, work 24 sc in ring, join rnd with a sl st in first sc.

Rnd 2 Ch 1, sc in same place as joining, *ch 4, dtr2tog over next 2 sts, in top of cluster just made work set of 3 leaves as follows: (ch 7, quadtr, ch 7, sc, ch 8, quintr, ch 8, sc, ch 7, quadtr, ch 7, sl st), ch 4, sc in next st of rnd 1, ch 7, skip next 2 sts, sc in next st; rep from * around 3 more times, omitting sc at end of last rep, join rnd with a sl st in first sc. Fasten off.

Rnd 3 With RS facing, join yarn with a sl st in tip of 2nd Leaf of next set, in top of ch-8 before quintr work ch 1, sc in same place as joining, *ch 2, skip next quintr, sc in next ch, ch 5, in tip of 3rd Leaf of same

set sc just before and sc just after quadtr, ch 7, in tip of first Leaf of next set work sc just before and sc just after quadtr, ch 5, in tip of 2nd Leaf of same set work sc just before quintr; rep from * around 3 more times, omitting sc at end of last rep, join rnd with a sl st in first sc.

Rnd 4 Ch 1, sc in same place as joining, *work 3 sc in next ch-2 sp, sc in next sc, sc in next 5 ch, sc in next 2 sc, sc in next 7 ch, sc in next 2 sc, sc in next 5 ch, sc in next sc; rep from * around 3 times more, omitting sc at end of last rep, join rnd with a sl st in first sc.

Rnd 5 Sl st in next 2 sc to corner, ch 4 (counts and 1 dc and ch 1), dc in same place as ch-4, *[ch 1, skip next st, dc in next st] 13 times to next corner **, work [ch 1, dc] twice all in same st as last dc; rep from * around twice more, then from * to ** once, end ch 1, join rnd with a sl st in 3rd ch of beg ch-4.

Rnd 6 Ch 4 (counts as 1 dc and ch 1), dc in same place as joining, *[ch 1, dc in next ch-sp] 15 times, ch 1**, work (dc, ch 1, dc, ch 1, dc) in next corner st; rep from * around twice more, then from * to ** once, end dc in corner st, ch 1, join rnd with a sl st in 3rd ch of beg ch-4.

Rnd 7 Ch 3 (counts as 1 dc), dc in same place as joining, *ch 1, [dc in next ch-sp, dc in next dc, ch 1, skip next ch, dc in next dc, dc in next ch-sp, ch 1, skip next dc] 5 times, dc in next ch-sp, dc in next dc, ch 1, skip next ch, dc in next dc, dc in next ch-sp, ch 1**, work 3 dc in next corner st; rep from * around twice

more, then from * to ** once, end dc in corner st, join rnd with a sl st in top of beg ch-3.

Rnd 8 Ch 4 (counts as 1 dc and ch 1), dc in same place as joining, *dc in next dc, [ch 1, skip next ch, dc in next 2 sts] 13 times to next corner, ch 1**, work (dc, ch 1, dc) in same place as last dc; rep from * around twice more, then from * to ** once, join rnd with a sl st in 3rd ch of beg ch-4.

Rnd 9 Ch 1, work 2 sc in same place as joining, then sc in each ch-sp and dc around, working 3 sc in center st of next 3 corners, end sc in first corner, join rnd with a sl st in first sc.

Rnd 10 Ch 5 (counts as 1 dtr), dtr2tog in same place as joining (counts as dtr3tog), ch 2, dtr3tog in same place as last cluster, *ch 5, skip next 4 sts, work dtr3tog in next st, [ch 5, skip next 5 sts, work dtr3tog in next st] 6 times, ch 5, skip next 4 sts**, work (dtr3tog, ch 2, dtr3tog) in next corner st; rep from * around twice more, then from * to ** once, join rnd with a sl st in top of first cluster.

Rnd 11 Sl st to first ch-2 sp, ch 8, sc in 5th ch from hook, dc in same ch-2 sp, MP, *dc in next cluster, [MP, skip next 2 ch, dc in next ch, MP, skip next 2 ch, dc in next cluster] 8 times, MP**, work [dc, MP] twice in next corner ch-2 sp; rep from * around twice more, then from * to ** once, join rnd with a sl st in 3rd ch of beg ch-8. Fasten off.

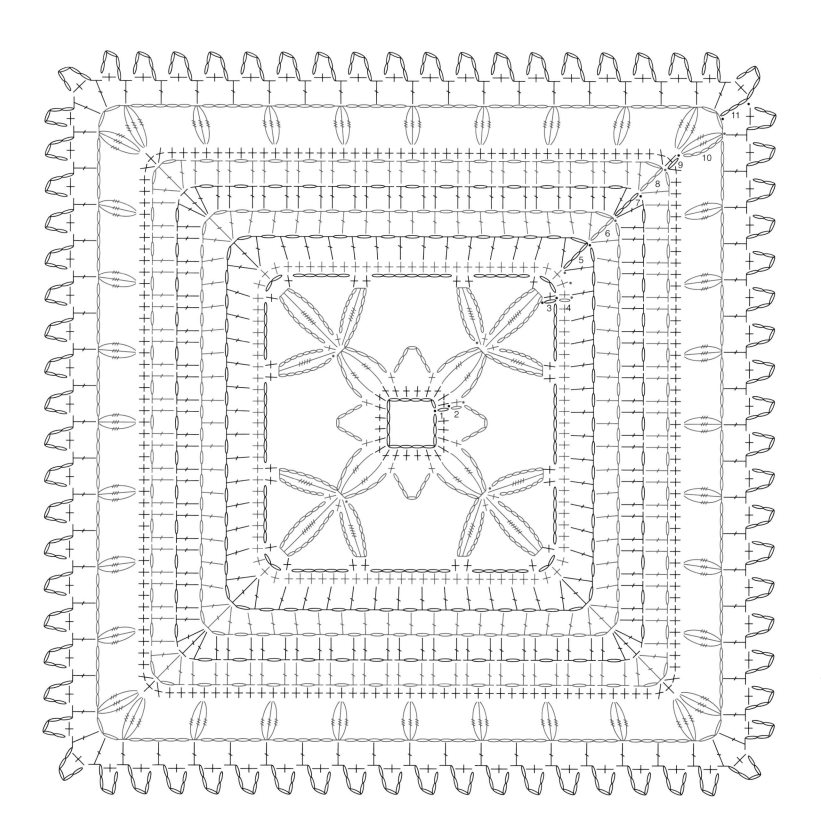

155

156

157

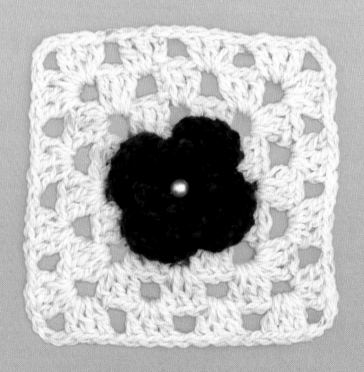

158

Grannies—*Floral*

155 *Begonia*

With A, chain 6. Join chain with a sl st, forming a ring.

Treble 3 together (tr3tog) In ring work [yo twice, insert hook in ring, yo and draw up a lp, (yo, draw through 2 lps on hook) twice] 3 times, yo and draw through all 4 lps on hook.

Treble 4 together (tr4tog) In ring work [yo twice, insert hook in ring, yo and draw up a lp, (yo, draw through 2 lps on hook) twice] 4 times, yo and draw through all 5 lps on hook.

Rnd 1 (RS) Ch 4 (counts as 1 tr), tr3tog in ring (counts as tr4tog), *ch 4, tr4tog in ring; rep from * around 6 times more, end ch 4, join rnd with a sl st in top of beg ch-4—8 ch-4 sps. Fasten off.

Rnd 2 With RS facing, join B with a sl st in any ch-sp, ch 3 (counts as 1 dc), work 4 dc in same sp, *work 5 dc in next ch-sp, ch 5, work 5 dc in next ch-sp; rep from * around twice more, end work 5 dc in last ch-sp, ch 5, join rnd with a sl st in top of beg ch-3.

Rnd 3 Ch 1, working through back lps only, sc in each st and ch around, working 3 sc in 3rd ch of each corner ch-5 lp, join rnd with a sl st in first sc. Fasten off.

156 *Cluster*

Chain 12. Join chain with a sl st, forming a ring.

Treble 3 together (tr3tog) [Yo twice, insert hook in sp, yo and draw up a lp, (yo, draw through 2 lps on hook) twice] 3 times, yo and draw through all 4 lps on hook.

Double treble 3 together (dtr3tog) [Yo 3 times, insert hook in specified st (or sp), yo and draw up a lp, (yo, draw through 2 lps on hook) 3 times] 3 times, yo and draw through all 4 lps on hook.

Double treble 4 together (dtr4tog) [Yo 3 times, insert hook in specified st (or sp), yo and draw up a lp, (yo, draw through 2 lps on hook) 3 times] 4 times, yo and draw through all 5 lps on hook.

Rnd 1 (RS) Ch 1, work 24 sc in ring, join rnd with a sl st in first sc.

Rnd 2 Ch 5 (counts as 1 dtr), dtr3tog over next 3 sts (counts as 1 dtr4tog), [ch 7, dtr4tog over same st as last leg of previous cluster and next 3 sts] 7 times, ch 7, join rnd with a sl st in top of first cluster.

Rnd 3 Ch 1, sc in same place as joining, *[ch 3, skip next ch, sc in next ch] 3 times, ch 3, skip next ch, sc in top of next cluster; rep from * around 7 times, omitting sc at end of last rep, join rnd with a sl st in first sc.

Rnd 4 Sl st in first 2 ch of first ch-3 sp, ch 1, sc in same ch-3 sp, *ch 3, sc in next ch-3 sp; rep from * around, omitting sc at end of last rep, join rnd with a sl st in first sc.

Rnd 5 Rep rnd 4.

Rnd 6 Sl st in first 2 ch of first ch-3 sp, ch 1, sc in same ch-3 sp, *[ch 3, sc in next ch-3 sp] 4 times, ch 3, skip next ch-3 sp, work (tr3tog, ch 5, dtr4tog, ch 4, sl st in top of last cluster, ch 5, tr3tog) in next ch-3 sp, ch 3, skip next ch-3 sp, sc in next ch-3 sp; rep from * around 3 times more, omitting sc at end of last rep, join rnd with a sl st in first sc. Fasten off.

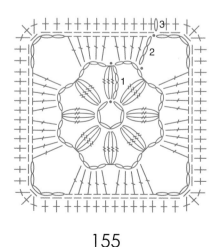

155

156

With A, chain 8. Join chain with a sl st, forming a ring.

Treble 5 together (tr5tog) [Yo twice, insert hook in next st, yo and draw up a lp, (yo, draw through 2 lps on hook) twice] 5 times, yo and draw through all 6 lps on hook.

Treble 6 together (tr6tog) [Yo twice, insert hook in next st, yo and draw up a lp, (yo, draw through 2 lps on hook) twice] 6 times, yo and draw through all 7 lps on hook.

Note When changing colors, draw new color through when you sl st to join rnd.

Rnd 1 (RS) Ch 4 (counts as 1 tr), work 5 tr in ring, *ch 3, work 6 tr in ring; rep from * around twice more,

end ch 3, join rnd with a sl st in top of beg ch-4.

Rnd 2 Ch 5, tr5tog, *ch 5, sl st in next 3 ch, ch 5, tr6tog; rep from * around twice more, end ch 5, sl st in last 3 ch. Fasten off.

Rnd 3 With RS facing, join B with a sl st in top of any cluster, * work (3 tr, ch 1, 3 tr, ch 2, 3 tr, ch 1, 3 tr) in next ch-3 sp of rnd 1, sl st in top of next cluster; rep from * around 3 times more, end last rep with join rnd with a sl st in first sl st changing to A.

Rnd 4 Ch 4 (counts as 1 tr), work 5 tr in same place as joining, *work (6 tr, ch 2, 6 tr) in next ch-2 sp, work 6 tr in sl st at top of next cluster; rep from * around twice more, end work (6 tr, ch 2, 6 tr) in last

ch-2 sp, join rnd with a sl st in top of beg ch-4 changing to C.

Rnd 5 Ch 1, sc in next 5 tr, dc in ch-1 sp between two 3 tr groups of rnd 3, *sc in next 6 tr, work 3 sc in next corner ch-2 sp, [sc in next 6 tr, dc in ch-1 sp between two 3 tr groups of rnd 3] twice; rep from * around twice more, end sc in next 6 tr, work 3 sc in last corner ch-2 sp, sc in last 6 tr, dc in ch-1 sp between last two 3 tr groups of rnd 3, join rnd with a sl st in first sc.

Rnd 6 Ch 3 (counts as 1 dc), dc in each st around, working 3 dc in center sc of each corner, join rnd with a sl st in top of beg ch-3. Fasten off.

To make an adjustable ring, use A to make a slipknot 10"/25.5cm from free end of yarn. Place slipknot on hook, then wrap free end of yarn twice around your first and second fingers on your left hand. Then work with yarn coming from ball as follows:

Flower

First row of petals

Rnd 1 (RS) Ch 2 (counts as 1 dc), work 3 dc in ring, sl st in ring, *work 4 dc in ring, sl st in ring; rep from * around twice more, pull free end of yarn to close circle, then join rnd with a sl st in top of beg ch-2—4 petals. Fasten off.

Second row of petals

With WS facing, join A with a sl st through base of any 3rd dc of rnd 1.

Rnd 2 (WS) Ch 4, *sl st through base of next 3rd dc of next group, ch 4; rep from * around twice more, join rnd with a sl st in first sl st—4 ch-4 lps. Turn.

Rnd 3 (RS) *Work (sc, 5 dc, sl st) in next ch-4 lp; rep from * around 3 times more. Fasten off.

Background

With RS facing, fold second row of petals towards you, join B with a sl st around post of any sc of rnd 3.

Rnd 4 Ch 6, *sl st around post of next sc, ch 6; rep from * around twice more, join rnd with a sl st in first sl st—4 ch-6 lps.

Rnd 5 Sl st in first ch-6 lp, ch 3 (counts as 1 dc), work (2 dc, ch 3, 3 dc) into same ch-6 lp, *ch 1, work (3 dc, ch 3, 3 dc) in next ch-6 lp; rep from * around twice more, end ch 1, join rnd with a sl st in top of

beg ch-3—4 corner ch-3 sps.

Rnd 6 Ch 4 (counts as 1 dc and ch 1), work (3 dc, ch 3, 3 dc) in first corner ch-3 sp, *ch 1, work 3 dc in next ch-1 sp, ch 1, work (3 dc, ch 3, 3 dc) in next corner ch-3 sp; rep from * around twice more, end ch 1, work 2 dc in last ch-1 sp, join rnd with a sl st in 3rd ch of beg ch-4.

Rnd 7 Ch 3 (counts as 1 dc), work 2 dc in first ch-1 sp, ch 1, *work (3 dc, ch 3, 3 dc) in next corner ch-3 sp, ch 1, [work 3 dc in next ch-1 sp, ch 1] twice; rep from * around twice more, end work (3 dc, ch 3, 3 dc) in last corner ch-3 sp, ch 1, work 3 dc in last ch-1 sp, ch 1, join rnd with a sl st in top of beg ch-3. Fasten off.

Finishing

Sew a bead to center of flower.

159

Flowers are made by first making four separate rings that form the centers of the flowers. The inner rnd (rnd 1) works one petal in each ring and also connects the flowers around the inner edge. The outer rnd (rnd 2) works three petals in each ring and also connects the flowers around the outer edge.

Flower centers (make 4)

Chain 5. Join chain with a sl st, forming a ring. Fasten off. Do not fasten off after making 4th ring.

Inner petals

Rnd 1 (RS) Ch 4 (counts as 1 tr), work 3 tr in ring, [work 4 tr in next ring] 3 times, join rnd with a sl st in top of beg ch-4. Fasten off.

Outer petals

Rnd 2 With RS facing, join yarn with a sl st in any ring, ch 4 (counts as 1 tr, work (3 tr, ch 4, sl st in ring, ch 4, 4 tr, ch 4, sl st in ring, ch 4, 4 tr) in same ring, [work (4 tr, ch 4, sl st in ring, ch 4, 4 tr, ch 4, sl st, ch 4, 4 tr) in next ring] 3 times, join rnd with a sl st in top of beg ch-4.

Border

You will now be working into the four petal points of each flower. The first point is at the upper left corner of the first outer petal. The second is at the upper right corner of the second outer petal. The third is at the upper left corner of the second outer petal. The fourth is at the upper right corner of the third outer petal.

Rnd 3 (RS) Sl st in first 4 sts of first outer petal to upper left corner, ch 1, sc in same place as last sl st, *ch 4, sc in next petal point; rep from * around, end ch 1, join rnd with a dc in first sc (counts as 1 ch-4)—16 ch-4 sps.

Rnd 4 Ch 1, sc in first ch-sp (made at end of rnd 3), ch 5, sc in next ch-sp, ch 5, work (sc, ch 5, sc) in corner ch-sp, *[ch 5, sc in next ch-sp] 3 times, ch 5, work (sc, ch 5, sc) in next corner ch-sp; rep from * around twice more, end ch 5, sc in last ch-sp, ch 2, join rnd with a dc in first sc (counts as 1 ch-5).

Rnd 5 Ch 1, sc in first ch-sp (made at end of rnd 4), [ch 5, sc in next ch-sp] twice, ch 5, work (sc, ch 5, sc) in corner ch-sp, *[ch 5, sc in next ch-sp] 4 times, ch 5, work (sc, ch 5, sc) in next corner ch-sp; rep from * around twice more, end ch 5, sc in last ch-sp, ch 5, join rnd with a sl st in first sc. Fasten off.

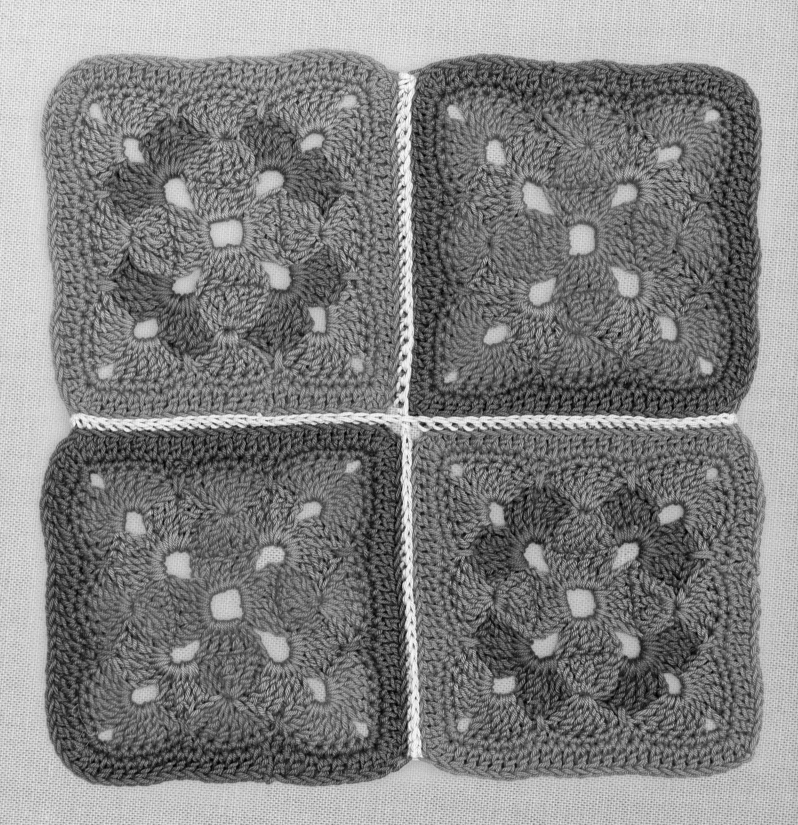

160

Motif I

Work rnds 1–6 as for tricolor.

Motif II

Work rnds 1–6 as for tricolor in color sequence as follows: **Rnds 1 and 2** C. **Rnd 3** A. **Rnd 4** C. **Rnds 5** and **6** B.

Joining

Place motifs I and II tog, WS facing. With RS facing you, join a contrasting color with a sl st in back lp of motif in front. Ch 1, working in back lp of motif in front and in front lp of motif in back, sc across. Working in the same manner, cont to sc motifs tog to form strips, then sc strips tog.

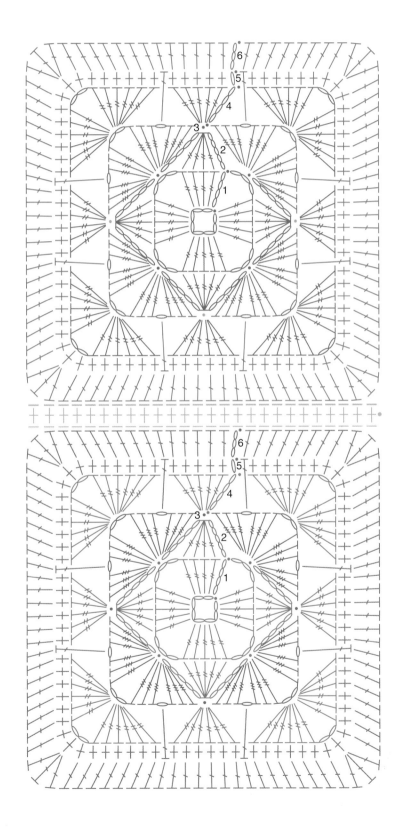

161

Chain 4. Join chain with a sl st, forming a ring.

Treble 4 together (tr4tog) [Yo twice, insert hook in next st, yo and draw up a lp, (yo, draw through 2 lps on hook) twice] 4 times, yo and draw through all 5 lps on hook.

Treble 5 together (tr5tog) [Yo twice, insert hook in next st, yo and draw up a lp, (yo, draw through 2 lps on hook) twice] 5 times, yo and draw through all 6 lps on hook.

Make picot (MP) Ch 3, sl st in same ch (or st) as last sl st.

Rnd 1 (RS) Ch 5 (counts as 1 dc and ch 2), [dc in ring, ch 2] 7 times, join rnd with a sl st in 3rd ch of beg ch-5—8 ch-2 sps.

Rnd 2 Sl st in first ch of first ch-2 sp, ch 3 (counts as 1 dc), work 4 dc in same sp, [work 5 dc in next ch-2 sp] 7 times, join rnd with a sl st in top of beg ch-3—40 dc.

Rnd 3 Ch 3 (counts as 1 dc), dc in next 4 sts, ch 1, [dc in next 5 sts, ch 1] 7 times, join rnd with a sl st jn top of beg ch-3.

Rnd 4 Ch 4 (counts as 1 tr), tr4tog (counts as 1 tr5tog), *ch 4, dc in next ch-1 sp, ch 4, tr5tog; rep from * around, end ch 4, dc in last ch-1 sp, ch 1, join rnd with a dc in top of first tr4tog (counts as 1 ch-4 sp).

Rnd 5 Ch 1, sc in first ch-sp (made at end of rnd 4), *ch 5, sc in next ch-sp; rep from * around, end ch 2, join rnd with a dc in top of first sc (counts as 1 ch-5 sp).

Rnd 6 Ch 1, sc in first ch-sp (made at end of rnd 5), *ch 5, work (3 dc, ch 2, 3 dc) in next ch-sp, [ch 5, sc in next ch-sp] 3 times; rep from * around twice more, end ch 5, work (3 dc, ch 2, 3 dc) in next ch-sp, [ch 5, sc in next ch-sp] twice, ch 2, join rnd with a dc in first sc (counts as 1 ch-5 sp).

Rnd 7 Ch 1, sc in first ch-sp (made at end of rnd 6), ch 5, sc in next ch-sp, *ch 5, work (3 dc, ch 2, 3 dc) in next corner ch-2 sp, [ch 5, sc in next ch-sp] 4 times; rep from * around twice more, end ch 5, work (3 dc, ch 2, 3 dc) in last corner ch-2 sp, [ch 5, sc in next ch-sp] twice, ch 2, join rnd with a dc in first sc (counts as 1 ch-5 sp).

Rnd 8 Ch 1, sc in first ch-sp (made at end of rnd 7), [ch 5, sc in next ch-sp] twice, *ch 5, work (3 dc, ch 5, 3 dc) in next corner ch-2 sp, [ch 5, sc in next ch-sp] 5 times; rep from * around twice more, end ch 5, work (3 dc, ch 5, 3 dc) in last corner ch-2 sp, [ch 5, sc in next ch-sp] twice, ch 5, join rnd with a sl st in first sc.

Rnd 9 Sl st in first 3 ch of first ch-5 sp, ** *MP, sl st in next 6 ch or sts*; rep from * to * before next corner ch-5 sp, work (MP in 3rd dc of first 3-dc group, sl st in next 3 ch, MP, sl st in next 3 sts, MP in first dc of second 3-dc group), sl st in next 6 ch (and or sts); rep from ** around, join rnd with a sl st in first sl st. Fasten off.

Finishing

Sew a bead to center of magnolia.

162

163

With A, chain 8. Join chain with a sl st, forming a ring.

Popcorn Work 3 dc in same st, drop lp from hook. Working from front to back, insert hook into both lps of first dc, pick up dropped lp and draw through dc, then ch 1 to secure popcorn.

Rnd 1 (RS) Ch 1, work 12 sc in ring, join rnd with a sl st in first sc.

Rnd 2 Ch 3 (counts as 1 dc), work 2 dc in same place as joining, drop lp from hook, working from front to back, insert hook into top of beg ch-3, pick up dropped lp and draw through ch, then ch 1 to secure popcorn (beg popcorn made), ch 2, [work popcorn in next sc, ch 2] 11 times, join rnd with a sl st in top of beg popcorn—12 popcorns. Fasten off.

Rnd 3 With RS facing, join B with a sl st in any ch-2 sp, ch 3 (counts as 1 dc), work (dc, ch 2, 2 dc) in same sp, *[work 3 dc in next ch-2 sp] twice, work (2 dc, ch 2, 2 dc) in next ch-2 sp; rep from * around twice more, end [work 3 dc in next ch-2 sp] twice, join rnd with a sl st in top of beg ch-3. Fasten off.

Rnd 4 With RS facing, join C with a sl st in any corner ch-2 sp, ch 3 (counts as 1 dc), work (dc, ch 2, 2 dc) in same sp, *[work 3 dc between next 2 dc groups] 3 times, work (2 dc, ch 2, 2 dc) in next corner ch-2 sp; rep from * around twice more, end [work 3 dc between next 2 dc groups] 3 times, join rnd with a sl st in top fo beg ch-3. Fasten off.

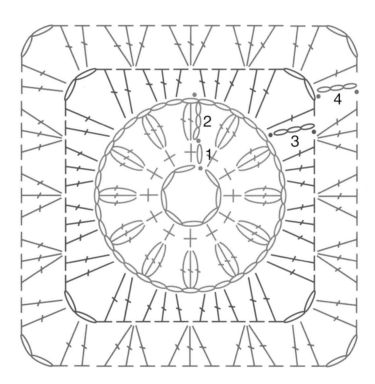

With A, chain 12. Join chain with a sl st, forming a ring.

Make picot (MP) Ch 3, sl st down through top of last sc made.

Rose

First row of petals

Rnd 1 (RS) Ch 1, work 18 sc in ring, join rnd with a sl st in first sc.

Rnd 2 Ch 1, sc in same place as joining, ch 3, skip next 2 sc, [sc in next sc, ch 3, skip next 3 sc] 5 times, join rnd with a sl st in first sc.

Rnd 3 Ch 1, [work (sc, ch 3, 5 dc, ch 3, sc) in next ch-3 sp] 6 times, join rnd with a sl st in first sc.

Second row of petals

Rnd 4 Ch 1, sc between 2 sc directly below joining, ch 5 behind petal of rnd 3, [sc between next 2 sc, ch 5 behind petal of rnd 3] 5 times, join rnd with a sl st in first sc.

Rnd 5 Ch 1, [work (sc, ch 3, 7 dc, ch 3, sc) in next ch-5 sp] 6 times, join rnd with a sl st in first sc. Fasten off.

Background

Rnd 6 With RS facing, join B with a sl st between any 2 sc of rnd 5, ch 1, sc between same 2 sc, ch 6 behind petal of rnd 5, [sc between next 2 sc, ch 6 behind petal of rnd 5] 5 times, join rnd with a sl st in first sc.

Rnd 7 Sl st in first ch-6 lp, ch 3 (counts as 1 dc), *work (4 dc, ch 2, dc) in same ch-6 lp, work 6 dc in next ch-5 lp, work (2 dc, ch 2, 4 dc) in next ch-6 lp**, dc in next ch-6 lp; rep from * to ** once more, join rnd with a sl st in top of beg ch-3.

Rnd 8 Ch 3 (counts as 1 dc), dc in each dc around, working (2 dc, ch 2, 2 dc) in each corner ch-2 sp, join rnd with a sl st in top of beg ch-3. Fasten off.

Rnd 9 With RS facing, join C with a sl st in same place as joining, ch 1, sc in same place as joining, *[MP, sc in next st] twice, sc in next 2 sts, [sc in next st, MP] twice, work (sc, ch 7, sc) in next corner ch-2 sp, [sc in next st, MP] twice, sc in next 2 sts, [sc in next st, MP] twice, sc in next st; rep from * around 3 times more omitting sc at end of last rep, join rnd with a sl st in first sc.

Rnd 10 Sl st across to top of first picot, ch 1, sc in same picot, *ch 5, sc in first picot, ch 5, work (sc, ch 7, sc) in next corner ch-7 lp, (ch 5, skip next picot, sc in next picot) twice, ch 5, sc in first picot; rep from * around 3 times more omitting sc at end of last rep, join rnd with a sl st in first sc. Fasten off.

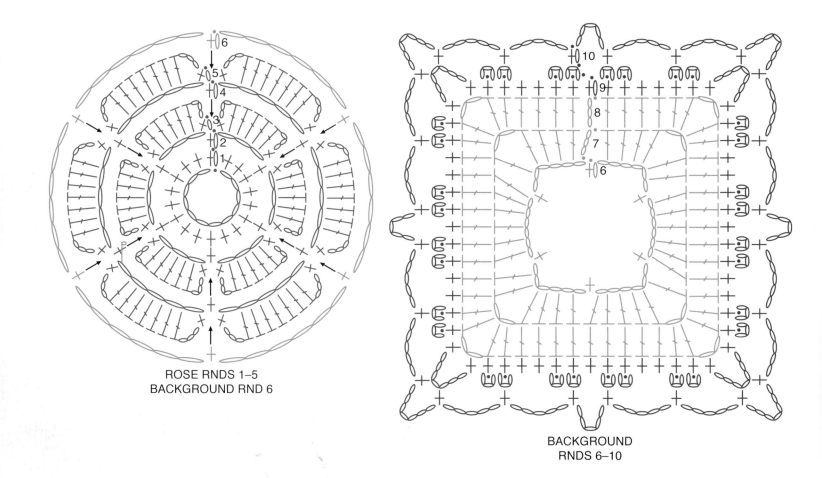

ROSE RNDS 1–5
BACKGROUND RND 6

BACKGROUND
RNDS 6–10

flowers

Chapter 5

164

Rose

With A, chain 65.

Row 1 (RS) Skip first 6 ch (counts as 1 hdc, skip 1 ch and ch 3), hdc in 7th ch from hook, *ch 3, skip next ch, hdc in next ch; rep from * across. Turn.

Row 2 Ch 3 (counts as 1 dc), work (dc, ch 3, 2 dc) in first ch-3 sp, ch 1, *work (2 dc, ch 3, 2 dc) in next ch-3 sp, ch 1; rep from * across, omitting ch-1 at end of last rep. Turn.

Row 3 Ch 3, work 7 dc in first ch-3 sp, sl st in next ch-1 sp, *work 7 dc in next ch-3 sp, sl st in next ch-1 sp; rep from * across, end work 7 dc in last ch-3 sp, sl st in top of ch-3 t-ch of row below. Fasten off. Do not turn.

Row 4 With RS facing, join B with a sl st in first dc, ch 1, sc in same st as joining, *sc loosely in next dc; rep from * across. Fasten off.

Leaf (make 3)

With B, chain 17.

Row 1 (RS) Skip first 2 ch (counts as 1 sc and ch-1 t-ch), sc in next 14 ch, work 3 sc in last ch, turn to bottom lps of beg ch, sc in next 15 bottom lps. Turn.

Rows 2–6 Ch 1 (counts as 1 sc), skip first st, sc in each st to center st of point, work 3 sc in center st, sc in each st to within last 3 sts and t-ch. Turn.

Row 7 Rep row 2. Fasten off.

Stem

With B, chain 22.

Joining leaves

Row 1 (RS) Sl st in center base of first leaf, turn, sc in next 5 ch, join second leaf as foll: *insert hook through center base of leaf and in next ch, yo and draw up a lp, yo and draw through both lps on hook; rep from * for third leaf, then sc in each ch to end. Fasten off.

Finishing

Shape rose strip in a spiral forming a flower that has three rows of petals. Tack together in center of flower to secure petals. Sew a bead to center of rose. Sew leaves to back of rose.

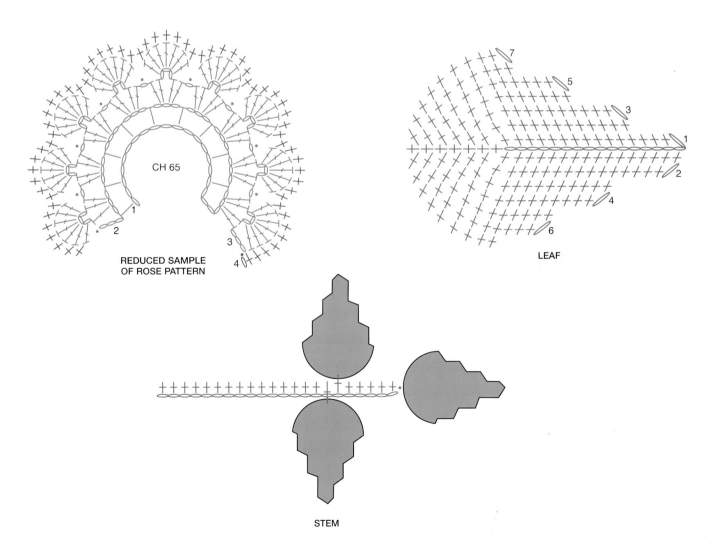

CH 65

1

2

3

4

REDUCED SAMPLE OF ROSE PATTERN

7

5

3

1

2

4

6

LEAF

STEM

165

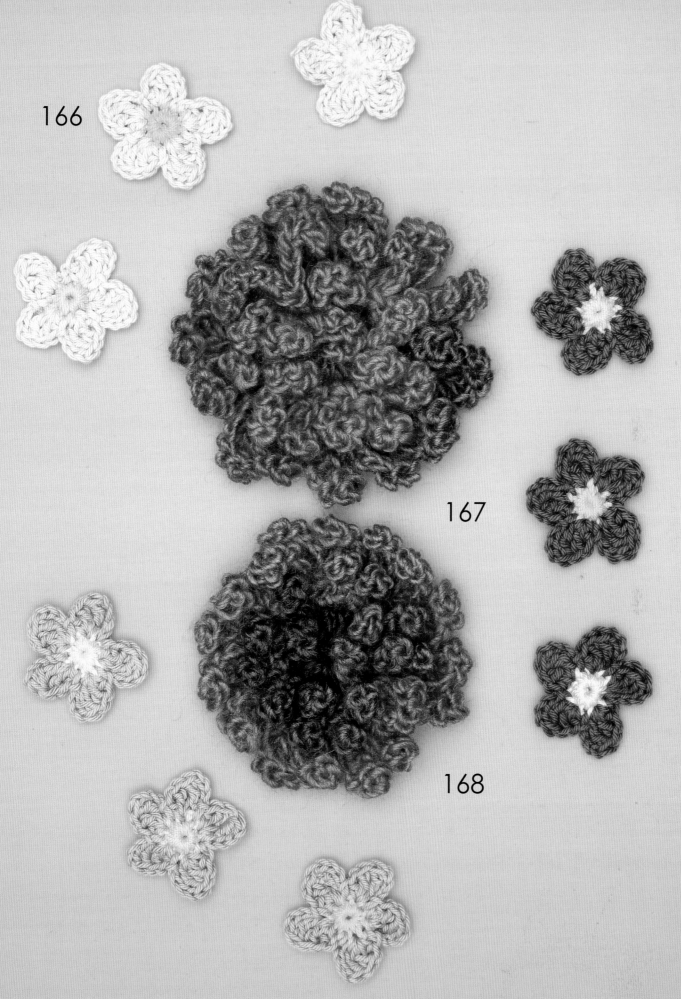

166

167

168

Wild rose

With A, chain 6. Join chain with a sl st, forming a ring.

Rnd 1 (RS) Ch 1, work 12 sc in ring, join rnd with a sl st in first st—12 sc.

Rnd 2 Ch 1, sc in first st, ch 12, *sc in next st, ch 12; rep from *around, join rnd with a sl st in first st—12 petals. Fasten off.

Finishing

Place one flower on top of the other. Tack flowers together by sewing a running stitch around inner edges of rnd 1. Pull yarn to gather, then fasten off securely. Sew a pearl to center of flower.

Leaf

With B, chain 17.

Row 1 (RS) Skip first 2 ch (counts as 1 sc and ch-1 t-ch), sc in next 13 ch, work 2 sc in last ch (2nd sc in the center st of the point), turn to bottom lps of beg ch, sc in next 16 bottom lps. Turn.

Row 2 Ch 1 (counts as 1 sc), skip first st, working through *front* lps only, sc in each st to center st of point, work 3 sc in center st, sc in each st to within last 3 sts and t-ch. Turn.

Row 3 Ch 1 (counts as 1 sc), skip first st, working through *back* lps only, sc in each st to center st of point, work 3 sc in center st, sc in each st to within last 3 sts and t-ch. Turn.

Rows 4 and 6 Rep row 2.

Rows 5 and 7 Rep row 3. Fasten off.

Finishing

Sew point of leaf to underside of wild rose.

WILD ROSE

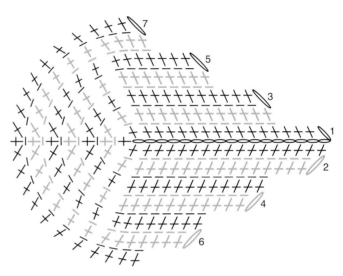

LEAF

To make an adjustable ring, use A to make a slipknot 10"/25.5cm from free end of yarn. Place slipknot on hook, then wrap free end of yarn twice around your first and second fingers on your left hand. Then work with yarn coming from ball as follows:

Rnd 1 (RS) Ch 1, work 10 sc in ring, pull free end of yarn to close circle, then join rnd with a sl st in first sc—10 sc. Fasten off.

Rnd 2 With RS facing, join B with a sl st in any st, *ch 4, work (tr, dc, hdc) in next st, sl st in next st; rep from *around 4 times more, join rnd with a sl st in first ch of beg ch-4—5 petals. Fasten off.

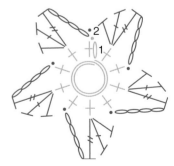

FORGET-ME-NOT

167 *Large Chrysanthemum*

To make an adjustable ring, make a slipknot 10"/25.5cm from free end of yarn. Place slipknot on hook, then wrap free end of yarn twice around your first and second fingers on your left hand. Then work with yarn coming from ball as follows:
Rnd 1 (RS) Ch 2 (counts as 1 hdc), work 16 hdc in ring, pull free end of yarn to close circle, then join rnd with a sl st in top of beg ch-2—17 hdc.

Inner row of petals

Rnd 2 Working in front lps only, ch 1, sc in same place as joining, ch 5, sc in 2nd ch from hook, then sc in next 3 ch, sc in side of first sc, *sc in next st, ch 5, sc in 2nd ch from hook, then sc in next 3 ch, sc in side of first sc at beg of rep; rep from * around, join rnd with a sl st in first sc—17 petals.

Outer row of petals

Rnd 3 Working in free back lps of rnd 1, ch 1, sc in same place as joining, ch 8, hdc in 3rd ch from hook, then hdc in next 5 ch, sc in side of first sc made, *sc in next st, ch 8, hdc in 3rd ch from hook, then hdc in next 5 ch, sc in side of first sc at beg of rep; rep from * around, join rnd with a sl st in first sc—17 petals. Fasten off.

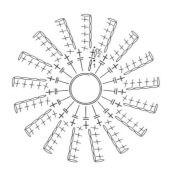

INNER ROW OF PETALS

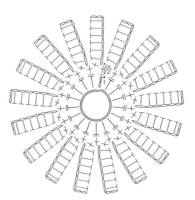

OUTER ROW OF PETALS

168 *Small Chrysanthemum*

To make an adjustable ring, make a slipknot 10"/25.5cm from free end of yarn. Place slipknot on hook, then wrap free end of yarn twice around your first and second fingers on your left hand. Then work with yarn coming from ball as follows:
Rnd 1 (RS) Ch 2 (counts as 1 hdc), work 16 hdc in ring, pull free end of yarn to close circle, then join rnd with a sl st in top of beg ch-2—17 hdc.

Inner row of petals

Rnd 2 Working in front lps only, ch 1, sc in same place as joining, ch 3, sc in 2nd ch from hook, then sc in next ch, sc in side of first sc, *sc in next st, ch 3, sc in 2nd ch from hook, then sc in next ch, sc in side of first sc at beg of rep; rep from * around, join rnd with a sl st in first sc—17 petals.

Outer row of petals

Rnd 3 Working in free back lps of rnd 1, ch 1, sc in same place as joining, ch 6, hdc in 3rd ch from hook, then hdc in next 3 ch, sc in side of first sc made, *sc in next st, ch 6, hdc in 3rd ch from hook, then hdc in next 3 ch, sc in side of first sc at beg of rep; rep from * around, join rnd with a sl st in first sc—17 petals. Fasten off.

INNER ROW OF PETALS

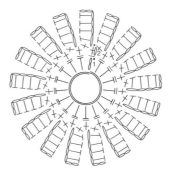

OUTER ROW OF PETALS

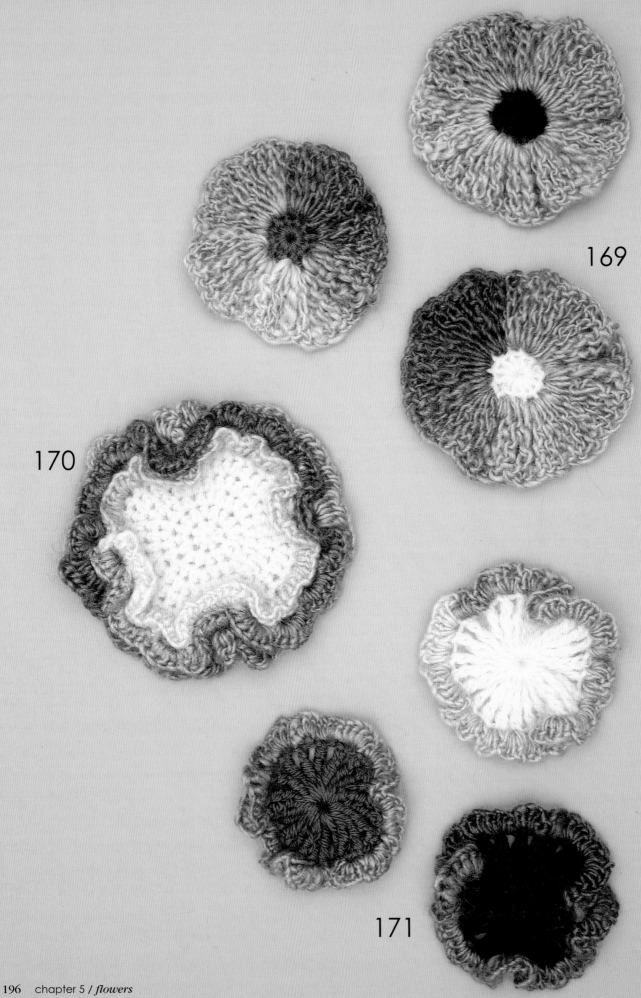

169

170

171

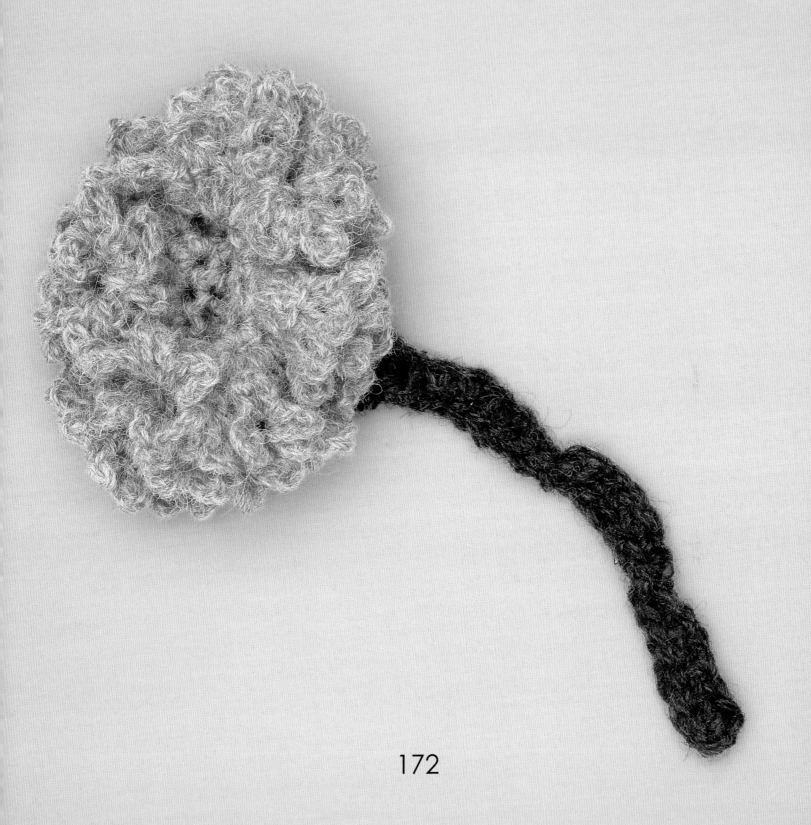

172

169 *Fungus I*

To make an adjustable ring, use A to make a slipknot 10"/25.5cm from free end of yarn. Place slipknot on hook, then wrap free end of yarn twice around your first and second fingers on your left hand. Then work with yarn coming from ball as follows:

Note The WS is the RS of the fungus.

Rnd 1 (RS) Ch 1 (counts as 1 hdc), work 12 hdc in ring, pull free end of yarn to close circle, then join rnd with a sl st in top of beg ch-2—13 hdc. Fasten off.

Rnd 2 With RS facing, join B with a sl st in any st, ch 5 (counts as 1 dtr), work 4 dtr in same st, *work 5 dtr in next st; rep from * around, join rnd with a sl st in top of beg ch-4. Fasten off.

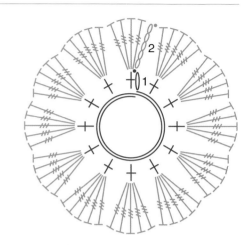

170 *Fungus II*

To make an adjustable ring, use A to make a slipknot 10"/25.5cm from free end of yarn. Place slipknot on hook, then wrap free end of yarn twice around your first and second fingers on your left hand. Then work with yarn coming from ball as follows:

Rnd 1 (RS) Ch 5 (counts as 1 dtr), work 25 dtr in

ring, pull free end of yarn to close circle, then join rnd with a sl st in top of beg ch-4—26 dtr. Fasten off. Turn to WS.

Rnd 2 With WS facing, join B with a sl st in any st, ch 1, work 5 sc in same st as joining, *work 5 sc in next st; rep from * around, join rnd with a sl st in first sc. Fasten off.

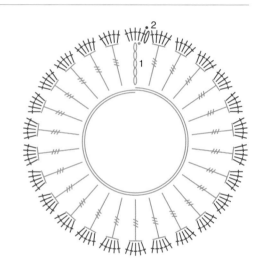

171 *Fungus III*

To make an adjustable ring, use A to make a slipknot 10"/25.5cm from free end of yarn. Place slipknot on hook, then wrap free end of yarn twice around your first and second fingers on your left hand. Then work with yarn coming from ball as follows:

Rnd 1 (RS) Ch 1, work 8 sc, pull free end of yarn to close circle, then join rnd with a sl st in first sc.

Rnd 2 Ch 1, work 2 sc in each st around, join rnd with a sl st in first st—16 sc.

Rnd 3 Ch 1, work 2 sc in first st, sc in next st, *work 2 sc in next st, sc in next st; rep from * around, join

rnd with a sl st in first st—24 sc.

Rnd 4 Ch 1, work 2 sc in first st, sc in next 2 sts, *work 2 sc in next st, sc in next 2 sts; rep from * around, join rnd with a sl st in first st—32 sc.

Rnd 5 Ch 1, work 2 sc in first st, sc in next 3 sts, *work 2 sc in next st, sc in next 3 sts; rep from * around, join rnd with a sl st in first st—40 sc.

Rnd 6 Ch 1, sc in each st around, join rnd with a sl st in first st. Fasten off.

First ruffle

Rnd 7 With RS facing, join B with a sl st in any st, ch 1, work 3 sc in same st as joining; *work 3 sc in

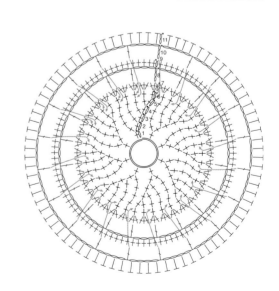

next st and every st around, join rnd with a sl st in first st—120 sc. Fasten off.

Second ruffle

Rnd 8 Working in back of first ruffle, join B with a sl st around post of any st on rnd 6, ch 6 (counts as 1 dc and ch 3), skip next st on rnd 6, dc around post of next st on rnd 6, *ch 3, skip next st on rnd 6, dc around post of next st on rnd 6; rep from * around, end ch 3, join rnd with a sl st in 3rd ch of beg ch-6—20 ch-3 lps.

Rnd 9 Ch 1, *work 5 sc in next ch-3 lp; rep from * around, join rnd with a sl st in first st. Fasten off.

Third ruffle

Rnd 10 Working in back of second ruffle, join B with a sl st around post of any of the same sts on rnd 6 as second ruffle, ch 7 (counts as 1 dc and ch 4), skip next st on rnd 6, dc around post of next st on rnd 6, *ch 4, skip next st on rnd 6, dc around post of next st on rnd 6; rep from * around, end ch 4, join rnd with a sl st in 3rd ch of beg ch-7—20 ch-4 lps.

Rnd 11 Ch 2, *work 4 hdc in next and every ch-4 lp around, join rnd with a sl st in top of beg ch-2. Fasten off.

172 *Carnation*

Linked double crochet (LDC) Insert hook down through horizontal loop round stem of last st made, yo, draw up a loop; insert hook to make st and complete in the usual manner.

Note At the beginning of the round, to make the first LDC, treat the 2nd ch of the starting ch as the horizontal loop.

Linked double treble crochet (LDTR) Insert hook down through uppermost of 3 horizontal loops around stem of last st made, yo, draw up a loop, [insert hook down through next lower horizontal loop, yo, draw up a loop through] twice; insert hook to make st and complete in the usual manner.

Note At the beginning of the round, to make the first LDTR, treat the 2nd, 3rd and 4th ch of the starting ch as horizontal loops.

Calyx

With A, chain 4. Join chain with a sl st, forming a ring.

Rnd 1 (RS) Ch 3 (counts as 1 dc), work 5 LDC in ring, join rnd with a sl st in top of beg ch-3—6 sts.

Rnd 2 Ch 5 (counts as 1 dtr), LDTR in first st, [work 2 LDTR in next st] 5 times, join rnd with a sl st in top of beg ch-5—12 sts. Fasten off.

Flower head

Rnd 3 With RS facing, join B with a sl st in any st, ch 1, sc in same st as joining, sc in next 11 sts, join rnd with a sl st in first st—12 sts.

Rnd 4 Ch 1, sc in each st around, join rnd with a sl st in first st.

Rnd 5 Ch 1, work 2 sc in first st, [work 3 sc in next st] 11 times, work sc in same st as first st, join rnd with a sl st in first st—36 sts.

Rnd 6 Ch 3 (counts as 1 dc), work 2 dc in first st, *work 3 dc in next st; rep from * around, join rnd with a sl st in top of beg ch-3—108 sts. Turn.

Rnd 7 (WS) Ch 1, sc in first st, ch 5, *sc in next st, ch 5; rep from * around, join rnd with a sl st in first st—108 ch-5 lps. Fasten off.

Stem

With RS facing, join A with a sl st in foundation ring at base of calyx, ch 22 and work as foll: sc in 2nd ch from hook and in each ch to end, join stem with a sl st in opposite side of foundation ring at base of calyx. Turn, then sl st in each st down stem, twisting the stem every 5 or 6 sts to add textural interest. Fasten off.

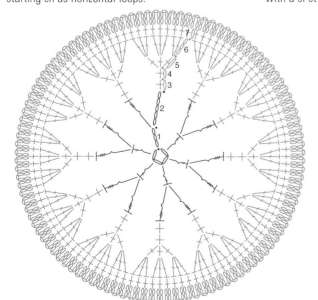

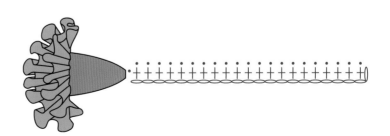

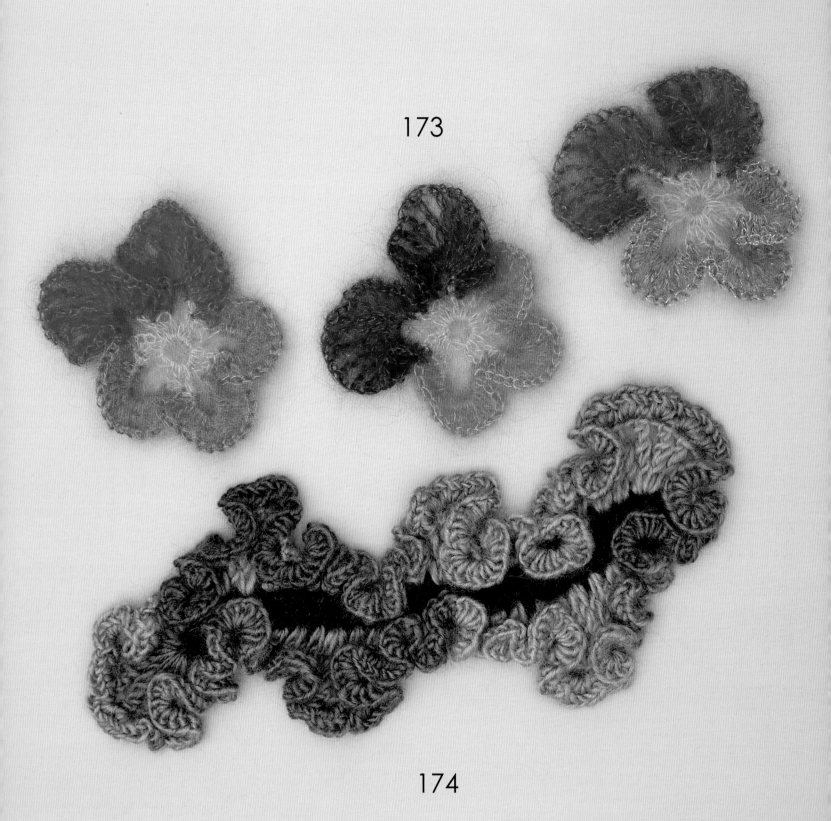

173

174

173 *Pansy*

With A, chain 6. Join chain with a sl st, forming a ring.

Flower center

Rnd 1 (RS) Ch 3 (counts as 1 dc), work 2 dc in ring, [ch 7, work 3 dc in ring] 4 times, ch 7, join rnd with a sl st in top of beg ch-3—5 ch-7 lps. Fasten off.

Small petals

Rnd 2 (RS) With RS facing, join B with a sl st in 3rd dc of any 3-dc group, ch 3 (counts as 1 dc), work 15 tr in next ch-7 lp, [skip next dc, dc in next dc, skip next dc, work 15 tr in next ch-7 lp] twice, dc in next dc. Fasten off.

Large petals

Rnd 2 (RS) With RS facing, skip next dc after last dc of small petals, join C with a sl st in next dc, ch 3 (counts as 1 dc), ch 1, *in next ch-7 lp work: [tr, ch 1] twice, [dtr, ch 1] 3 times, [ttr, ch 1] 5 times, [dtr, ch 1] 3 times, [tr, ch 1] twice*, dc in next dc, skip next dc, dc in next dc, ch 1; rep from * to *, end dc in next dc, skip next dc, join to small petals with a sl st in top of beg ch-3 of small petals. Fasten off.

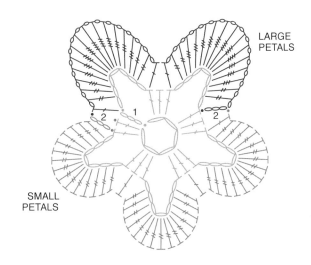

LARGE PETALS

SMALL PETALS

174 *Lichen*

With A, chain 35.

Note When changing colors, draw new color through when you sl st to join rnd.

Rnd 1 (RS) Sc in 2nd ch from hook and in next 32 ch, work 3 sc in last ch, turn to bottom lps of chain, sc in each lp to last lp, work 4 sc in last lp, join rnd with a sl st in first st changing to B—74 sc.

Rnd 2 Sl st in first st, *work 2 sc in next st, work 2 hdc in next st, work 2 dc in next st, work 2 tr in next st, work 3 dtr in next st, work 2 tr in next st, work 2 dc in next st, work 2 hdc in next st, work 2 sc in next st, sl st in next st; rep from * around, end sl st in last st, join rnd with a sl st in first sl st.

Rnd 3 Ch 1, work 5 sc in each st around (chart shows only the first 7 increases). Join rnd with a sl st in first st. Fasten off.

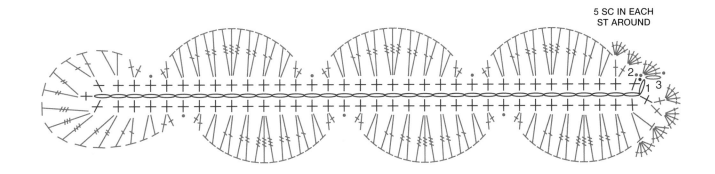

5 SC IN EACH ST AROUND

175

176

177

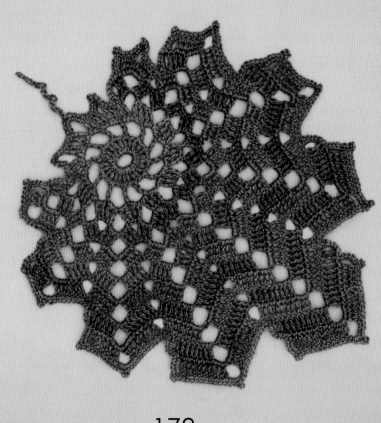

178

179

175 *Cherries*

Cherry (make 2)

To make an adjustable ring, use A to make a slipknot 10"/25.5cm from free end of yarn. Place slipknot on hook, then wrap free end of yarn twice around your first and second fingers on your left hand. Then work with yarn coming from ball as follows:

Rnd 1 (RS) Ch 1, work 6 sc in ring, pull free end of yarn to close circle, then join rnd with a sl st in first st—6 sc.

Rnd 2 Ch 1, work 2 sc in each st around, join rnd with a sl st in first st—12 sc.

Rnds 3-6 Ch 1, sc in each st around, join rnd with a

sl st in first st. Stuff cherry with a small ball of A.

Rnd 7 Ch 1, *skip next st, sc in next st; rep from * around, join rnd with a sl st in first st—6 sc.

Rnd 8 Rep rnd 7—3 sc. Fasten off, leaving a long tail. Thread tail in tapestry needle and weave through last rnd of sts. Pull tight to gather. Fasten off securely.

Short stem

With B, chain 21.

Fasten off, leaving a long tail for sewing.

Long stem

With B, chain 27.

Fasten off, leaving a long tail for sewing.

Leaf (make 3)

With B, chain 14.

Rnd 1 (RS) Sc in 2nd ch from hook, sc in next 3 ch, dc in next 5 ch, sc in next 3 ch, work 2 sc in last ch, turn to bottom lps of ch and work as foll: sc in first 4 lps, dc in next 5 lps, sc in last 4 lps, join rnd with a sl st in first st. Fasten off, leaving a long tail for sewing.

Finishing

Sew a stem to a cherry as foll: thread tapestry needle with stem tail. Insert needle through the cherry from top to bottom, then back again. Fasten off securely. Sew three leaves together, then sew tops of stems to base where leaves are joined.

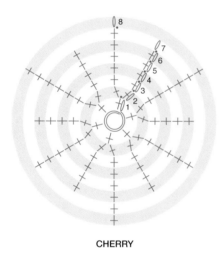

CHERRY

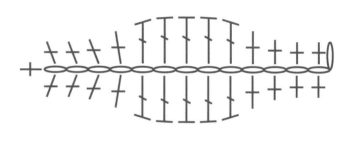

LEAF

176 *Seed Pod*

Note The WS is the RS of the leaves and seed pod.

Leaf (make 3)

Chain 15.

Rnd 1 (RS) Sc in 2nd ch from hook, hdc in next ch, dc in next 3 ch, tr in next 4 ch, dc in next 3 ch, hdc in next ch, sc in last ch, ch 3, turn to bottom lps of foundation ch, sc in first lp, hdc in next lp, dc in next

3 lps, tr in next 4 lps, dc in next 3 lps, hdc in next lp, sc in last lp, ch 3, join rnd with a sl st in first sc. Fasten off, leaving a long tail for sewing.

Seed pod (make 1)

Chain 22.

Rnd 1 (RS) Sc in 2nd ch from hook, hdc in next 2 ch, dc in next 3 ch, tr in next 3 ch, dtr in next 3 ch, tr in

next 3 ch, dc in next 3 ch, hdc in next 2 ch, sc in last ch, ch 3, turn to bottom lps of foundation ch, sc in first lp, hdc in next 2 lps, dc in next 3 lps, tr in next 3 lps, dtr in next 3 lps, tr in next 3 lps, dc in next 3 lps, hdc in next 2 lps, sc in last lp, ch 3, join rnd with a sl st in first sc. Fasten off, leaving a long tail for sewing.

Tendril (make 1)

Chain 30.

Row 1 (RS) Work 2 sc in 2nd ch from hook, *work 3 sc in next ch; rep from * across. Fasten off, leaving a long end for sewing pieces together.

Finishing

For seed pod, bring side edges at top of pod together so they meet. Beg at top of pod, sew edges together for 1½"/4cm; fasten off securely. Sew a line of pearls or beads down center of seed pod, as shown. Sew leaves to top of seed pod, then sew end of tendril to top side edge of seed pod.

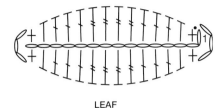

LEAF

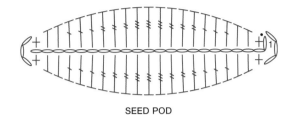

SEED POD

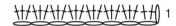

REDUCED SAMPLE
OF TENDRIL

177 *Water Lily*

Single crochet 2 together (sc2tog) [Insert hook in next st, yo and draw up a lp] twice, yo and draw through all 3 lps on hook.

Flower center

With A, chain 5. Join chain with a sl st, forming a ring.

Rnd 1 (RS) Ch 1, work 8 sc in ring, join rnd with a sl st in first st—8 sc.

Rnd 2 Ch 1, working in front lps only of rnd 1, work [sc, ch 5, sc] twice in each st around, join rnd with a sl st in first st.

Rnd 3 Ch 1, working in back lps only of rnd 1, work 2 sc in each st around, join rnd with a sl st in first st—16 sc.

Rnd 4 Ch 1, working in front lps only of rnd 3, work [sc, ch 5, sc] twice in each st around, join rnd with a sl st in first st. Fasten off.

Rnd 5 Ch 1, working in back lps only of rnd 3, sc in each st around, join rnd with a sl st in first st—16 sc.

Rnd 6 Ch 1, work 2 sc in each st of rnd 5, join rnd with a sl st in first—32 sc.

Rnd 7 Ch 1, working in back lps only of rnd 6, sc in each st around, join rnd with a sl st in first st—32 sc.

Rnd 8 Ch 1, sc in each st of rnd 7, join rnd with a sl st in first—32 sc.

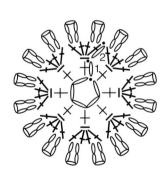

FLOWER CENTER
RNDS 1–2

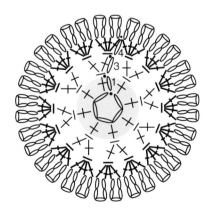

FLOWER CENTER
RNDS 3–4

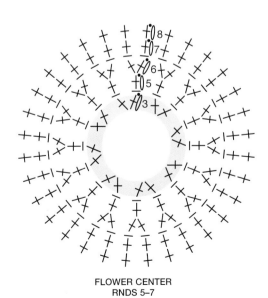

FLOWER CENTER
RNDS 5–7

Small petals

First petal (make 1)

Row 1 (RS) With RS of flower center facing, join B with a sl st in any free front lp of rnd 6, ch 1, work 3 sc in same lp as joining. Turn.

Row 2 Ch 1, work 2 sc in each st—6 sts. Turn.

Row 3 Ch 1, work 2 sc in first st, sc in each st to last st, work 2 sc in last st—8 sts. Turn.

Row 4 Ch 1, sc in each st across. Turn.

Row 5 Ch 1, sc2tog over first 2 sts, sc in each st across—7 sc. Turn.

Rows 6–10 Rep row 5—2 sc. Turn.

Row 11 Ch 1, sc2tog—1 sc. Fasten off.

Second petal (make 7)

Row 1 (RS) With RS of flower center facing, skip next 3 free front lps of rnd 6, join B with a sl st in next free lp, ch 1, work 3 sc in same lp as joining. Turn. Rep rows 2–10 as for first petal. Working in this manner, join and make 6 more petals.

Large petals

First petal (make 1)

With C, chain 2.

Row 1 (RS) Work 3 sc in 2nd ch from hook. Turn.

Row 2 Ch 1, work 2 sc in each st—6 sts. Turn.

Row 3 Ch 1, work 2 sc in first st, sc in each st to last st, work 2 sc in last st—8 sts. Turn.

Rows 4 and 5 Rep row 3—12 sc. Turn.

Rows 6 and 7 Ch 1, sc in each st across. Turn.

Row 8 Ch 1, sc2tog over first 2 sts, sc in each st across—11 sc. Turn.

Rows 9–17 Rep row 8—2 sc. Turn.

Row 18 Ch 1, sc2tog—1 sc. Fasten off.

Second petal (make 7)

Work as for first petal until row 6 is completed. Turn.

Joining

Row 7 (RS) With RS of first petal facing, sl st in left side edge of row 7 of first petal, ch 1, sc in each st across second petal. Turn. Cont to work as for first petal through row 18. Fasten off. Working in this manner, make and join 6 more petals, joining last petal to first petal at end of row 7, forming a circle.

Finishing

With RS of flower center/small petals facing, place on top of RS of large petal ring. Line up small petals with large petals, matching tips of petals. On WS, use C threaded through a tapestry needle to tack the bottom tip of each large petal to rnd 8 of flower center.

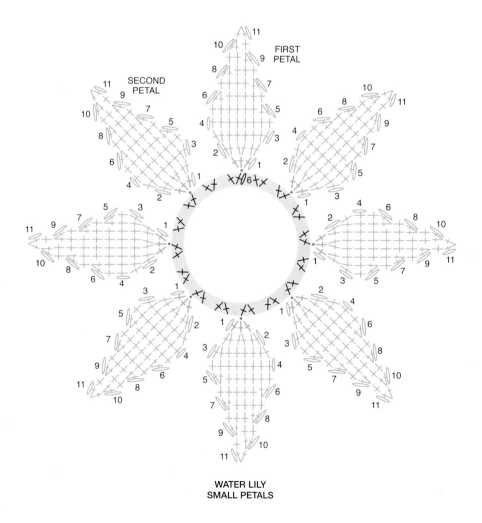

WATER LILY
SMALL PETALS

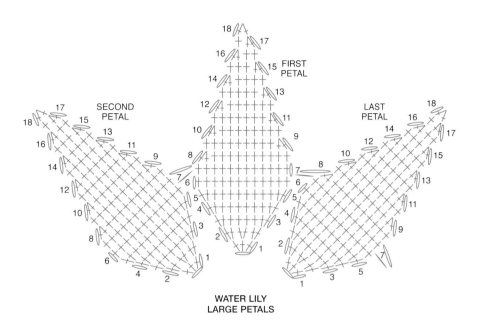

FIRST PETAL

SECOND PETAL

LAST PETAL

WATER LILY
LARGE PETALS

178 *Latvian Leaf*

Chain 10. Join chain with a sl st, forming a ring.

Make picot (MP) Ch 3, sl st in 3rd ch from hook.

Rnd 1 (RS) Ch 4 (counts as 1 tr), work 23 tr in ring, join rnd with a sl st in top of beg ch-4—24 tr.

Rnd 2 Ch 8 (counts as 1 tr and ch 4), skip first st, tr in next st, ch 4, *skip next st, tr in next st, ch 4; rep from * around, join rnd with a sl st in 4th ch of beg ch-8—12 ch-4 lps.

Rnd 3 Sl st in first ch-lp, ch 4 (counts as 1 tr), tr in same to ch-4 lp, *ch 6, work 2 tr in same ch-4 lp as last 2 tr, ch 1, work 2 tr in next ch-4 lp; rep from * around, end ch 1, join rnd with a sl st in top of beg ch-4 —12 ch-6 lps.

Now work in rows as foll:

Row 1 (RS) Sl st in first ch of ch-6 lp, ch 4 (counts as 1 tr), work (2 tr, ch 6, 3 tr) in same ch-6 lp, *work (3 tr, ch 6, 3 tr) in next ch-6 lp; rep from * around 7 times more—9 ch-6 lps. Turn.

Row 2 Sl st in first 3 tr, ch 4 (counts as 1 tr), *work (3 tr, ch 6, 3 tr) in next ch-6 lp, tr in next tr, skip next 4 tr, tr in next tr; rep from * 8 times more, omitting (skip next 4 tr, tr in next tr) at end of last rep—9 ch-6 lps. Turn.

Row 3 Sl st in first 4 tr, 6 ch and next 7 tr, ch 4 (counts as 1 tr), tr in next tr, *work (3 tr, ch 6, 3 tr) in next ch-6, tr in next 2 tr, skip next 4 tr, tr in next 2 tr; rep from * 6 times more, omitting (skip next 4 tr, tr in next 2 tr) at end of last rep—7 ch-6 lps. Turn.

Row 4 Sl st in first 3 tr, ch 4 (counts as 1 tr), tr in next 2 tr, *work (3 tr, ch 6, 3 tr) in next ch-6, tr in next 3 tr, skip next 4 tr, tr in next 3 tr; rep from * 6 times more, omitting (skip next 4 tr, tr in next 3 tr) at end of last rep—7 ch-6 lps. Turn.

Row 5 Sl st in first 6 tr, 6 ch and next 9 tr, ch 4 (counts as 1 tr), tr in next 3 tr, *work (3 tr, ch 6, 3 tr) in next ch-6, tr in next 4 tr, skip next 4 tr, tr in next 4 tr; rep from * 4 times more, omitting (skip next 4 tr, tr in next 3 tr) at end of last rep—5 ch-6 lps. Turn.

Row 6 Sl st in first 3 tr, ch 4 (counts as 1 tr), tr in next 4 tr, *work (3 tr, ch 6, 3 tr) in next ch-6, tr in next 5 tr, skip next 4 tr, tr in next 5 tr; rep from * 4 times more, omitting (skip next 4 tr, tr in next 5 tr) at end of last rep—5 ch-6 lps. Turn.

Row 7 Sl st in first 8 tr, 6 ch and next 11 tr, ch 4 (counts as 1 tr), tr in next 5 tr, *work (3 tr, ch 6, 3 tr) in next ch-6, tr in next 6 tr, skip next 4 tr, tr in next 6 tr; rep from * twice more, omitting (skip next 4 tr, tr in next 6 tr) at end of last rep—3 ch-6 lps. Turn.

Row 8 Sl st in first 3 tr, ch 4 (counts as 1 tr), tr in next 6 tr, *work (3 tr, ch 6, 3 tr) in next ch-6, tr in next 7 tr, skip next 4 tr, tr in next 7 tr; rep from * twice more, omitting (skip next 4 tr, tr in next 7 tr) at end of last rep—3 ch-6 lps. Turn.

Row 9 Sl st in first 10 tr, 6 ch and next 13 tr, ch 4 (counts as 1 tr), tr in next 7 tr, work (3 tr, ch 6, 3 tr) in next ch-6, tr in next 8 tr—1 ch-6 lp. Turn.

Row 10 Sl st in first 3 tr, ch 4 (counts as 1 tr), tr in next 8 tr, work (3 tr, ch 6, 3 tr) in ch-6, tr in next 9 tr—1 ch-6 lp. Fasten off.

Picot edging and stem

Note To work evenly, sc in each st and work 4 sc over each tr and ch-4 t-ch at side edge of leaf. With RS facing, join yarn with a sl st in center ch-6 lp at bottom of leaf.

Rnd 1 (RS) Ch 1, work 3 sc in same lp as joining, sc in each st to next ch-6 lp, work (3 sc, MP 3 sc) in ch-6 lp, *sc evenly along side edge of next leaf tip to top right corner before next ch-6 lp, MP, sc in each st to ch-6 lp, work (3 sc, MP 3 sc) in ch-6 lp; rep from * 4 times more. Cont along opposite side of leaf as foll: **Sc in each st to top left corner of same leaf tip, MP, sc evenly to next ch-6 lp, work (3 sc, MP, 3 sc) in ch-6 lp; rep from ** 4 times more, end sc in each st to next ch-6 lp, work (3 sc, MP, 3 sc) in ch-6 lp, sc in each st to center ch-6 lp at bottom, work 3 sc in ch-6 lp, join rnd with a sl st in first sc, ch 20 (or desired amount) for stem. Fasten off.

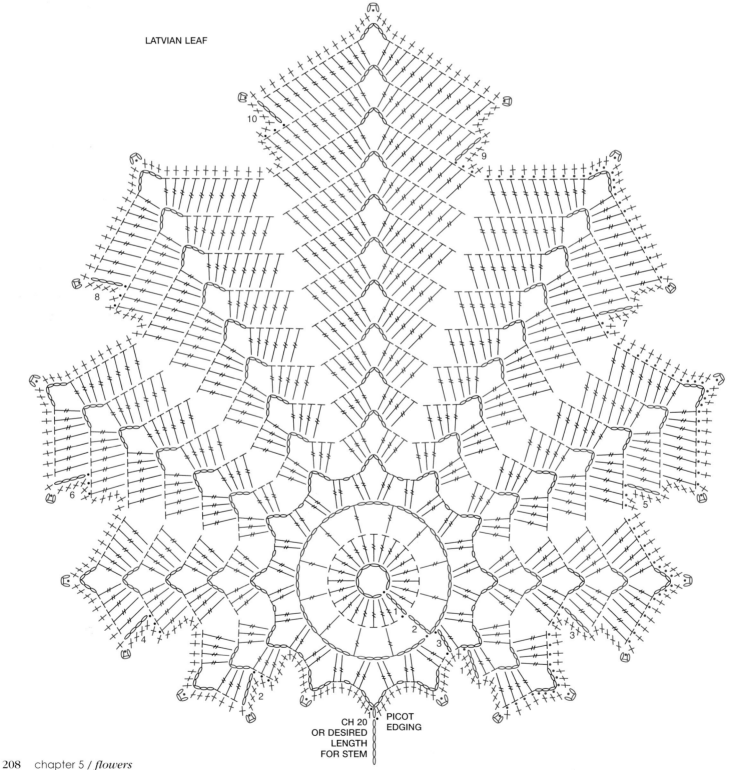

LATVIAN LEAF

CH 20
OR DESIRED
LENGTH
FOR STEM

PICOT
EDGING

Flower center

To make an adjustable ring, use A to make a slipknot 10"/25.5cm from free end of yarn. Place slipknot on hook, then wrap free end of yarn twice around your first and second fingers on your left hand. Then work with yarn coming from ball as follows:

Rnd 1 (RS) Ch 1, work 8 sc in ring, pull free end of yarn to close circle, then join rnd with a sl st in first sc—8 sc. Fasten off.

Rnd 2 Ch 1, work 2 sc in each st around, join rnd with a sl st in first st—16 sc.

Rnd 3 Ch 1, work 2 sc in first st, sc in next st, *work 2 sc in next st, sc in next st; rep from * around, join rnd with a sl st in first st—24 sc.

Rnd 4 Ch 1, work 2 sc in first st, sc in next 2 sts, *work 2 sc in next st, sc in next 2 sts; rep from * around, join rnd with a sl st in first st—32 sc.

Rnd 5 Ch 1, work 2 sc in first st, sc in next 3 sts, *work 2 sc in next st, sc in next 3 sts; rep from * around, join rnd with a sl st in first st—40 sc.

Rnd 6 Ch 1, sc in each st around, join rnd with a sl st in first st. Fasten off.

Large petal (make 8)

With A, chain 15.

Row 1 (RS) Sc in 2nd ch from hook, sc in next 12 ch, work 5 sc in last ch, turn to bottom lps of ch and and sc in 13 lps across—31 sc. Turn.

Row 2 Ch 1, sc in next 15 sts, work 3 sc in next st, sc in last 15 sts—33 sc. Turn.

Row 3 Ch 1, sc in next 16 sts, work 3 sc in next st, sc in last 16 sts—35 sc. Turn.

Row 4 Ch 1, sc in next 17 sts, work 3 sc in next st, sc in last 17 sts—37 sc. Fasten off.

Small petal (make 8 each using B and C)

With B, chain 10.

Row 1 (RS) Sc in 2nd ch from hook, sc in next 7 ch, work 5 sc in last ch, turn to bottom lps of ch and sc in 8 lps across—21 sc. Turn.

Row 2 Ch 1, sc in next 10 sts, work 3 sc in next st, sc in last 10 sts—23 sc. Turn.

Row 3 Ch 1, sc in next 11 sts, work 3 sc in next st, sc in last 11 sts—25 sc. Turn.

Row 4 Ch 1, sc in next 12 sts, work 3 sc in next st, sc in last 12 sts—27 sc. Fasten off.

Finishing

Steam-block petals flat. For each large petal, bring side edges at bottom of petal together so they meet. Beg at base of petal, sew edges together for ¾"/2cm; fasten off securely. Sew base of each large petal to outer edge of flower center, spacing them evenly around. For each small B petal, bring side edges at bottom of petal together so they meet. Beg at base of petal, sew edges together for ¾"/2cm; fasten off securely. Sew base of each small petal to rnd 5 of flower center, spacing petals evenly around and placing them between large petals. Sew base of each small petal to rnd 3 of flower center, spacing petals evenly around and placing them between small B petals. Make a 1¾"/4.5-diameter pompom using D. Sew to center of flower.

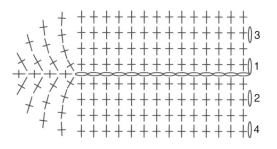

SUNFLOWER

LARGE PETAL

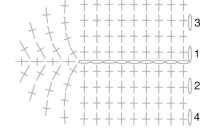

SMALL PETAL

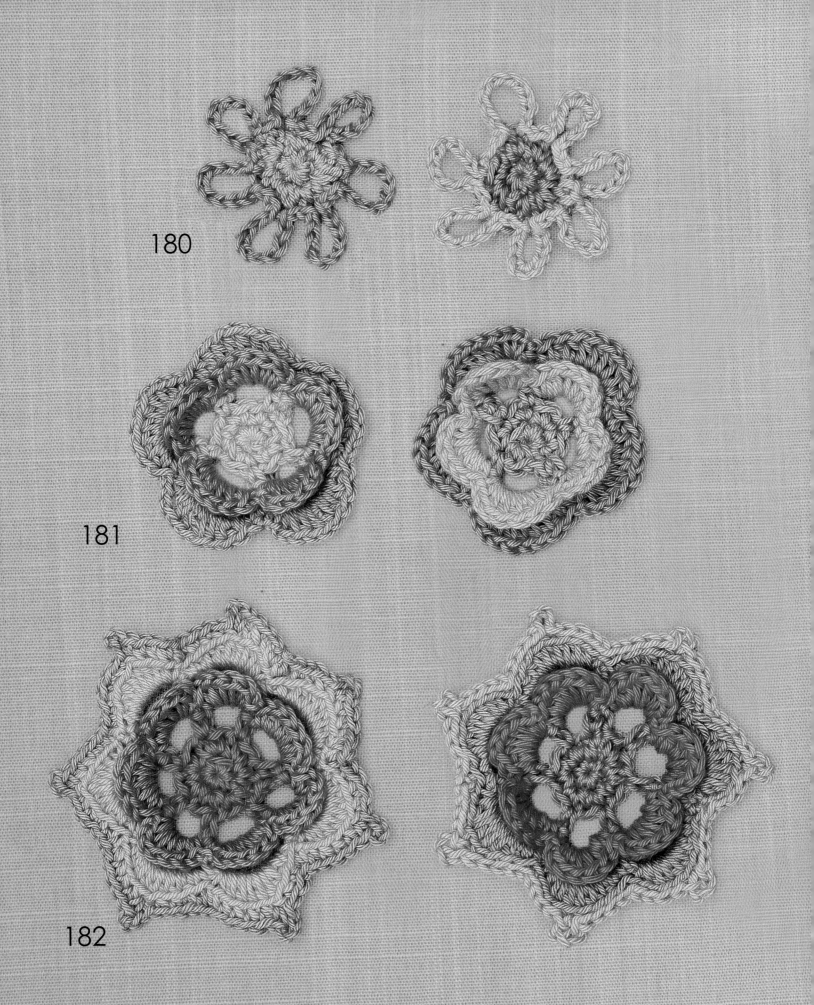

180

181

182

Flowers—*Fantasy*

180 *Lazy Daisy*

To make an adjustable ring, use A to make a slipknot 10"/25.5cm from free end of yarn. Place slipknot on hook, then wrap free end of yarn twice around your first and second fingers on your left hand. Then work with yarn coming from ball as follows:

Rnd 1 (RS) Ch 1, work 7 sc in ring, pull free end of yarn to close circle, then join rnd with a sl st in first sc—7 sc.

Rnd 2 Ch 1, work 2 sc in each st around, join rnd with a sl st in first st—14 sc. Fasten off.

Rnd 3 With RS facing, join B with a sl st in any st, ch 9, sl st in same st as joining, *sl st in next 2 sts, ch 9, sl st in same st as last sl st; rep from * around 5 times more, end sl st in last st—7 petals. Fasten off.

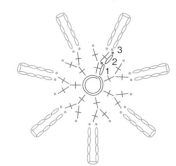

181 *Five-Petal Flower*

To make an adjustable ring, use A to make a slipknot 10"/25.5cm from free end of yarn. Place slipknot on hook, then wrap free end of yarn twice around your first and second fingers on your left hand. Then work with yarn coming from ball as follows:

Rnd 1 (RS) Ch 1, work 5 sc in ring, pull free end of yarn to close circle, then join rnd with a sl st in first sc—5 sc.

Rnd 2 Ch 1, work 2 sc in each st around, join rnd with a sl st in first st—10 sc.

Rnd 3 Ch 1, sc in first st, ch 5, skip next st, [sc in next st, ch 5, skip next st] 4 times, join rnd with a sl st in first st—5 ch-5 lps. Fasten off.

Rnd 4 With RS facing, join B with a sl st in any ch-5 lp, ch 1, work (sc, 5 hdc, sc) in same ch-5 lp, [work (sc, 5 hdc, sc) in next ch-5 lp] 4 times, join rnd with a sl st in first sc—5 petals. Fasten off.

Rnd 5 With RS facing, fold any petal forward to work on WS of flower, join C with a sl st around first sc of petal on rnd 4, ch 1, sc around same st, ch 6, [sc around first sc of next petal on rnd 4, ch 6] 4 times, join rnd with a sl st in first sc—5 ch-6 lps.

Rnd 6 Sl st in first ch-6 lp, work (sc, 7 hdc, sc) in same ch-6 lp, [work (sc, 7 hdc, sc) in next ch-6 lp] 4 times, join rnd with a sl st in first sc. Fasten off.

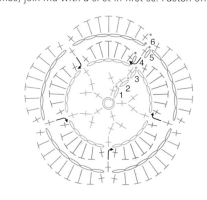

182 *Seven-Petal Flower*

To make an adjustable ring, use A to make a slipknot 10"/25.5cm from free end of yarn. Place slipknot on hook, then wrap free end of yarn twice around your first and second fingers on your left hand. Then work with yarn coming from ball as follows:

Rnd 1 (RS) Ch 1, work 7 sc in ring, pull free end of yarn to close circle, then join rnd with a sl st in first sc—7 sc.

Rnd 2 Ch 1, work 2 sc in each st around, join rnd with a sl st in first st—14 sc.

Rnd 3 Ch 1, sc in first st, ch 5, [skip next st, sc in next st, ch 5] 6 times, join rnd with a sl st in first st—7 ch-5 lps. Fasten off.

Rnd 4 With RS facing, join B with a sl st in any ch-5 lp, ch 1, work (sc, 5 hdc, sc) in same ch-5 lp, [work (sc, 5 hdc, sc) in next ch-5 lp] 6 times, join rnd with a sl st in first sc—7 petals. Fasten off.

Rnd 5 With RS facing, fold any petal forward to work on WS of flower, join C with a sl st around first sc of petal on rnd 4, ch 1, sc around same st, ch 6, [sc around first sc of next petal on rnd 4, ch 6] 7 times, join rnd with a sl st in first sc—7 ch-6 lps.

Rnd 6 Sl st in first ch-6 lp, work (sc, 7 hdc, sc) in same ch-6 lp, [work (sc, 7 hdc, sc) in next ch-6 lp] 6 times, join rnd with a sl st in first sc. Fasten off.

Rnd 7 With RS facing, join D with a sl st in back lp of first sc of any petal, working in back lp only, sl st in next 4 sts, [ch 3, sl st in same place as last sl st (picot made), sl st in next 9 sts] 6 times, sl st in last 4 sts, join rnd with a sl st in first sl st. Fasten off.

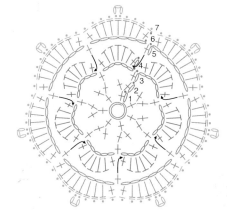

183

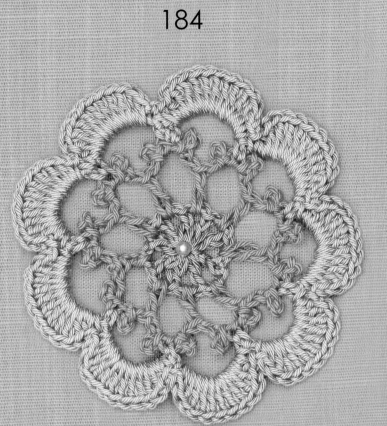

184

185

186

187

183 *Amanda Whorl*

With A, chain 13. Join chain with a sl st, forming a ring.

Note When changing colors, draw new color through last 2 lps on hook to complete last st.

Segment I

Row 1 (RS) Ch 4 (counts as 1 tr), [tr in ring, ch 6, dc in top of tr just made, tr in ring] 3 times, tr in ring, ch 2, work 10 tr in ring. Turn.

Row 2 Work a picot of (ch 5, sl st in 5th ch from hook), sc in next 9 tr, changing to B. Turn.

Segment II

Ch 1, sc in same place as ch 1, ch 3, skip next 3 sc, sc in next sc, ch 9, sl st in first sc to complete joined base ring.

Row 1 Rep row 1 of segment I.

Row 2 Ch 2, sc in picot of previous segment, ch 3, sl st to first ch of row to complete picot, continue as for segment I changing to C. Work 5 more segments as for segment I using C, D, A, B and C, changing to D at the end of segment VII.

Segment VIII

Using D, work as for previous segments, except join to segment I as you work row 2 as follows: ch 2, sc in picot of segment VII, ch 1, sc in picot of segment I, ch 2, sl st to first ch of row to complete picot, skip first tr, sc in next 5 tr, sl st to segment I, sc in next 4 tr, sl st to segment I. Fasten off.

Center ring

With RS facing, join A with a sl st in any sc along inner edge.

Rnd 1 Ch 1, sc in same place as joining, [sc in next picot, sc in side of next sc] 7 times, sc in next picot, join rnd with a sl st in first sc. Fasten off.

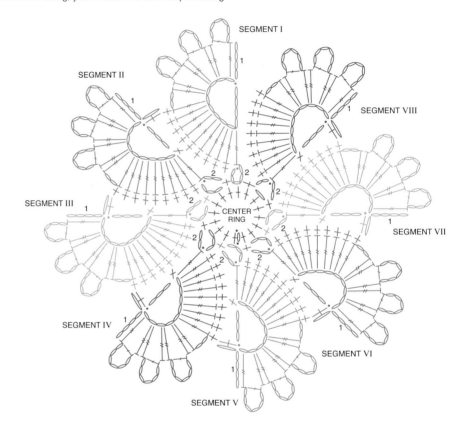

184 *Picot Rose*

With A, chain 3. Join chain with a sl st, forming a ring.

Rnd 1 (RS) Ch 5 (counts as 1 dc and ch 2), [dc in ring, ch 2] 7 times, join rnd with a sl st in 3rd ch of beg ch-5—8 ch-2 sps. Fasten off.

Rnd 2 With RS facing, join B with a sl st in any ch-2 sp, ch 8 (counts as 1 dc and ch-5 for picot), sl st in 5th ch from hook (picot made), ch 5, sl st in 4th ch from hook (picot made), ch 1, *dc in next ch-2 sp, [ch 5, sl st in 4th ch from hook] twice, ch 1; rep from * around 6 times more, join rnd with a sl st in 3rd ch of beg ch-9. Fasten off.

Rnd 3 With RS facing, join C with a sl st in ch between any 2 picots, ch 1, sc in same place as joining, *ch 7, skip next (picot, dc, picot), sc in ch between next 2 picots; rep from * around 7 times more, omitting sc at end of last rep, join rnd with a sl st in first sc.

Rnd 4 Sl st in next ch, ch 1, *work (sc, hdc, 9 dc, hdc, sc) in next ch-7 lp; rep from * around 7 times more, join rnd with a sl st in first sc. Fasten off.

Finishing

Sew a bead to center of rose.

185 *Popcorn*

To make an adjustable ring, use A to make a slipknot 10"/25.5cm from free end of yarn. Place slipknot on hook, then wrap free end of yarn twice around your first and second fingers on your left hand. Then work with yarn coming from ball as follows:

Popcorn (PC) Work 5 dc in same st, drop lp from hook. Working from front to back, insert hook into both lps of first dc, pick up dropped lp and draw through dc, then ch 1 to secure popcorn.

Rnd 1 (RS) Ch 1, work 12 sc in ring, pull free end of

yarn to close circle, then join rnd with a sl st in first sc—12 sc.

Rnd 2 Ch 4 (counts as 1 dc and ch 1), PC in next st, *dc in next st, ch 1, PC in next st; rep from * around, join rnd with a sl st in 3rd ch of beg ch-4—6 petals. Fasten off.

Rnd 3 With RS facing, join B with a sl st in any dc, ch 3 (counts as 1 dc) work 4 dc in same dc as joining, drop lp from hook, working from front to back, insert hook into top of beg ch-3, pick up

dropped lp and draw through ch, then ch 1 to secure popcorn (beg popcorn made), ch 3, PC in top of next PC, ch 3, *PC in next dc, ch 3, PC in top of next PC, ch 3; rep from * around, join rnd with a sl st in top of beg popcorn—12 petals. Fasten off.

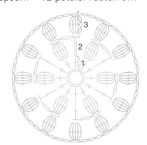

186 *Moorish*

To make an adjustable ring, use A to make a slipknot 10"/25.5cm from free end of yarn. Place slipknot on hook, then wrap free end of yarn twice around your first and second fingers on your left hand. Then work with yarn coming from ball as follows:

Spike single crochet (SSC) Insert hook between 2 sts of rnd 1, yo, draw up a lp that is the same height as the working row, yo and draw through both lps on hook.

Make picot (MP) Ch 3, sl st in same st as last sc.

Note When changing colors, draw new color through when you sl st to join rnd.

Rnd 1 (RS) Ch 1, work 16 sc in ring, pull free end of

yarn to close circle, then join rnd with a sl st in first sc—16 sc.

Rnd 2 Ch 1, sc in same place as joining, sc in next st, *work (sc, ch 9, sc) in next st**, sc in next 3 sts; rep from * around twice more, then from * to ** once, end sc in last st, join rnd with a sl st in first st changing to B.

Rnd 3 Ch 1, sc in same place as joining, *skip next 2 sts, work (2 hdc, 2 dc, 2 tr, 2 dtr, 5 ttr, 2 dtr, 2 tr, 2 dc, 2 hdc) in next ch-9 lp, skip next 2 sts, sc in next st; rep from * around 3 times more, omitting sc at end of last rep, join rnd with a sl st in first st changing to C.

Rnd 4 Ch 1, work SSC, *ch 4, skip next 4 sts, sc in

next st, MP, [ch 3, skip next 2 sts, sc in next st, MP] 4 times, ch 4, skip next 4 sts, work SSC; rep from * around 3 times more, omitting SSC at end of last rep, join rnd with a sl st in top of beg SSC. Fasten off.

187 *Shell*

To make an adjustable ring, use A to make a slipknot 10"/25.5cm from free end of yarn. Place slipknot on hook, then wrap free end of yarn twice around your first and second fingers on your left hand. Then work with yarn coming from ball as follows:

Rnd 1 (WS) Ch 4 (counts as 1 tr), work 4 tr in ring, ch 2, [work 5 tr in ring, ch 2] 4 times, pull free end of

yarn to close circle, then join rnd with a sl st in top of beg ch-4—5 5-tr groups. Fasten off. Turn.

Rnd 2 (RS) With RS facing, join B with a sl st in 3rd st of any 5-tr group, ch 1, sc in same st as joining, work 9 tr in first ch-2 sp, *sc in 3rd st of next 5-tr group, work 9 tr in next ch-2 sp; rep from * around 4 times more, join rnd with a sl st in first sc. Fasten off.

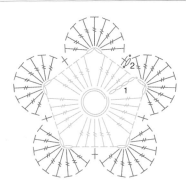

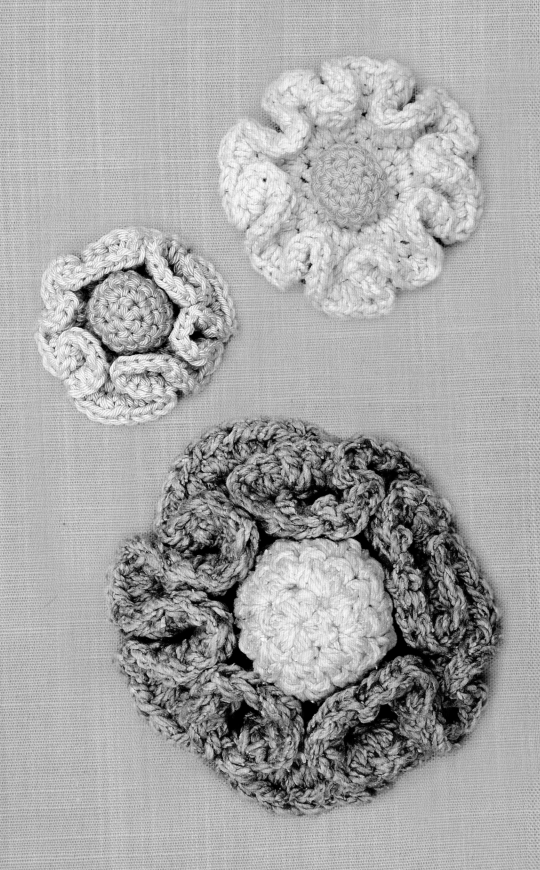

188

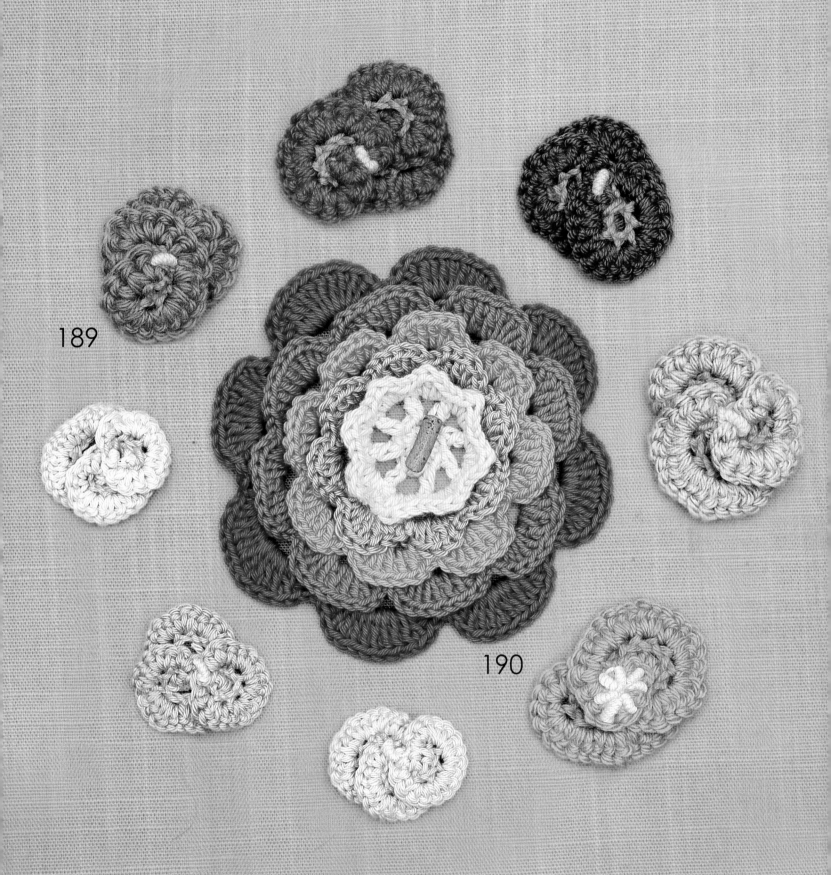

189

190

188 *Ruffle*

To make an adjustable ring, use A to make a slipknot 10"/25.5cm from free end of yarn. Place slipknot on hook, then wrap free end of yarn twice around your first and second fingers on your left hand. Then work with yarn coming from ball as follows:

Petals

Rnd 1 (RS) Ch 1, work 8 sc in ring, pull free end of yarn to close circle, then join rnd with a sl st in first sc—8 sc.

Rnd 2 Ch 1, work 2 sc in each around, join rnd with a sl st in first st—16 sc.

Rnd 3 Rep rnd 2—32 sc.

Rnd 4 Rep rnd 2—64 sc.

Rnd 5 Rep rnd 2—128 sc. Fasten off.

Flower center

Make an adjustable ring.

Rnd 1 (RS) Ch 1, work 6 sc in ring, pull free end of yarn to close circle, then join rnd with a sl st in first sc—6 sc.

Rnd 2 Ch 1, work 2 sc in each around, join rnd with a sl st in first st—12 sc.

Rnds 3 and 4 Ch 1, sc in each st around, join rnd with a sl st in first st. Wind a small ball of B and

insert into flower center.

Rnd 5 Ch 1, *skip next st, sc in next st; rep from * all round. Fasten off leaving a long tail. Thread tail in tapestry needle and weave through last rnd of sts. Pull tight to gather, fasten off securely.

Finishing

Sew flower center to center of petals.

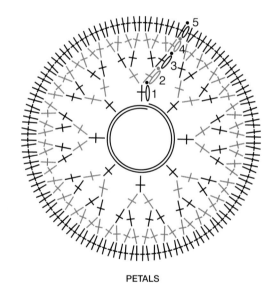

PETALS

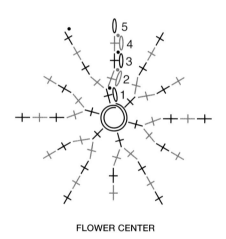

FLOWER CENTER

189 *Squiggle*

With A, chain 12. Fasten off, then turn chain.

Note The WS is the RS of the flower.

Row 1 (RS) With RS facing, join B, skip first ch, work 2 sc in next ch, *work 3 sc in next ch; rep from * to end. Fasten off.

Finishing

Twist squiggle into a 3-petal flower. Tack together in center of flower to secure petals. In center of flower, embroider one or more French knots or bullion stitches using C.

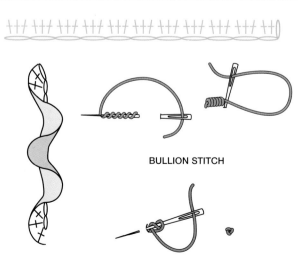

BULLION STITCH

FRENCH KNOT

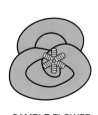

SAMPLE FLOWER

SAMPLE FLOWER

With A, chain 8. Join chain with a sl st, forming a ring.

Note When changing colors, draw new color through last 2 lps on hook to complete last st.

Rnds 1 and 2 Rep rnds 1 and 2 as for Irish rose (see page 223).

Rnd 3 Rep rnd 3, changing to B as you join the rnd.

Rnd 4 Rep rnd 4.

Rnd 5 Rep rnd 5, changing to C as you join the rnd.

Rnd 6 Rep rnd 6.

Rnd 7 Rep rnd 7, changing to D as you join the rnd.

Rnd 8 Rep rnd 8.

Rnd 9 Rep rnd 9, changing to E as you join the rnd.

Rnds 10 and 11 Rep rnds 10 and 11. Fasten off.

Finishing

Sew a bead to center of rose.

191

192

193

194

195

196

Large petals (make 3)

With A, chain 15.

Row 1 (RS) Sc in 2nd ch from hook, sc in next 12 ch, work 5 sc in last ch, turn to bottom lps of beg ch, sc in next 13 bottom lps—31 sts. Turn.

Row 2 Ch 1, sc in first 15 sts, work 3 sc in next st, sc in last 15 sts—33 sts. Turn.

Row 3 Ch 1, sc in first 16 sts, work 3 sc in next st, sc in last 16 sts—35 sts. Turn.

Row 4 Ch 1, sc in first 17 sts, work 3 sc in next st, sc in last 17 sts—37 sts. Fasten off. Do not turn.

Row 5 With WS facing, join B with a sl st in first st, then sl st in each st to end. Fasten off.

Small petal (make 3)

With A, chain 10.

Row 1 (WS) Sc in 2nd ch from hook, sc in next 7 ch, work 5 sc in last ch, turn to bottom lps of beg ch, sc in next 8 bottom lps—21 sts. Turn.

Row 2 Ch 1, sc in first 10 sts, work 3 sc in next st, sc in last 10 sts—23 sts. Turn.

Row 3 Ch 1, work 4 sc in first st, *work 5 sc in next st; rep from * to end. Fasten off.

Flower base

To make an adjustable ring, use C to make a slipknot 10"/25.5cm from free end of yarn. Place slipknot on hook, then wrap free end of yarn twice around your first and second fingers on your left hand. Then work with yarn coming from ball as follows:

Rnd 1 (RS) Ch 1, work 8 sc in ring, pull free end of yarn to close circle, then join rnd with a sl st in first sc—8 sts.

Rnd 2 Ch 1, work 2 sc in each st around, join rnd with a sl st in first st—16 sts.

Rnds 3–5 Ch 1, sc in each st around, join rnd with a sl st in first st.

Rnd 6 Rep rnd 3. Fasten off, leaving a long tail for sewing.

Flower stem

With C, chain 31.

Row 1 (WS) Sc in 2nd ch from hook and in each ch across. Fasten off.

Finishing

With RS facing, sew 3 large petals evenly spaced inside flower base, forming a fan. Wind a small ball of C and insert into flower center, then sew to secure. Sew bottom edges of 3 small petals to flower center, then tack petals together halfway along the petals, forming the crest. Sew stem to flower base.

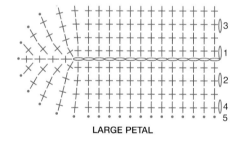

LARGE PETAL

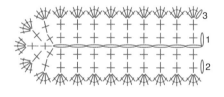

SMALL PETAL

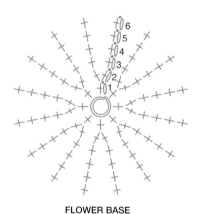

FLOWER BASE

STEM

Chain 8. Join chain with a sl st, forming a ring.

Rnd 1 (RS) Ch 1, work 16 sc in ring, join rnd with a sl st in first st—16 sc.

Rnd 2 Ch 5 (counts as 1 dc and ch 2), skip next st, [dc in next st, ch 2, skip next st] 7 times, join rnd with a sl st in 3rd ch of beg ch-5—8 ch-2 sps.

Rnd 3 Sl st in first ch-2 sp, ch 1, [work (sc, hdc, dc, hdc, sc) in next ch-2 sp] 8 times, join rnd with a sl st in first sc—8 petals.

Rnd 4 Working behind each petal, sl st in base of next 2 sts, ch 1, sc in base of same dc as last sl st, [ch 3, skip next 4 sts, sc in base of next dc] 7 times, ch 3, join rnd with a sl st in first sc—8 ch-3 lps.

Rnd 5 Sl st in first ch-3 lp, ch 1, work (sc, hdc, 3 dc, hdc, sc) in each ch-3 lp around, join rnd with a sl st in first sc—8 petals.

Rnd 6 Working behind each petal, sl st in base of next 3 sts, ch 1, sc in base of same dc as last sl st, [ch 5, skip next 6 sts, sc in base of next dc] 7 times, ch 5, join rnd with a sl st in first sc—8 ch-5 lps.

Rnd 7 Sl st in first ch-5 lp, ch 1, work (sc, hdc, 5 dc, hdc, sc) in each ch-5 lp around, join rnd with a sl st in first sc—8 petals.

Rnd 8 Working behind each petal, sl st in base of next 4 sts, ch 1, sc in base of same dc as last sl st, [ch 7, skip next 8 sts, sc in base of next dc] 7 times, ch 7, join rnd with a sl st in first sc—8 ch-7 lps.

Rnd 9 Sl st in first ch-7 lp, ch 1, work (sc, hdc, 7 dc, hdc, sc) in each ch-7 lp around, join rnd with a sl st in first sc—8 petals.

Rnd 10 Working behind each petal, sl st in base of next 5 sts, ch 1, sc in base of same dc as last sl st, [ch 9, skip next 10 sts, sc in base of next dc] 7 times, ch 9, join rnd with a sl st in first sc—8 ch-9 lps.

Rnd 11 Sl st in first ch-9 lp, ch 1, work (sc, hdc, 9 dc, hdc, sc) in each ch-9 lp around, join rnd with a sl st in first sc—8 petals. Fasten off.

Finishing

Sew a bead to center of rose.

193 *Button I*

Note The WS is the RS of the flower.

To make an adjustable ring, make a slipknot 10"/25.5cm from free end of yarn. Place slipknot on hook, then wrap free end of yarn twice around your first and second fingers on your left hand. Then work with yarn coming from ball as follows:

Rnd 1 (RS) Ch 3 (counts as 1 dc), work 17 dc in ring, pull free end of yarn to close circle, then join rnd with a sl st in first sc—18 dc.

Rnd 2 Ch 1, work 2 sc in each st around, join rnd with a sl st in first st—36 sc.

Rnd 3 Sl st in first st, *skip next 2 sts, work 7 dc in next st, skip next 2 sts, sl st in next st; rep from * around 5 times more, omitting sl st at end of last rep, join rnd with a sl st in first sl st—6 petals. Fasten off.

Finishing

Turn flower over to WS. Sew a button to center of flower.

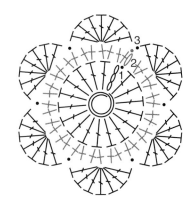

194 *Button II*

Note The WS is the RS of the flower.

To make an adjustable ring, use A to make a slipknot 10"/25.5cm from free end of yarn. Place slipknot on hook, then wrap free end of yarn twice around your first and second fingers on your left hand. Then work with yarn coming from ball as follows:

Rnd 1 (RS) Ch 1, work 8 sc in ring, pull free end of yarn to close circle, then join rnd with a sl st in first sc—8 sc.

Rnd 2 Ch 1, work 2 sc in each st around, join rnd with a sl st in first st—16 sc.

Rnd 3 Ch 1, work 2 sc in first st, sc in next st, *work 2 sc in next st, sc in next st; rep from * around, join rnd with a sl st in first st—24 sc.

Rnd 4 Ch 1, work 2 sc in first st, sc in next 2 sts, *work 2 sc in next st, sc in next 2 sts; rep from * around, join rnd with a sl st in first st—32 sc.

Rnd 5 Ch 1, work 2 sc in first st, sc in next 3 sts, *work 2 sc in next st, sc in next 3 sts; rep from * around, join rnd with a sl st in first st—40 sc. Fasten off.

Rnd 6 With RS facing, join B with a sl st in any st, ch 1, sc in same st as joining, sc in each st around, join rnd with a sl st in first st. Fasten off.

Rnd 7 With RS facing, join C with a sl st in any st, ch 1, work 5 sc in same st as joining, work 5 sc in next st; join rnd with a sl st in first st. Fasten off.

Finishing

Turn flower over to WS. Sew a button to center of flower.

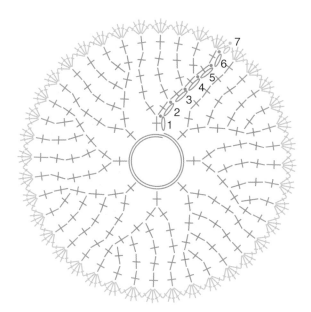

195 *Prudence Whorl*

Bullion stitch Wrap yarn around hook 5 times, insert hook into st (or ring), yo and draw up a lp, yo and draw through all lps on hook one at a time.

To make an adjustable ring, use A to make a slipknot 10"/25.5cm from free end of yarn. Place slipknot on hook, then wrap free end of yarn twice around your first and second fingers on your left hand. Then work with yarn coming from ball as follows:

Rnd 1 (RS) Ch 3 (counts as 1 dc), work bullion st in ring, [dc in ring, work bullion st] 5 times, pull free end of yarn to close circle, then join rnd with a sl st in top of beg ch-3—6 bullion sts. Fasten off.

Rnd 2 With RS facing, join B with a sl st in top of any dc, ch 3 (counts as 1 dc), [work (bullion st, dc) in next st] 11 times, bullion st in same dc as joining, join rnd with a sl st in top of beg ch-3. Fasten off.

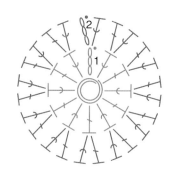

196 *Scallop Flower*

Spike slip stitch (SPSL) Insert hook in same st as sl st on rnd 2, yo, draw up a lp that is the same height as the working row and draw through both lps on hook.

Note The SPSL *does not* replace another st.

To make an adjustable ring, use A to make a slipknot 10"/25.5cm from free end of yarn. Place slipknot on hook, then wrap free end of yarn twice around your first and second fingers on your left hand. Then work with yarn coming from ball as follows:

Rnd 1 (RS) Ch 1, work 8 sc in ring, pull free end of yarn to close circle, then join rnd with a sl st in first sc—8 sc. Fasten off.

Rnd 2 With RS facing, join B with a sl st in any st, ch 9, [sl st in next st, ch 9] 7 times, join rnd with a sl st in first sl st—8 ch-9 lps.

Rnd 3 *Work (2 sc, 2 hdc, 2 dc, 3 tr, 2 dc, 2 hdc, 2 sc) in next ch-9 lp; rep from * around, join rnd with a sl st in first sc—8 petals. Fasten off.

Rnd 4 With RS facing, join A with a sl st in 3rd st of any petal, working through back lps only, sl st in next 12 sts, *work SPSL (see Note), skip next 2 sts, sl st in 3rd st of next petal, working through back lps only, sl st in next 12 sts; rep from * around, end SPSL, skip last 2 sts, join rnd with a sl st in first sl st. Fasten off.

Finishing

Sew a bead to center of flower.

projects
_____

Chapter 6

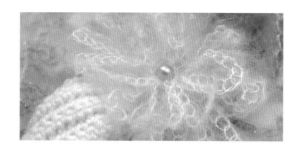

Gossamer Wrap
with Wild Rose Embellishments

intermediate

FINISHED MEASUREMENTS

• Approx 22"/56cm wide x 84"/213.5cm long (excluding roses and leaves)

MATERIALS

• 3 .88oz/25g balls (each approx 227yd/208m) of Rowan/Westminster Fibers, Inc. *Kidsilk Night* (mohair/silk/polyester/nylon) in #608 moonlight (MC)
• 1 .88oz/25g ball (each approx 229yd/210m) of Rowan/Westminster Fibers, Inc. *Kidsilk Haze* (mohair/silk) in #580 grace (A)
• 1 .88oz/25g ball (each approx 197yd/180m) of RYC/Westminster Fibers, Inc. *Cashsoft 4 Ply* (wool/microfiber/cashmere) in #433 cream (B)
• Sizes C/2 and E/4 (2.75 and 3.5mm) crochet hooks *or size to obtain gauge*
• Eight 6mm pearls
• Sewing needle
• Sewing thread to match roses

GAUGE

3 ch-7 lps and 9 rows to 4"/10cm over picot trellis using larger crochet hook.
Wild rose to 3"/7.5cm diameter using smaller crochet hook.
Take time to check gauge.

CHARTS

See Wild Rose and Leaf (p. 194) for charts.

WRAP

With larger hook and MC, ch 97.

Foundation row (RS) Sc in 2nd ch from hook and in each ch across—96 sts. Turn.

Row 1 *Ch 7, skip next 5 sts, work (sl st, ch 3, sl st—picot made) into next st; rep from * across. Turn.

Row 2 *Ch 7, work a picot in 4th ch of next ch-7 lp; rep from * across. Turn.

Rep row 2 for picot trellis until piece measures approx 82"/208cm from beg, end with a WS row.

Next row (RS) *Ch 7, sl st in 4th ch of next ch-7 lp; rep from * across. Turn.

Last row Ch 1, sc in each ch and st across—96 sts. Turn.

Shell edging

Row 1 (RS) Ch 1, *skip next 2 sts, work 5 dc in next st, skip next 2 sts, sc in next st; rep from * across. Fasten off.

With RS facing, turn to bottom lps of beg ch. Join MC with a sl st in first bottom lp.

Row 1 (RS) Ch 1, skip first st, work 5 dc in next st, skip next 2 sts, sc in next st, *skip next 2 sts, work 5 dc in next st, skip next 2 sts, sc in next st; rep from * across. Fasten off.

WILD ROSES (make 16 pieces)

With smaller hook and A, chain 6. Join chain with a sl st forming a ring.

Rnd 1 (RS) Ch 1, work 12 sc in ring, join rnd with a sl st in first st—12 sc.

Rnd 2 Ch 1, sc in first st, ch 12, *sc in next st, ch 12; rep from *around, join rnd with a sl st in first st—12 petals. Fasten off.

LEAVES (make 8)

With smaller hook and B, chain 17.

Row 1 (RS) Skip first 2 ch (counts as 1 sc and ch-1 t-ch), sc in next 13 ch, work 2 sc in last ch (2nd sc in the center st of the point), turn to bottom lps of beg ch, sc in next 16 bottom lps. Turn.

Row 2 Ch 1 (counts as 1 sc), skip first st, working through front lps only, sc in each st to center st of point, work 3 sc in center st, sc in each st to within last 3 sts and t-ch. Turn.

Row 3 Ch 1 (counts as 1 sc), skip first st, working through back lps only, sc in each st to center st of point, work 3 sc in center st, sc in each st to within last 3 sts and t-ch. Turn.

Rows 4 and 6 Rep row 2.

Rows 5 and 7 Rep row 3. Fasten off.

FINISHING

On RS, place markers for 4 roses along shell edging at top edge of wrap, with the first and last ½"/1.3cm from side edges and the others evenly spaced between. Rep along shell edging at bottom edge of wrap. Place one rose on top of the other. Using needle and thread, tack roses together by sewing a running stitch around inner edges of rnd 1. Pull yarn to gather, fasten securely, then sew to shell edging at a marker. Using needle and thread, sew a pearl to center of rose, then sew a leaf to underside of rose.

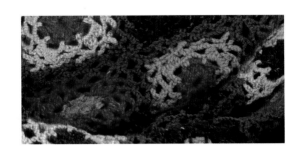

Cranesbill Lace Wrap

intermediate

FINISHED MEASUREMENTS

• Approx 28"/71cm wide x 82"/223cm long

MATERIALS

• 4 1¾oz/50g balls (each approx 137yd/125 m) of Jaeger/Westminster Fibers, Inc. *Pure Silk DK* (silk) in #008 cameo (A)

• 3 1¾oz/50g balls (each approx 191yd/175m) of Rowan/Westminster Fibers, Inc. *Felted Tweed* (wool/alpaca/viscose) in #154 ginger (B), 2 balls in #151 bilberry (C)

• 5 1¾oz/50g balls (each approx 142yd/130m) of RYC/Westminster Fibers, Inc. *Cashsoft DK* (wool/microfiber/cashmere) in #524 evergreen (E), 2 balls in #522 cashew (D)

• Size F/5 (3.75mm) crochet hook *or size to obtain gauge*

GAUGE

One cranesbill lace motif to 3½"/9cm using size F/5 (3.75mm) crochet hook.

Take time to check gauge.

CHARTS

See Cranesbill Lace (p. 160–161) for chart.

STITCH GLOSSARY

Beg cluster In same sp work, [yo, insert hook in sp, yo and draw up a lp, yo, draw through 2 lps on hook] twice, yo and draw through all 3 lps on hook.

Cluster In same sp, [yo, insert hook in sp, yo and draw up a lp, yo, draw through 2 lps on hook] 3 times, yo and draw through all 4 lps on hook.

MOTIF I (make 20)

With A, ch 6. Join chain with a sl st, forming a ring.

Rnd 1 (RS) Ch 3 (counts as 1 dc), work beg cluster in ring (counts as 1 cluster), [ch 2, work cluster in ring] 7 times, ch 2, join rnd with a sl st in top of first cluster. Fasten off.

Rnd 2 With RS facing, join B with a sl st in any ch-3 sp, ch 1, sc in same ch-3 sp, [ch 5, sc in next ch-3 sp] 7 times, ch 2, join rnd with a dc in first sc.

Rnd 3 *Ch 5, work (cluster, ch 3, cluster) in next ch-5 lp**, ch 5, sc in next ch-5 sp; rep from * around twice more, then from * to ** once, end ch 2, to join rnd, dc in dc that joined rnd 2.

Rnd 4 *Ch 5, sc in next ch-5 lp, ch 5, work (sc, ch 5, sc) in next corner ch-3 sp, ch 5, sc in next ch-5 lp; rep from * around 3 times more, ending last rep sc in dc that joined rnd 3 (instead of next ch-5 lp), join rnd

with a sl st in first ch of beg ch-5. Fasten off.

MOTIF II (make 15)

Work as for motif I in color sequence as follows:

Rnd 1 C.

Rnds 2–4 D.

MOTIF III (make 20)

Work as for motif I in color sequence as follows:

Rnd 1 D.

Rnds 2–4 B.

MOTIF IV (make 18)

Work as for motif I in color sequence as follows:

Rnd 1 C.

Rnds 2–4 A.

MOTIF V (make 16)

Work as for motif I in color sequence as follows:

Rnd 1 A.

Rnds 2–4 C.

MOTIF VI (make 20)

Work as for motif I in color sequence as follows:

Rnd 1 B.

Rnds 2–4 D.

MOTIF VII (make 14)

Work as for motif I in color sequence as follows:

Rnd 1 D.

Rnds 2–4 C.

MOTIF VIII (make 17)

Work as for motif I in color sequence as follows:

Rnd 1 B.

Rnds 2–4 A.

JOINING

Row 1

Motif I—Rnd 5 With RS of a motif I facing, join E with a sl st in center ch-5 lp of any side, ch 1, sc in same place as joining, ch 5, sc in next ch-5 lp, ch 5, *work (sc, ch 5, sc) in next corner ch-5 lp, [ch 5, sc in next ch-5 lp] 3 times, ch 5; rep from * around twice more, end work (sc, ch 5, sc) in last corner ch-5 lp, ch 5, sc in next ch-5 lp, ch 5, join rnd with a sl st in first sc. Fasten off.

Motif II—Rnd 5 With RS of a motif II facing, join E with a sl st in center ch-5 lp of any side, ch 1, sc in same place as joining, ch 5, sc in next ch-5 lp, ch 5, *work (sc, ch 5, sc) in next corner ch-5 lp, [ch 5, sc in next ch-5 lp] 3 times, ch 5; rep from * once more, sc in next corner ch-5 lp, ch 2, sl st in corner ch-5 lp of motif I, ch 2, sc in same corner ch-5 lp of motif II, [ch 2, sl st in next ch-5 lp of motif I, ch 2, sc in next ch-5 lp of motif II] 3 times, ch 2, sl st in next ch-5 lp of motif I, end ch 2, sc in last corner ch-5 lp of motif II, ch 2, sl st in corner ch-5 lp of motif I, ch 2, sc in

same corner ch-5 lp of motif II, ch 5, sc in next ch-5 lp of motif II, ch 5, join rnd with a sl st in first sc. Fasten off. Working in the same manner and referring to placement diagram, cont to join motifs forming a strip.

Row 2

Motif IV—Rnd 5 With RS of a motif IV facing, join E with a sl st in center ch-5 lp of any side, ch 1, sc in same place as joining, ch 5, sc in next ch-5 lp, ch 5, work (sc, ch 5, sc) in next corner ch-5 lp, [ch 5, sc in next ch-5 lp] 3 times, ch 5, sc in next corner ch-5 lp, ch 2, sl st in corner ch-5 lp of motif I of row below, ch 2, sc in same corner ch-5 lp of motif IV, [ch 2, sl st in next ch-5 lp of motif I, ch 2, sc in next ch-5 lp of motif IV] 3 times, ch 2, sl st in next ch-5 lp of motif I, ch 2, sc in next corner ch-5 lp of motif IV, ch 2, sl st in corner ch-5 lp of motif I, ch 2, sl st in same corner ch-5 lp of motif IV, [ch 5, sc in next ch-5 lp of motif IV] 3 times, ch 5, work (sc, ch 5, sc) in last corner ch-5 lp, ch 5, sc in next ch-5 lp, ch 5, join rnd with a sl st in first sc. Fasten off.

Motif V—Rnd 5 With RS of a motif V facing, join E with a sl st in center ch-5 lp of any side, ch 1, sc in same place as joining, ch 5, sc in next ch-5 lp, ch 5, work (sc, ch 5, sc) in next corner ch-5 lp, [ch 5, sc in next ch-5 lp] 3 times, ch 5, sc in next corner ch-5 lp, ch 2, sl st in corner joining of motifs II and III of row below, ch 2, sc in same corner ch-5 lp of motif V, [ch 2, sl st in next ch-5 lp of motif II, ch 2, sc in next ch-5 lp of motif V] 3 times, ch 2, sl st in next ch-5 lp of motif II, ch 2, sc in next corner ch-5 lp of motif V, ch 2, sl st in corner joinings of motifs I and II of row below, ch 2, sl st in same corner ch-5 lp of motif V,

[ch 2, sl st in next ch-5 lp of motif IV, ch 2, sc in next ch-5 lp of motif V] 3 times, ch 2, sl st in next ch-5 lp of motif IV, ch 2, sc in next corner ch-5 lp of motif V, ch 2, sl st in corner ch-5 lp of motif IV, ch 2, sl st in same corner ch-5 lp of motif V, ch 5, sc in next ch-5 lp of motif V, ch 5, join rnd with a sl st in first sc. Fasten off. Working in the same manner and referring to placement diagram, cont to join motifs to the row below and to each other until 20 rows have been completed and 140 motifs have been joined.

FINISHING

Edging

Rnd 1 (RS) With RS facing, join D with a sl st in back lp of 3rd ch of any ch-5 corner lp, ch 1, sc in back lp of same place as joining, working through back lps only, sc in each ch around (skipping all sc), working 3 sc in 3rd ch of each ch-5 corner lp, join rnd with a sl st in first sc. Fasten off.

Rnd 2 With RS facing, join B with a sl st in back lp of center sc of any corner, ch 1, sc in back lp of same place as joining, working through back lps only, sc in each sc around, working 3 sc in center sc of each corner, join rnd with a sl st in first sc. Fasten off.

Rnd 3 Rep rnd 2 using C.

Rnd 4 (WS) With WS facing, join E with a sl st in center sc of any corner, ch 3, sl st in same place as joining (picot made), sl st in next 2 sts, *work (sl st, ch 3, sl st) in next st (picot made), sl st in next 2 sts; rep from * around, join rnd with a sl st in firt sl st. Fasten off.

PLACEMENT DIAGRAM

VIII	VII	VI	V	IV	VII	IV	Row 20
I	IV	III	II	I	VIII	III	Row 19
VI	V	VIII	VII	VI	V	IV	Row 18
III	II	I	IV	III	II	I	Row 17
IV	VII	VI	V	VIII	V	VI	Row 16
I	VIII	III	II	I	IV	III	Row 15
VI	V	IV	VII	VI	V	VIII	Row 14
III	II	I	VIII	III	II	I	Row 13
VIII	VII	VI	V	IV	VII	VI	Row 12
I	IV	III	II	I	VIII	III	Row 11
VI	V	VIII	VII	VI	V	IV	Row 10
III	II	I	IV	III	II	I	Row 9
IV	VII	VI	V	VIII	VII	VI	Row 8
I	VIII	III	II	I	IV	III	Row 7
VI	V	IV	VII	VI	V	VIII	Row 6
III	II	I	VIII	III	II	I	Row 5
VIII	VII	VI	V	IV	VII	VI	Row 4
I	IV	III	II	I	VIII	III	Row 3
VI	V	VIII	VII	VI	V	IV	Row 2
III	II	I	IV	III	II	I	Row 1

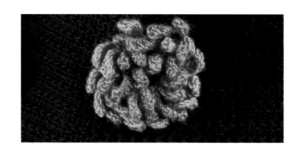

Chrysanthemum Bag

intermediate

FINISHED MEASUREMENTS

• Approx 13"/34.5cm wide x 12"/30.5cm high (excluding strap)

MATERIALS

• 5 1¾oz/50g balls (each approx 123yd/113m) of Rowan/Westminster Fibers, Inc. *Wool Cotton* (wool/cotton) in #956 coffee rich (MC)

• 1 1¾oz/50g ball (each approx 131yd/120m) of Rowan/Westminster Fibers, Inc. *Tapestry* (wool/soybean protein fiber) in #172 potpourri (CC)

• Sizes D/3 and E/4 (3.25 and 3.5mm) crochet hooks *or size to obtain gauge*

• Two 2"/50mm brass rings

• Tapestry needle

GAUGE

23 sts and 19 rows to 4"/10cm over sc daisy st using smaller crochet hook.

Large chrysanthemum to 4½"/11.5cm diameter using larger crochet hook.

Small chrysanthemum to 3¼"/8cm diameter using larger crochet hook.

Take time to check gauge.

CHARTS

See Single Crochet Daisy—Solid (p.17) for Daisy Cluster chart, and p. 195 for Large Chrysanthemum and Small Chrysanthemum charts

STITCH GLOSSARY

Daisy cluster (DCL) Insert hook into bottom lp of ch 1 just made, yo and draw up a lp, draw up a lp in same st as last lp of daisy cluster just made, draw up a lp in each of next 2 ch (or sts), yo and draw through all 5 lps on hook.

BAG

With MC, ch 81.

Foundation row (RS) Draw up a lp in 2nd, 3rd, 4th and 5th ch from hook, yo and draw through all 5 lps on hook, ch 1, *work DCL, ch 1; rep from * across. Turn.

Row 1 Ch 1, sc in each st and ch across. Turn.

Row 2 Ch 3, draw up a lp in 2nd ch from hook, then in 3rd ch from hook, draw up a lp in each of next 2 sts, yo and draw through all 5 lps on hook, ch 1, *work DCL, ch 1; rep from * across. Turn. Rep rows 1 and 2 for sc daisy st and work even until piece measures 24"/61cm from beg. Fasten off.

LARGE CHRYSANTHEMUM (make 1)

To make an adjustable ring, use CC to make a slipknot 10"/25.5cm from free end of yarn. Place slipknot on hook, then wrap free end of yarn twice around your first and second fingers on your left hand. Then work with yarn coming from ball as follows:

Rnd 1 (RS) Ch 2 (counts as 1 hdc), work 16 hdc in ring, pull free end of yarn to close circle, then join rnd with a sl st in top of beg ch-2—17 hdc.

Inner row of petals

Rnd 2 Working in front lps only, ch 1, sc in same place as joining, ch 5, sc in 2nd ch from hook, then sc in next 3 ch, sc in side of first sc, *sc in next st, ch 5, sc in 2nd ch from hook, then sc in next 3 ch, sc in side of first sc at beg of rep; rep from * around, join rnd with a sl st in first sc—17 petals.

Outer row of petals

Rnd 3 Working in free back lps of rnd 1, ch 1, sc in same place as joining, ch 8, hdc in 3rd ch from hook, then hdc in next 5 ch, sc in side of first sc made, *sc in next st, ch 8, hdc in 3rd ch from hook, then hdc in next 5 ch, sc in side of first sc at beg of rep; rep from * around, join rnd with a sl st in first sc—17 petals. Fasten off.

SMALL CHRYSANTHEMUM (make 2)

To make an adjustable ring, make a slipknot 10"/25.5cm from free end of yarn. Place slipknot on hook, then wrap free end of yarn twice around your

first and second fingers on your left hand. Then work with yarn coming from ball as follows:

Rnd 1 (RS) Ch 2 (counts as 1 hdc), work 16 hdc in ring, pull free end of yarn to close circle, then join rnd with a sl st in top of beg ch-2—17 hdc.

Inner row of petals

Rnd 2 Working in front lps only, ch 1, sc in same place as joining, ch 3, sc in 2nd ch from hook, then sc in next ch, sc in side of first sc, *sc in next st, ch 3, sc in 2nd ch from hook, then sc in next ch, sc in side of first sc at beg of rep; rep from * around, join rnd with a sl st in first sc—17 petals.

Outer row of petals

Rnd 3 Working in free back lps of rnd 1, ch 1, sc in same place as joining, ch 6, hdc in 3rd ch from hook, then hdc in next 3 ch, sc in side of first sc made, *sc in next st, ch 6, hdc in 3rd ch from hook, then hdc in next 3 ch, sc in side of first sc at beg of rep; rep from * around, join rnd with a sl st in first sc—17 petals. Fasten off.

FINISHING

Block bag to measurements. Fold bag in half and sew side seams.

Ring tabs (make 2)

With RS facing and smaller hook, join MC with a sl st in st ½"/1.3cm from right side seam.

Foundation row (RS) Ch 1, sc in same st as joining, sc in next 4 sts—5 sts. Turn.

Row 1 Ch 1, sc in each st across. Turn. Rep row 1 for sc until piece measures 2"/5cm from beg. Fasten off, leaving a long tail for sewing. Thread crocheted tab through brass ring. Sew end of tab to top edge of opposite side of bag, then sew through both thicknesses of tab close to top edge of bag. In the same way, make and sew another tab on other side of bag. Sew large chrysanthemum to front of bag.

Twisted cord strap

Cut four 8½yd/7.5m strands of MC and five 8½yd/7.5m strands CC. Put strands together and fold in half. Tie ends into a knot. Holding the knot in your hand, slip the loop over a hook and pull tight. Slip a pencil through the knotted end, then rotate the pencil, continue without releasing the tension, twisting the cord until it starts to double back on itself. Put one finger in center of cord and carefully fold in half, letting the two ends of the cord twist together. Make a knot 4"/10cm from each end, then trim off ends 2"/5cm from base of knots. Thread strap through brass rings, then tie ends in an overhand knot.

Flower tassel cord

Cut two 65"/165cm strands of MC. Make twisted cord as for strap, making a knot 2"/5cm from each end. Trim off ends 1"/2.5cm from base of knots. Sew a small chrysanthemum to each end of cord. Fold tassel cord in half. Thread folded end through a brass ring, then the thread ends of the cord through the folded end. Adjust and tighten cord so one end is longer than the other.

1920's Flapper Cap

intermediate

FINISHED MEASUREMENTS

• Head circumference 22"/56cm

MATERIALS

• 1 1¾oz/50g ball (each approx 191yd/175m) of Rowan/Westminster Fibers, Inc. *Felted Tweed* (wool/alpaca/viscose) in #151 bilberry (MC)

• 1 .88oz/25g ball (each approx 120yd/110) of Rowan/Westminster Fibers, Inc. *Scottish Tweed 4 Ply* (wool) each in #10 brilliant pink (A) and #05 lavender (B)

• 1 1¾oz/50g ball (each approx 197yd/180m) of RYC/Westminster Fibers, Inc. *Cashsoft 4 Ply* (wool/microfiber/cashmere) in #436 fennel (C)

• Size D/3 (3.25mm) crochet hook *or size to obtain gauge*

• One 4mm pearl

• Sewing needle

• Sewing thread

GAUGE

19 sts and 21 rnds to 4"/10cm over sc using size D/3 (3.25mm) crochet hook.

Scallop flower to 3¾"/9.5cm diameter using size D/3 (3.25mm) crochet hook.

Take time to check gauge.

CHARTS

See Scallop Flower (p.225) for flower chart and Cherries (p.204) for the leaf chart.

STITCH GLOSSARY

Spike slip stitch (SPSL) Insert hook in same st as sl st on rnd 2, yo, draw up a lp that is the same height as the working row and draw through both lps on hook.

Note The SPSL does not replace another st.

CAP

To make an adjustable ring, use MC to make a slipknot 10"/25.5cm from free end of yarn. Place slipknot on hook, then wrap free end of yarn twice around your first and second fingers on your left hand. Then work with yarn coming from ball as follows:

Rnd 1 (RS) Ch 1, work 8 sc in ring, join rnd with a sl st in first st.

Rnd 2 Ch 1, work 2 sc in each st around, join rnd with a sl st in first st—16 sts.

Rnd 3 Ch 1, sc in each st around, join rnd with a sl st in first st.

Rnd 4 Ch 1, *sc in next st, work 2 sc in next st; rep from * around, join rnd with a sl st in first st—24 sts.

Rnd 5 Rep rnd 3.

Rnd 6 Ch 1, *sc in next 2 sts, work 2 sc in next st; rep from * around, join rnd with a sl st in first st—32 sts.

Rnd 7 Rep rnd 3.

Rnd 8 Ch 1, *sc in next 3 sts, work 2 sc in next st; rep from * around, join rnd with a sl st in first st—40 sts.

Rnd 9 Rep rnd 3.

Rnd 10 Ch 1, *sc in next 4 sts, work 2 sc in next st; rep from * around, join rnd with a sl st in first st—48 sts.

Rnd 11 Rep rnd 3.

Rnd 12 Ch 1, *sc in next 5 sts, work 2 sc in next st; rep from * around, join rnd with a sl st in first st—56 sts.

Rnd 13 Rep rnd 3.

Rnd 14 Ch 1, *sc in next 6 sts, work 2 sc in next st; rep from * around, join rnd with a sl st in first st—64 sts.

Rnd 15 Rep rnd 3.

Rnd 16 Ch 1, *sc in next 7 sts, work 2 sc in next st; rep from * around, join rnd with a sl st in first st—72 sts.

Rnd 17 Rep rnd 3.

Rnd 18 Ch 1, *sc in next 8 sts, work 2 sc in next st; rep from * around, join rnd with a sl st in first st—80 sts.

Rnd 19 Rep rnd 3.

Rnd 20 Ch 1, *sc in next 9 sts, work 2 sc in next st; rep from * around, join rnd with a sl st in first st—88 sts.

Rnd 21 Rep rnd 3.

Rnd 22 Ch 1, *sc in next 10 sts, work 2 sc in next st; rep from * around, join rnd with a sl st in first st—96 sts.

Rnd 23 Rep rnd 3.

Rnd 24 Ch 1, *sc in next 11 sts, work 2 sc in next st; rep from * around, join rnd with a sl st in first st—104 sts.

Rnd 25 Rep rnd 3.

Beg shell st pat:

Rnd 26 Ch 3, work 4 dc in next st, *skip next 2 sts, sl st in next st, skip next 2 sts, work 5 dc in next st (shell made); rep from * around, end skip next 2 sts, join rnd with a sl st in last st.

Rnd 27 Ch 3 (counts as 1 dc), work 4 dc in same place as rnd 26 joining, *sl st in 3rd st of next shell, work 5 dc in next sl st; rep from * around, end sl st in 3rd st of last shell.

Rnds 28–35 Rep rnd 27.

Rnd 36 *Work 5 dc in next sl st, sl st in 3rd st of next shell, ch 5, skip next 5 sts, sl st in 3rd st of next shell; rep from * around, end work 5 dc in last sl st.

Rnd 37 Sl st across next 3 sts, *ch 7, sc in 3rd ch of next ch-5, ch 7, sc in 3rd st of next shell; rep from * around.

Rnd 38 *Sl st in each ch to 4th ch of next ch-7 lp, ch 3, sl st in next ch (picot made); rep from * around, end sl st in each st to end of rnd. Fasten off.

SCALLOP FLOWER

To make an adjustable ring, use A to make a slipknot 10"/25.5cm from free end of yarn. Place slipknot on hook, then wrap free end of yarn twice around your first and second fingers on your left hand. Then work with yarn coming from ball as follows:

Rnd 1 (RS) Ch 1, work 8 sc in ring, pull free end of yarn to close circle, then join rnd with a sl st in first sc—8 sc. Fasten off.

Rnd 2 With RS facing, join B with a sl st in any st, ch 9, [sl st in next st, ch 9] 7 times, join rnd with a sl st in first sl st—8 ch-9 lps.

Rnd 3 *Work (2 sc, 2 hdc, 2 dc, 3 tr, 2 dc, 2 hdc, 2 sc) in next ch-9 lp; rep from * around, join rnd with a sl st in first sc—8 petals. Fasten off.

Rnd 4 With RS facing, join A with a sl st in 3rd st of any petal, working through back lps only, sl st in next 12 sts, *work SPSL (see Note), skip next 2 sts, sl st in 3rd st of next petal, working through back lps only, sl st in next 12 sts; rep from * around, end SPSL, skip last 2 sts, join rnd with a sl st in first sl st. Fasten off.

LEAVES (make 2)

With C, chain 14.

Rnd 1 (RS) Sc in 2nd ch from hook, sc in next 3 ch, dc in next 5 ch, sc in next 3 ch, work 2 sc in last ch, turn to bottom lps of ch and work as foll: sc in first 4 lps, dc in next 5 lps, sc in last 4 lps, join rnd with a sl st in first st. Fasten off leaving a long tail for sewing.

FINISHING

Sew on flower to front of cap. Sew pearl to center of flower. Sew leaves to cap, underneath flower petals, as shown.

Woven Scarf

intermediate

FINISHED MEASUREMENTS

• Approx 7"/18cm wide x 64"/163cm long (excluding fringe)

MATERIALS

• 2 1¾oz/50g balls (each approx 191yd/175m) of Rowan/Westminster Fibers, Inc. *Felted Tweed* (wool/alpaca/viscose) in #142 melody (A)

• 2 1¾oz/50g balls (each approx 137yd/125m) of Jaeger/Westminster Fibers, Inc. *Pure Silk DK* (silk) in #002 dawn (C)

• 1 ball in #001 chalk (B)

• 1 1¾oz/50g ball (each approx 142yd/130m) of RYC/Westminster Fibers, Inc. *Cashsoft DK* (wool/microfiber/cashmere) in #509 lime (D)

• Size E/4 (3.5mm) crochet hook *or size to obtain gauge*

• Large-eye yarn needle

GAUGE

23 sts and 15 rows to 4"/10cm over basic mesh st using size E/4 (3.5mm) crochet hook (before weaving).
Take time to check gauge.

NOTE When changing colors, draw new color through last 2 lps on hook to complete last st, then turn. Cut and join colors as needed.

SCARF

Background mesh

With A, ch 44.

Foundation row (RS) Dc in 6th ch (counts as 1 dc, ch 1 and skip 1 ch) from hook, *ch 1, skip next ch, dc in next ch; rep from * across—20 ch-1 sps. Turn.

Row 1 Ch 4 (counts as 1 dc and ch 1), skip first dc, *dc in next dc, ch 1; rep from *, end dc in 3rd ch of t-ch of row below. Turn. Rep row 1 for basic mesh st and work in stripe pat as follows: *3 rows B, 2 rows A, 3 rows C, 2 rows A, 3 rows D, 2 rows A, 3 rows C, 2 rows A; rep from * until piece measures approx 64"/163cm, end with 2 rows A. Fasten off.

FINISHING

Weaving

Cut three 76"/193cm strands of yarn for each vertical row of weaving. Working color sequence from right to left, weave rows from bottom edge to top edge as follows: 2 rows C, 2 rows A, 2 rows B, 2 rows A, 4 rows D, 2 rows A, 2 rows B, 2 rows A, 2 rows C. Even up strands so 6"/15cm extends beyond bottom and top edges.

Fringe

With RS of bottom edge facing, and working from right to left, divide the first six strands of C into three groups of two strands. Braid for 3½"/9cm, make an overhand knot just below braiding, then trim 1"/2.5cm below knot. Cont to work in this manner across bottom and top edges.

Squiggle Scarf

intermediate

FINISHED MEASUREMENTS

• Approx 7"/17.5cm wide x 42"/106.5cm long (excluding fringe)

MATERIALS

• 3 1¾oz/50g balls (each approx 151yd/140m) of Rowan/Westminster Fibers, Inc. *Kid Classic* (lambswool/mohair/nylon) in #853 spruce (MC)

• 1 .88oz/25g ball (each approx 229yd/210m) of Rowan/Westminster Fibers, Inc. *Kidsilk Haze* (mohair/silk) each in #577 elegance (A), #578 swish (B) and #597 jelly (C)

• Size G/6 (4mm) crochet hook *or size to obtain gauge*

• 1½"/38mm pompom maker

GAUGE

19 sts to 5"/12.5cm and 11 rows to 4"/10cm over dc pat st using size G/6 (4mm) crochet hook.
Take time to check gauge.

NOTE Scarf is made horizontally.

SCARF

With MC, ch 165 loosely.

Row 1 (WS) Dc in 4th ch from hook and in each ch across—162 sts. Ch 3, turn.

Row 2 Working through back loops only, dc in each st across. Ch 3, turn.

Row 3 Working through front loops only. dc in each st across. Ch 3, turn. Rep rows 2 and 3 7 times more, then rep row 2 once—18 rows and 17 horizontal ridges of free loops. Fasten off.

FINISHING

Block scarf lightly to measurements.

Picot edging

With RS facing, join MC with a sl st in first st of row 18, ch 3, sl st in same st as joining, sl in next 3 sts, *ch 3, sl st in same st as last st, sl st in next 3 sts; rep from * across. Fasten off. Turn to bottom edge of foundation ch. With RS facing, join MC with a sl st in first bottom loop of foundation ch, ch 3, sl st in same loop as joining, sl in next 3 loops, *ch 3, sl st in same loop as last st, sl st in next 3 loops; rep from * across. Fasten off.

Fringe and squiggle embellishments

For first fringe/squiggle, join MC with a sl st in right side edge of center horizontal ridge of free loops; ch 20 and fasten off. Rep on left side edge. Join A with a sl st in first ch at right edge.

Row 1 Ch 1, work 2 sc in same ch as joining, [work 2 sc in next ch] 19 times. Fold scarf along ridge of free loops, *work 2 sc in next free loop; rep from * to ch at left edge, [work 2 sc in next ch] 20 times. Ch 1, turn.

Row 2 Work 2 sc in each st across. Fasten off.

For second fringe/squiggle, skip 2 horizontal ridges up from first fringe/squiggle and join MC with a sl st in right side edge of next horizontal ridge; ch 20 and fasten off. Rep on left side edge. Cont to work as for first fringe/squiggle using B.

For third fringe/squiggle, skip 2 horizontal ridges down from first fringe/squiggle and cont to work as for second fringe/squiggle.

For fourth fringe/squiggle, skip 2 horizontal ridges up from second fringe/squiggle and join MC with a sl st in right side edge of next horizontal ridge; ch 20 and fasten off. Rep on left side edge. Cont to work as for first fringe/squiggle using C.

For fifth fringe/squiggle, skip 2 horizontal ridges down from third fringe/squiggle and cont to work as for fourth fringe/squiggle.

Pompoms (make 10 pieces)

With B, make 2 pompoms 1½"/4cm in diameter. Sew one to each end of first fringe. Make 4 pompoms using C and sew one to each end of second and third fringes. Make 4 pompoms using A and sew one to each end of fourth and fifth fringes.

Ruffle Flower Pincushion

intermediate

FINISHED MEASUREMENTS

• Approx 5"/13cm diameter (excluding leaves)

MATERIALS

• 1 3½oz/100g ball (each approx 186yd/170m) of Rowan/Westminster Fibers, Inc. *Scottish Tweed Aran* (wool) each in #005 lavender (A), and #002 machair (C)

• Size H/8 (5mm) crochet hook *or size to obtain gauge*

• 1 .88oz/25g ball (each approx 120yd/110m) of Rowan/Westminster Fibers, Inc. *Scottish Tweed 4 Ply* (wool) in #10 brilliant pink (B)

GAUGE

16 sts and 8 rnds to 4"/10cm over sc using size H/8 (5mm) crochet hook.

Take time to check gauge.

CHARTS

See Ruffle (p.218) for Ruffle Flower chart and Cherries (p.204) for the leaf chart.

RUFFLE FLOWER

To make an adjustable ring, use A to make a slipknot 10"/25.5cm from free end of yarn. Place slipknot on hook, then wrap free end of yarn twice around your first and second fingers on your left hand. Then work with yarn coming from ball as follows:

Petals

Rnd 1 (RS) Ch 1, work 8 sc in ring, pull free end of yarn to close circle, then join rnd with a sl st in first sc—8 sc.

Rnd 2 Ch 1, work 2 sc in each around, join rnd with a sl st in first st—16 sc.

Rnd 3 Rep rnd 2—32 sc.

Rnd 4 Rep rnd 2—64 sc.

Rnd 5 Rep rnd 2—128 sc. Fasten off.

Flower center

Cut a 6 yd/5.5m length of B and set aside for stuffing.

To make an adjustable ring, use B to make a slipknot 10"/25.5cm from free end of yarn. Place slipknot on hook, then wrap free end of yarn twice around your first and second fingers on your left hand. Then work with 3 strands held tog as follows:

Rnd 1 (RS) Ch 1, work 6 sc in ring, pull free end of yarn to close circle, then join rnd with a sl st in first sc—6 sc.

Rnd 2 Ch 1, work 2 sc in each around, join rnd with a sl st in first st—12 sc.

Rnds 3 and 4 Ch 1, sc in each st around, join rnd with a sl st in first st. Using 6 yd/5.5m length of B, wind a firm ball that's large enough to fit snugly inside of flower center. Insert into flower center.

Rnd 5 Ch 1, *skip next st, sc in next st; rep from * all round. Fasten off, leaving a long tail. Thread tail in tapestry needle and weave through last rnd of sts. Pull tight to gather, fasten off securely.

LEAVES (make 3)

With C, chain 14.

Rnd 1 (RS) Sc in 2nd ch from hook, sc in next 3 ch, dc in next 5 ch, sc in next 3 ch, work 2 sc in last ch, turn to bottom lps of ch and work as foll: sc in first 4 lps, dc in next 5 lps, sc in last 4 lps, join rnd with a sl st in first st. Fasten off, leaving a long tail for sewing.

FINISHING

Sew flower center to center of petals. Sew leaves in a group to underside of flower.

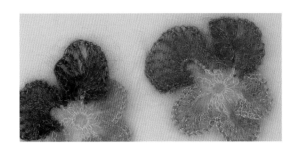

Pansy Choker

intermediate

MATERIALS

- 1 .88oz/25g ball (each approx 229yd/210m) of Rowan/Westminster Fibers, Inc. *Kidsilk Haze* (mohair/silk) each in #578 swish (A), #583 blushes (B), #606 candy girl (C), #596 marmalade (D), #595 liqueur (E) and #578 splendour (G)
- 1 .88oz/25g ball (each approx 227yd/208m) of Rowan/Westminster Fibers, Inc. *Kidsilk Night* (mohair/silk/polyester/nylon) in #612 fountain (F)
- Size C/2 (2.75mm) crochet hook *or size to obtain gauge*
- 17"/43cm of 1"/25mm-wide velvet ribbon
- Five-hole antique gold cast pewter clasp with end bars and chain
- One 6mm and six 4mm pearls
- Sewing needle
- Sewing thread to match ribbon

GAUGE

Pansy motif to 3"/7.5cm x 3 1/2"/9cm using size C/2 (2.75mm) crochet hook.

Take time to check gauge.

CHARTS

See Pansy (p.201) for Pansy chart.

PANSY I (make 3)

Flower center

With A, chain 6. Join chain with a sl st forming a ring.

Rnd 1 (RS) Ch 3 (counts as 1 dc), work 2 dc in ring, [ch 7, work 3 dc in ring] 4 times, ch 7, join rnd with a sl st in top of beg ch-3—5 ch-7 lps. Fasten off.

Small petals

Rnd 2 (RS) With RS facing, join B with a sl st in 3rd dc of any 3-dc group, ch 3 (counts as 1 dc), work 15 tr in next ch-7 lp, [skip next dc, dc in next dc, skip next dc, work 15 tr in next ch-7 lp] twice, dc in next dc. Fasten off.

Large petals

Rnd 2 (RS) With RS facing, skip next dc after last dc of small petals, join C with a sl st in next dc, ch 3 (counts as 1 dc), ch 1, *in next ch-7 lp work: [tr, ch 1] twice, [dtr, ch 1] 3 times, [ttr, ch 1] 5 times, [dtr, ch 1] 3 times, [tr, ch 1] twice*, dc in next dc, skip next dc, dc in next dc, ch 1; rep from * to *, end dc in next dc, skip next dc, join to small petals with a sl st in top of beg ch-3 of small petals. Fasten off.

PANSY II (make 2)

Work as for pansy I using A for center, D for small petals and E for large petals.

PANSY III (make 2)

Work as for pansy I using A for center, F for small petals and G for large petals.

FINISHING

Use needle and thread for all sewing. Turn one end of ribbon 1"/2.5cm to WS twice. Sew inner folded edge in place. Rep for opposite end. Position right end bar of clasp on RS of right end of ribbon, so top edge of end bar is even with top edge of ribbon; sew in place. Rep for left end bar and opposite end of ribbon. Sew a pansy I in center of ribbon. Sew a pansy II on either side of the center flower. Sew a pansy III on either side of the three center flowers. Sew a pansy I to either side of the five center flowers. Sew the 6mm pearl to center of center flower, then sew a 4mm pearl to center of each remaining flower.

Flower Shower Tunic

intermediate

SIZES

Instructions are written for size Small. Changes for Medium and Large are in parentheses.

FINISHED MEASUREMENTS

- Bust 36 (40, 45)"/91.5 (101.5, 114.5)cm
- Length 22 (22½, 23)"/56 (57, 58.5)cm
- Upper arm 14 (15,16)"/35.5 (38, 40.5)cm

MATERIALS

- 8 (9,10) 1¾oz/50g balls (each approx 186yd/170m) of Rowan/Westminster Fibers, Inc. *4 Ply Cotton* (cotton) in #132 bloom (MC), 1 ball each in #133 cheeky (A), #146 violetta (B), #120 orchid (C) and #142 mandarine (D)
- Size C/2 (2.75mm) crochet hook *or size to obtain gauge*
- Twelve 4mm beads
- Sewing needle
- Sewing thread

GAUGE

24 sts and 15 rows to 4"/10cm over mesh pat using size C/2 (2.75mm) crochet hook.

Take time to check gauge.

CHARTS

See Tiny Flowers (p.47) for Tiny Flowers chart.

BACK

With MC, ch 133 (145, 163).

Foundation row (RS) Hdc in the 7th ch (counts as 1 hdc, ch 2 and skip 2 ch) from hook, *ch 2, skip next 2 ch, hdc in next ch; rep from * across—43 (47, 53) ch-2 sps. Turn.

Row 1 Ch 4 (counts as 1 hdc and ch 2), skip first hdc, *hdc in next hdc, ch 2; rep from *, end hdc in 2nd ch of t-ch of row below. Turn.

Rep row 1 for mesh pat until piece measures 22 (22½, 23)"/56 (57, 58.5)cm from beg. Fasten off.

FRONT

Work as for back.

SLEEVE

With MC, ch 103 (109, 115).

Foundation row (RS) Hdc in the 7th ch (counts as 1 hdc, ch 2 and skip 2 ch) from hook, *ch 2, skip next 2 ch, hdc in next ch; rep from * across—33 (35, 37) ch-2 sps. Turn.

Row 1 Ch 4 (counts as 1 hdc and ch 2), skip first hdc, *hdc in next hdc, ch 2; rep from *, end hdc in 2nd ch of t-ch of row below. Turn.

Rep row 1 for mesh pat until piece measures 20"/51cm from beg. Fasten off.

FINISHING

Lightly steam-block pieces to measurements.

Tiny flowers

Back

Refer to placement diagram for back. With RS of back facing, count 22 (23, 27) ch-2 sps from RH edge, then count 3 ch-2 sps down from top edge, join A with a sl st in top bar of the 4th mesh square from the top edge, leaving a 6"/15cm-long tail.

First petal Ch 3 (counts as 1 dc), work (2 dc, sl st) over same bar. Turn work counterclockwise to bar at left.

Second petal Work (sl st, ch 3, 2 dc, sl st) over same bar. Turn work counterclockwise to bar at left.

Third petal Work as for second petal. Turn work counterclockwise to bar at left.

Fourth petal Work as for second petal. Join round with a sl st in first sl st. Fasten off. On WS, use yarn tail to close center of flower. Working from right to left, cont to follow placement diagram for size being made. Work placement diagram in reverse, omitting the center mesh column of flowers to complete the other side.

Front

Work as for back.

Sleeves

Refer to placement diagram for sleeve. With RS of back facing, count 17 (18, 19) ch-2 sps from RH edge, then count 3 ch-2 sps up from bottom edge, join B with a sl st in top bar of the 4th mesh square from the top edge, leaving a 6"/15cm long tail. Cont to work flower as for back. Work from right to left, cont to follow placement diagram for size being made. Work placement diagram in reverse, omitting the center mesh column of flowers, to complete the other side. Sew a 1 (2, 3¼)"/2.5 (5, 8)cm shoulder seam each side. Place markers 7 (7½, 8)"/17.5 (19, 20.5)cm down from shoulders on back and front. Sew sleeves to armholes between markers. Sew side seams, leaving last 6½"/16.5cm open for side slits. Sew sleeve seams.

Neck edging

With RS facing, join B with a sl st in left shoulder seam.

Rnd 1 (RS) Ch 1, sc in each st and ch around entire neck edge, join rnd with a sl st in first st.

Rnd 2 Sl st in first 2 sts, *work (sl st, ch 3, sl st) in next st (picot made), sl st in next 2 sts; rep from * around, join rnd with a sl st in first sl st. Fasten off.

Bottom edging

With RS facing, join B with a sl st in left side seam.

Rnd 1 (RS) Ch 1, sc in each st and ch around entire bottom edge, working 3 sc in each outer corner, join rnd with a sl st in first st. Rep rnd 2 as for neck edging.

Sleeve edging

With RS facing, join B with a sl st in underarm seam. Rep rnds 1 and 2 as for neck edging.

Twisted cord shoulder ties (make 2)

Cut one 6yd/5.5m strand of B. Fold strand in half. Tie ends into a knot. Holding the knot in your hand, slip the loop over a hook and pull tight. Slip a pencil through the knotted end, then rotate the pencil twisting the cord until it starts to double back on itself. Put one finger in center of cord and carefully fold in half, letting the two ends of the cord to twist together. Make a knot 4"/10cm from each end, then

trim off ends 3"/7.5cm from base of knots forming tassels. Thread each cord through top ch-2 sps on front and back, 4"/10cm from sleeve seam. Tie cord in a square knot at shoulder.

Cord flowers (make 12)

To make an adjustable ring, use A to make a slipknot 10"/25.5cm from free end of yarn. Place slipknot on hook, then wrap free end of yarn twice around your first and second fingers on your left hand. Then work with yarn coming from ball as follows:

Rnd 1 (RS) Working in ring, [ch 3, 2 dc, ch 3, sl st] 4 times, pull free end of yarn to close circle—4 petals. Fasten off leaving a long tail. Weave in tail securely. Make 3 more flowers using A, then 4 each using B and C. Sew beads to center of flowers using needle and thread. At the end of each tie, sew 3 flowers (one of each color) in a ring around cord, just above the tassel.

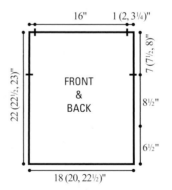 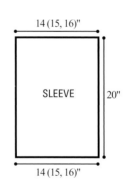

PLACEMENT DIAGRAM FOR BACK

CENTER
MESH

TOP EDGE

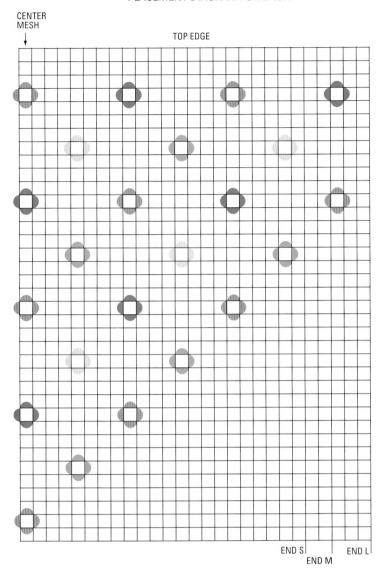

END S
END M
END L

PLACEMENT DIAGRAM FOR SLEEVE

Color Key

Cheeky (A)

Violetta (B)

Orchid (C)

Mandarine (D)

size L only

BOTTOM EDGE

END S
END M
END L

CENTER
MESH

Flower Motif Belt

intermediate

SIZES

Instructions are written for size Small. Changes for Medium and Large are in parentheses.

FINISHED MEASUREMENTS

• Approx 1½"/4cm wide x 32½ (34½ , 36½)"/82.5 (87.5, 92.5)cm (excluding tassel ties)

MATERIALS

• 1 1¾oz/50g ball (each approx 102yd/93m) of Rowan/Westminster Fibers, Inc. *Denim DK* (cotton) in #255 nashville (A)

• 1 1¾oz/50g ball (each approx 186yd/170m) of Rowan/Westminster Fibers, Inc. *4 Ply Cotton* (cotton) each in #133 cheeky (B) and #146 violetta (C)

• 1¾oz/50g ball (each approx 153yd/140m) of Jaeger/Westminster Fibers, Inc. *Sienna 4 Ply Cotton* (cotton) each in #425 chilli (D) and #423 petunia (E)

• Sizes C/2 and E/4 (2.75 and 3.5mm) crochet hooks *or size to obtain gauge*

• Tapestry needle

GAUGE

15 sts to 4"/10cm and 4 rows to 1½"/4cm over hdc using larger crochet hook.

Seven-petal flower to 3¼"/8cm diameter using smaller crochet hook.

Five-petal flower to 2¼"/5.5cm diameter using smaller crochet hook.

Lazy daisy to 2"/5cm diameter using smaller crochet hook.

Take time to check gauge.

CHARTS

See Seven-Petal Flower chart, Five-Petal Flower chart and Lazy Daisy chart all on p. 211.

BELT

With larger hook and A, ch 124 (132, 138).

Foundation row (RS) Hdc in 3rd ch from hook and in each ch across—122 (130, 136) sts. Ch 2, turn.

Row 1 Skip first st, working through both lps, hdc in each st across, end hdc in top of t-ch of row below. Ch 2, turn. Rep row 1 twice more. Fasten off.

SEVEN-PETAL FLOWER I

To make an adjustable ring, use B to make a slipknot 10"/25.5cm from free end of yarn. Place slipknot on smaller hook, then wrap free end of yarn twice around your first and second fingers on your left hand. Then work with yarn coming from ball as follows:

Rnd 1 (RS) Ch 1, work 7 sc in ring, pull free end of yarn to close circle, then join rnd with a sl st in first sc—7 sc.

Rnd 2 Ch 1, work 2 sc in each st around, join rnd with a sl st in first st—14 sc.

Rnd 3 Ch 1, sc in first st, ch 5, [skip next st, sc in next st, ch 5] 6 times, join rnd with a sl st in first st—7 ch-5 lps. Fasten off.

Rnd 4 With RS facing, join C with a sl st in any ch-5 lp, ch 1, work (sc, 5 hdc, sc) in same ch-5 lp, [work (sc, 5 hdc, sc) in next ch-5 lp] 6 times, join rnd with a sl st in first sc—7 petals. Fasten off.

Rnd 5 With RS facing, fold any petal forward to work on WS of flower, join E with a sl st around first sc of petal on rnd 4, ch 1, sc around same st, ch 6, [sc around first sc of next petal on rnd 4, ch 6] 7 times, join rnd with a sl st in first sc—7 ch-6 lps.

Rnd 6 Sl st in first ch-6 lp, work (sc, 7 hdc, sc) in same ch-6 lp, [work (sc, 7 hdc, sc) in next ch-6 lp] 6 times, join rnd with a sl st in first sc. Fasten off.

Rnd 7 With RS facing, join D with a sl st in back lp of first sc of any petal, working in back lp only, sl st in next 4 sts, [ch 3, sl st in same place as last sl st (picot made), sl st in next 9 sts] 6 times, sl st in last 4 sts, join rnd with a sl st in first sl st. Fasten off.

SEVEN-PETAL FLOWER II

Work as for seven-petal flower I in color sequence as follows:

Rnds 1–3 C.

Rnd 4 B.

Rnds 5 and 6 E.

Rnd 7 D.

FIVE-PETAL FLOWER I

To make an adjustable ring, use B to make a slipknot 10"/25.5cm from free end of yarn. Place slipknot on smaller hook, then wrap free end of yarn twice around your first and second fingers on your left hand. Then work with yarn coming from ball as follows:

Rnd 1 (RS) Ch 1, work 5 sc in ring, pull free end of yarn to close circle, then join rnd with a sl st in first sc—5 sc.

Rnd 2 Ch 1, work 2 sc in each st around, join rnd with a sl st in first st—10 sc.

Rnd 3 Ch 1, sc in first st, ch 5, skip next st, [sc in next st, ch 5, skip next st] 4 times, join rnd with a sl st in first st—5 ch-5 lps. Fasten off.

Rnd 4 With RS facing, join C with a sl st in any ch-5 lp, ch 1, work (sc, 5 hdc, sc) in same ch-5 lp, [work (sc, 5 hdc, sc) in next ch-5 lp] 4 times, join rnd with a sl st in first sc—5 petals. Fasten off.

Rnd 5 With RS facing, fold any petal forward to work on WS of flower, join D with a sl st around first sc of petal on rnd 4, ch 1, sc around same st, ch 6, [sc around first sc of next petal on rnd 4, ch 6] 4 times, join rnd with a sl st in first sc—5 ch-6 lps.

Rnd 6 Sl st in first ch-6 lp, work (sc, 7 hdc, sc) in same ch-6 lp, [work (sc, 7 hdc, sc) in next ch-6 lp] 4

times, join rnd with a sl st in first sc. Fasten off.

FIVE-PETAL FLOWER II

Work as for five-petal flower I in color sequence as follows:

Rnds 1–3 D.

Rnd 4 E.

Rnds 5 and 6 B.

LAZY DAISY I (make 7)

To make an adjustable ring, use D to make a slipknot 10"/25.5cm from free end of yarn. Place slipknot on smaller hook, then wrap free end of yarn twice around your first and second fingers on your left hand. Then work with yarn coming from ball as follows:

Rnd 1 (RS) Ch 1, work 7 sc in ring, pull free end of yarn to close circle, then join rnd with a sl st in first sc—7 sc.

Rnd 2 Ch 1, work 2 sc in each st around, join rnd with a sl st in first st—14 sc. Fasten off.

Rnd 3 With RS facing, join C with a sl st in any st, ch 9, sl st in same st as joining, *sl st in next 2 sts, ch 9, sl st in same st as last sl st; rep from * around 5 times more, end sl st in last st—7 petals. Fasten off.

LAZY DAISY II (make 6)

Work as for lazy daisy I in color sequence as follows:

Rnds 1 and 2 E.

Rnd 3 B.

LAZY DAISY III (make 2)

Work as for lazy daisy I in color sequence as follows:

Rnds 1 and 2 C.

Rnd 3 E.

FINISHING

On RS of belt, position seven-petal flower I, 1"/2.5cm from short edge and centered top to bottom; sew in place. At opposite end of belt, position seven-petal flower II in the same manner and sew in place. Sew five-petal flower I 1 (1¼, 1½)"/2.5 (3, 4)cm from seven-petal flower I. At opposite end of belt, sew five-petal II 1 (1¼, 1½)"/2.5 (3, 4)cm from seven petal flower II. Sew a lazy daisy I 1¼ (1¼, 1½)"/3 (3, 4)cm from each five-petal flower, then sew one in the center of the belt. Position a lazy daisy II and III between each pair of lazy daisy I's, spacing them evenly; sew in place.

Twisted cord tassel ties (make 2)

Cut one 3½yd/3.25m strand of A. Fold strand in half. Tie ends into a knot. Holding the knot in your hand, slip the loop over a hook and pull tight. Slip a pencil through the knotted end, then rotate the pencil, twisting the cord until it starts to double back on itself. Put one finger in center of cord and carefully fold in half, letting the two ends of the cord twist together. Make a knot 3"/7.5cm from each end, then trim off ends 2"/5cm from base of knots. Sew a tie to each short edge of belt, making the ends uneven in length. At the end of each tie, sew a lazy daisy I, back to back, to a lazy daisy II just above the tassel.

Mandala Sarong

intermediate

FINISHED MEASUREMENTS

- Approx 33½"/85cm wide x 48"/122cm long

MATERIALS

- 2 1¾oz/50g balls (each approx 153yd/140m) of Rowan/Westminster Fibers, Inc. *Kid Classic* (lambswool/ mohair/nylon) each in #828 feather (A) and #840 crystal (C)
- 4 1¾oz/50g balls (each approx 123 yd/113m) of Rowan/Westminster Fibers, Inc. *Wool Cotton* (wool/cotton) each in #953 august (B) and #909 french navy (D)
- Size E/4 (3.5mm) crochet hook *or size to obtain gauge*

GAUGE

Large motif I to 7½"/19cm diameter using size E/4 (3.5mm) crochet hook.
Small motif I to 3½"/9cm diameter using size E/4 (3.5mm) crochet hook.
Take time to check gauge.

CHARTS

See Mandala chart on p.103.

SARONG

First row

LARGE MOTIF I

To make an adjustable ring, with A, make a slipknot 10"/25.5cm from free end of yarn. Place slipknot on hook, then wrap free end of yarn twice around your first and second fingers on your left hand. Then work with yarn coming from ball as follows:

Rnd 1 (RS) Work 24 sc in ring, pull free end of yarn to close circle, then join rnd with a sl st in first sc.

Rnd 2 *Ch 5, sk next st, sl st in next st; rep from * around 10 times more, end ch 5, join rnd with a sl st in base of first ch-5—12 ch-5 lps.

Rnds 3–5 Sl st in first 3 ch of first ch-5 lp, *ch 5, sl st in next ch-5 lp; rep from * around 10 times more, end ch 5, join rnd with a sl st in 3rd sl st at beg of rnd—12 ch-5 lps. When rnd 5 is completed, fasten off.

Rnd 6 With RS facing, join yarn B with a sl st in any ch-5 lp, *ch 7, sl st in next ch-5 lp; rep from * around 10 times more, end ch 7, join rnd with a sl st in joining sl st—12 ch-7 lps.

Rnd 7 Sl st in first 4 ch of first ch-7 lp, *ch 7, sl st in next ch-7 lp; rep from * around 10 times more, end ch 7, join rnd with a sl st in 4th sl st at beg of rnd—12 ch-7 lps. Fasten off.

Rnd 8 With RS facing, join yarn C with a sl st in any ch-7 lp, *work 7 dc in next sl st, sl st in next ch-7 lp; rep from * around 10 times more, end work 7 dc in next sl st, join rnd with a sl st in joining sl st—12 shells. Fasten off.

Rnd 9 With RS facing, join yarn D with a sl st in 4th dc of any shell, *work 7 dc in next sl st, sl st in 4th dc of next shell; rep from * around 10 times more, end work 7 dc in next sl st, join rnd with a sl st in joining sl st—12 shells. Fasten off.

LARGE MOTIF II

Work as for large motif I in color sequence as follows:

Rnds 1–5 C, **Rnds 6 and 7** B. **Rnd 8** A.

JOINING

Row 1

Rnd 9 With RS facing, join yarn D with a sl st in 4th dc of any shell, *work 7 dc in next sl st, sl st in 4th dc of next shell; rep from * around 8 times more, join motifs as follows: work 3 dc in next sl st, sl st in 4th dc of a shell of motif I, work 3 more dc in same sl st of motif II, sl st in 4th dc of next shell of motif II, work 3 dc in next sl st, sl st in 4th dc of next shell of motif I, work 3 more dc in same sl st of motif II, sl st in 4th dc of next shell of motif II, end work 7 dc in next sl st, join rnd with a sl st in joining sl st—12 shells. Fasten off. Referring to placement and joining diagram, cont to make and join a large motif I to the previous large motif II, then a large motif II to the previous large motif I.

Row 2

Referring to placement and joining diagram, beg with a large motif II and join it to the first large motif I on row 1. Cont to make and join a large motif I to the previous large motif II and to the large motif II on row 1. **Note** Large motifs are always joined to one another in the 4th dc of two consecutive shells as shown on diagram. Cont to work in this manner until 6 rows of 4 motifs across have been completed —24 large motifs total (12 large motif I and 12 large motif II).

SMALL MOTIF I (make 15)

To make an adjustable ring, with B, make a slipknot 10"/25.5cm from free end of yarn. Place slipknot on hook, then wrap free end of yarn twice around your first and second fingers on your left hand. Then work with yarn coming from ball as follows:

Rnd 1 (RS) Ch 1, work 16 sc in ring, pull free end of yarn to close circle, then join rnd with a sl st in first sc.

Rnd 2 Skip first st, [work 7 dc in next st, skip next st, sl st in next st, skip next st] 3 times, work 7 dc in next st, skip next st, sl st in last st.

Joining

Referring to placement and joining diagram, fill in spaces between large motifs as follows:

Rnd 3 Sl st in first 4 sts of first shell of small motif, *ch 5, sl st in 4th dc of shell of large motif, ch 5, sl st in 4th dc of shell of small motif; rep from * around 3 more times. Fasten off.

SMALL MOTIF II (make 16)

Work as for small motif I through rnd 1.

Rnd 2 Skip first st, [work 7 dc in next st, skip next st,

sl st in next st, skip next st] twice, work 7 dc in next st, skip next st, sl st in next 5 sts.

Joining

Referring to placement and joining diagram, fill in spaces between large motifs around edge as follows:

Rnd 3 Sl st in first 4 sts of first shell of small motif, *ch 5, sl st in 4th dc of shell of large motif, ch 5, sl st in 4th dc of shell of small motif; rep from * around once more, sl st in next 4 sts. Fasten off.

FINISHING

Lightly steam-block piece to measurements.

Edging

With RS facing, join B with a sl st in 4th dc of a center shell of lower right corner.

Rnd 1 (RS) [Ch 7, sl st in 4th dc of next shell] twice, *ch 12, work 3 sl sts across bottom of next small motif II, ch 12, sl st in 4th dc of next shell, ch 5, sl st in 4th dc of next shell; rep from * 3 times more, ch 12, work 3 sl sts across bottom of next small motif II, ch 12, sl st in 4th dc of next shell, [ch 7, sl st in 4th dc of next shell] 4 times; rep from * to * twice, ch 12, work 3 sl sts across bottom of next small motif II, ch 12, sl st in 4th dc of next shell, [ch 7, sl st in 4th dc of next shell] 4 times; rep from * to * 4 times, ch 12, work 3 sl sts across bottom of next small motif II, ch 12, sl st in 4th dc of next shell, [ch 7, sl st in 4th dc of next shell] 4 times; rep from * to * twice, ch 12, work 3 sl sts across bottom of next small motif II, ch 12, end [sl st in 4th dc of next shell, ch 7] twice, join rnd with a sl st in first sl st.

Rnd 2 Ch 1, sc in each ch and sl st around, join rnd

with a sl st in first st.

Rnd 3 Rep rnd 2. Fasten off.

Rnd 4 With RS facing, join D with a sl st in center st of any side, ch 1, sc in same st as joining, * sc in each st to next corner, sc around corner inc 9 sts evenly spaced around corner; rep from * around, join rnd with a sl st in first st.

Rnd 5 Ch 1, sc in each st around, join rnd with a sl st in first st.

Rnd 6 Rep rnd 5. Fasten off.

Acknowledgments

First, a big thank you to my teachers: my mum, who taught me to crochet at the tender age of 4, and Pauline Turner, whose workshop at the beginning of 2006 taught me to let go and revel in the endless possibilities of the crochet medium. Many thanks to Tatiana Mirer, Prudence Mapstone, Margaret Hubert and James Walters.

Second, thank you to my dedicated staff: crochet ladies Rita Taylor and Jean Nicholas, secretary Beryl Smith, and finance director Lois Grindy. Thank you for putting up with my idiosyncrasies and supporting me through the twists and turns of this book's journey.

Third, thank you to Stephen Sheard and Kate Buller of Rowan/Jaeger Yarns for letting me crochet my way through their vast range of beautiful fibers. To Ann for sending me the yarn in next to no time, and Janine for her sense of humor.

Most importantly, thank you to the enthusiastic staff of Sixth&Spring Books: Trisha Malcolm for her faith in me, Erica Smith for her patience, Chi Ling Moy for her design sensibility, Tanis Gray and Elaine Silverstein.

Finally, to my design-devoted, fiber-fanatical fans who have supported me over the years—without you this book would not have been possible.

Resources

Jaeger Handknits
distributed by Westminster Fibers, Inc.

Rowan Yarns
distributed by Westminster Fibers, Inc.
www.knitrowan.com

RYC
distributed by Westminster Fibers, Inc.
www.knitrowan.com

Westminster Fibers, Inc.
4 Townsend West, Unit 8
Nashua, NH 03063
www.westminsterfibers.com

U.K. RESOURCES
Rowan Yarns
Green Lane Mill
Holmfirth
HD9 2DX England
www.knitrowan.com

For stockists in all other countries, please contact Rowan Yarns for details.

Books/Further Reading

300 Crochet Stitches
(The Harmony Guides, Vol 6).
London: Collins & Brown, 1999

220 More Crochet Stitches
(The Harmony Guides, Vol 7).
London: Collins & Brown, 1999

Hamilton-Hunt, Margaret. *Mon Tricot Knitting Dictionary.* New York: Crown Publishers, 1972

Mapstone, Prudence. *Bullions & Beyond: Tips and Techniques for the Crochet Bullion Stitch.*
Self-published, 2004

Righetti, Maggie.
Crocheting in Plain English.
New York: St. Martin's Press, 1988

Turner, Pauline. *How to Crochet.*
London: Collins & Brown, 2001

For details of the kits for crocheting my designs or custom crochet garments, write to:
Sasha Kagan
The Studio
Y Fron
Llawr-y-Glyn
Caersws
Powys, SY17 5RJ, UK
Phone: +44 (0)1686 430436
Email: sasha@sashakagan.co.uk

For further information about my workshops and lectures, go to:
www.sashakagan.co.uk